Jonathan Oswald

Reports of the United German Evangelical Luthern congregations

in North America, especially in Pennsylvania - Vol. 2

Jonathan Oswald

Reports of the United German Evangelical Luthern congregations
in North America, especially in Pennsylvania - Vol. 2

ISBN/EAN: 9783337103774

Printed in Europe, USA, Canada, Australia, Japan

Cover: Foto ©Lupo / pixelio.de

More available books at **www.hansebooks.com**

REPORTS

OF THE

United German Evangelical

Lutheran Congregations

IN

North America,

ESPECIALLY IN PENNSYLVANIA,

WITH A PREFACE BY

D. JOHN LUDWIG SCHULZE,

ORDINARY PROFESSOR OF THEOLOGY AND PHILOSOPHY IN THE ROYAL
PRUSSIAN FREDERICK'S UNIVERSITY, AS ALSO DIRECTOR OF THE
ORPHAN HOUSE AND ROYAL PÆDAGOGIUM.

PUBLISHED IN THE ORPHAN HOUSE, HALLE, A. D. 1750.

TRANSLATED FROM THE GERMAN BY
Rev. JONATHAN OSWALD, D. D.

No. 2.

PHILADELPHIA:
LUTHERAN PUBLICATION SOCIETY,
1881.

CHAPTER I.

Fifth Continuation of the Report of Several Evangelical Lutheran Congregations in America, Especially in Pennsylvania.............................. 5

CHAPTER II.

Continuation of the Report of Several Evangelical Lutheran Congregations in America, Especially in Pennsylvania..................... 220

CHAPTER III.

Sixth Continuation of the Report of Several Evangelical Lutheran Congregations in America, Especially in Pennsylvania 246

CHAPTER IV.

Several Letters from Pastor Brunnholtz, in Philadelphia, During the Years 1749 and 1750........... 391

CHAPTER V.

Extract from Pastor Handschuch's Diary from the 7th of September, 1748, to the 16th of May, 1750.. 415

A SHORT REPORT
OF SEVERAL
EVANGELICAL LUTHERAN CONGREGATIONS IN AMERICA.

CHAPTER I.

FIFTH CONTINUATION OF THE REPORT OF SEVERAL EVANGELICAL LUTHERAN CONGREGATIONS IN AMERICA, ESPECIALLY IN PENNSYLVANIA.

Continued report of Pastor Mühlenberg, concerning his official transactions.

DURING the winter months of 1747, I noted the following concerning the inward condition of one soul and another. A woman in New Hanover was suddenly seized with some sort of epilepsy. When I arrived, the paroxysm had just passed. I asked how it was with her heart and conscience before God, if she should be called into eternity? She answered: I glory alone in the bloody wounds which Jesus felt in his hands and in his feet; therein will I inwrap myself to live in a truly Christian manner, so that one day I may joyfully aspire to heaven. I replied: Many thousands of people in Christendom do this; with an unbroken and impenitent heart, they with their lips boast themselves of the bloody wounds of Jesus. Is it thus with you, also? She said: Oh! no, I feel myself a sinner, and because the dear Saviour receives sinners and rejects no one who comes unto him, he also will not reject, but receive me. The Lord Jesus was not wounded for the angels and other creatures, but for mankind who have sinned. When I acknowledge and feel myself a penitent sinner, I have a share in his wounds. I inquired: What is a penitent sinner? She answered: Whosoever truly knows and confesses his sins which he has committed from his youth up, in thought, word, and deed, and by the omission of that which is good, feels penitence and pain therefor, and would gladly have deliverance therefrom, he is a penitent sinner. I further asked: Is this your case? She answered: Yes; my sins are heavy and very great, and from my heart I repent of them—clear me of them, and through thy death and pains set me free, etc. When I further inquired: What are the wounds of Jesus? She answered: All the sufferings which my Jesus endured from his birth unto his death, and thereby obtained for all mankind an eternal redemption. On the question: What is it to inwrap one's self in the wounds of Jesus? her answer was: If I confess and repent of all my sins before God, God forgives me them for the sake of the sufferings of Christ, casts them into the depths of the sea, and looks upon me in his Son as if I had never sinned, and gives me strength also to follow my Jesus and the guidance of his Spirit. I asked: If as a penitent sinner you are so inwrapped, what must then follow? She answered: To inwrap myself therein is one thing, to live in a Christian manner is the other which follows. I added the question: Have you experienced all this? Whereupon she declared: That which I have not as yet experienced, the Lord will permit me yet to experience through grace. I inquired further: But you have forgotten one thing: tell me wherewith must we inwrap ourselves? Her answer was: Faith is the hand wherewith we lay hold and inwrap ourselves. On the question: Who worketh faith? her answer was: The Holy Ghost in a penitent heart. I asked finally: What is said in our hymn of faith? And she answered: The Holy Spirit renews the heart, reproves sin, worketh repentance and sorrow, gives a clear light concerning God's counsel, his Son and his grace. He it is who gives us faith and also sends down love to God into the heart, etc. I presented her case to God in prayer, who soon granted bodily recovery and still carries forward his work in her soul.

An aged woman, who has lost her sight, but in soul walks in the light, is indeed outwardly uncomely, but within in a fine condition. She has already often delighted me with her edifying conversation. Her daughter also fears the Lord, and before my time was joined in marriage to an excellent, quiet man, born in Moravia. The man holds to the Moravian congregation, but places no obstacle in the way of his wife. The mother, father, and daughter belong to our congregation. When the aged mother for the first time visited me, and at the door heard that I was instructing the young people, and asked the question on the passage Mark x. 16: *He that believeth and is baptized*, etc.: Children, can the Jews and the Gentiles be partakers of the salvation which is promised in this passage, as long as they continue in unbelief and blindness, and without baptism?—and the children answered: *He that believeth not shall be damned*, she afterwards said to me, her heart wept when she heard that I condemned the Jews and the Gentiles. The Jews, said she, are surely the kinsmen of our Lord Jesus, and the Gentiles are given unto him for an inheritance. I pray day and night that the dear Saviour may be a light to the Gentiles, and to the people of Israel a praise. I answered: Dear mother, that which you have said is partly correct, and it is well intended. The Jews are our dear Saviour's kinsmen according to the flesh, for Christ, *who is over all, God blessed forever*, Amen, Rom. ix. 15, came of the fathers, as concerning the flesh. Natural relationship, however, is not the ground of salvation, for those are not all children who have a natural descent from Abraham, but those who are of his faith, Rom. ix. 7, 8, and in Christ Jesus availeth neither circumcision, *i. e.* the Jews, nor uncircumcision, *i. e.* the Gentiles, but a *new creature*, Gal. vi. 15. Therefore Paul also says, 2 Cor. v. 16, 17: *Wherefore henceforth we know no man after the flesh*, etc. *Therefore, if any man be in Christ he is a new creature*, etc. The passage speaks, and therefore is true: *He that believeth and is baptized shall be saved, but he that believeth not shall be damned*, be he called Jew or Gentile. This is confirmed by John iii. 18: *He that believeth on him is not condemned, but he that believeth not is condemned already*, etc. Out of Christ, therefore, and without faith, neither Jew nor Gentile can expect the salvation which is promised in the Word of God; but the condemnation which is therein threatened. The heathen are given to our Lord Jesus Christ for an inheritance, and he has also, since his ascension to heaven, harvested a great multitude of them, and gathered them into his barn. But as many as held the truth in unrighteousness, and did not glorify God, but became vain in their own imaginations, esteemed themselves wiser, changed the truth of God into a lie, such God gave up, and permitted them to fall into the ruin which they desired and sought—Rom. i. 21-32. God has so arranged from the beginning, that no creature can justly accuse him. She said : But there are, for all that, so many thousands of poor people in all parts of the world who have already sat in darkness for some centuries, and who also, themselves without God, cannot come to the light. I replied : God has always presented to mankind the means and the way to their true happiness, and raised his standard high enough throughout all times, and every economy, and also yet holds faith before every one. Just think, there is scarcely a corner in the four quarters of the earth, no hidden place on the ocean, no gold or silver mine, no rare plant, no costly spices, no art or science, has been so high and hidden, but the nations and peoples have searched it out. Now, but for the wickedness of the hearts of mankind, in virtue of which they love darkness more than the light, there would be no people in the world who could not, from the beginning until now, have seen the light which was set up, and thereby have come to the light of faith. She answered: This is true; still we should think that those fathers, who in special visitations of God violently rejected the light, were the most guilty; for what could the children and descendants help for that, who in the various centuries are born in the thickest darkness, and know nothing else? Shall so many souls be lost because their ancestors thrust the light from them? Whereupon I answered: This is another question. In the first place, we must assign ourselves as dust into the deepest humility; that we have a little, low, imperfect, erring understanding and knowledge; that we do not even understand the very least part of those things which we daily carry in and about us; therefore we must believe it as an established truth, that our thoughts are not God's, and God's are not our thoughts. With your all, you cannot even measure the finite space between this and the most distant stars; and many thousand times less is it possible that you, with your finite little understanding, should measure the infinite understanding and wisdom of God. In the second place, we must diligently consider the attributes of God, which he, from great love, has revealed unto us in his Word, by his Son; especially compare his righteousness and his mercy with each other, and reflect that they all stand in the most perfect equality with each other. Then will we reach the infallible conclusion: God can and will eternally do unto his creatures, not too much, and also not too little, but exactly right. In the meanwhile remember it is seventeen hundred and odd years since God sent his most beloved Son himself among the Jews and invited them. Again, the Son of God sent whole troops of apostles, evangelists, shepherds, and teachers, among both the Jews and the Gentiles. Did they not scourge them, persecute them, drive them from one city to another, crucify and slay them? Now, if the omniscient God had permitted the people so to act, and yet forced one apostle and servant after the other upon them, how many thousand more righteous souls would the Jews and the Gentiles already have slain in the seventeen hundred years, and loaded upon themselves incalculably more innocent blood? With all this, the light of the gospel, in all this time, was never wholly extinguished, but has here and there stood upon the candle-stick, so that it might have shone into the eyes of all nations and peoples, if they had not wantonly closed them, and loved darkness and its works more than the light. Beyond this, God has already, again and anew, permitted a knocking at the door of both Jews and Gentiles; but they still resist mightily. Only you continue simply in the Word of God and therein nourish your soul: thus will the extravagant thoughts soon lose themselves. That you pray for the Jews and the heathen, you do well; I do it also, for it is our duty, and universal love demands it. May the Lord graciously arise; let the fullness of the Gentiles come in, and restore his Israel. She said: Oh! yes; we will lay our hand upon our mouth, and behold the goodness to those who stand, and the severity on them who have fallen.

On another occasion, she came to me and complained of the deep corruption of her heart. I embraced the opportunity, therefore, to inquire somewhat more particularly after her condition. On examination, I found that she was pretty well established in a knowledge of repentance, faith, and godliness, and experienced in practice. She was gradually enlightened, and attained a consciousness of her deep ruin, but also found the fountain of grace, where she obtained purification and refreshment for her poor soul, and continues in the renovation. She said, that in repentance her sins did not present themselves singly, but all together, so that they became for her as a heavy burden; too heavy, until she was enabled to cast them upon Christ, as the destroyer of sin. At first when the Lord through grace forgave her her transgressions, covered her sin, and imputed not her trespasses for the sake of her Kinsman, she was very joyful, and could draw near to the throne of grace with glad prayer. After this time, one sin after the other which she had committed from her youth up, came into her mind. Against these she presented to her dear Father in heaven the beautiful promises, as *e. g.*, *I will not remember thy sins*, etc. *But there is forgiveness with thee, that thou mayst be feared.* Now, although she perceived a hatred and aversion to all sinful conduct, the world and its lusts, and a longing desire after all good, yet some vanity was ever ready to spring up and grow from the root of sin, whereof the trunk and branches were cut off in repentance. When during the day, in quiet, she observed her heart and all thoughts which arose in it, she was ashamed and grieved, that so much impurity proceeded from it; now self-love and self-sufficiency, and then soon again other subtle inclinations would arise, insensibly to lead her astray. But on the other side, she was warned against this by the indwelling spirit of God, that she must contend against this, and pray, *Create in me a clean heart*, etc. Soon a storm came from without into the family, and would disquiet her. But that which came from without did not give her as much pain as that which came from within. What she had to suffer on this account from ignorant people, she did not regard at all, but thought they knew no better. I gave her the necessary admonition, and prayed with her, as the wants required. When I, on Sunday, repeated my sermon in church, by question and answer, she gave beautiful and clear answers, which served as an example to others for imitation. She gladly visits the sick, as much as her infirmity permits, and edifies them with the Word of God. Her chief concern is, that she, with her husband and daughter, may be saved.

Another woman in Providence, who is yet unmarried, gradually lost her sight, but, through the grace of God, attained to a clear knowledge of and faith in Jesus Christ. When she arrived in the country, she was in debt for the voyage, and her parents, on account of poverty, were unable to assist her. She worked from the first with the Mennonites at Skippack or Motecha, where one of our wardens lived. Now, as the Mennonites saw that she walked honorably and worked diligently, they desired much to persuade her to re-baptism. At that time, the Lutherans had as yet no preacher in Providence. She however adhered to the said warden, and was present when he, on Sundays, read a sermon for his family. After the congregation at Providence was gathered, and preparation made for divine service, she earnestly held to it, and by a diligent use of the means of grace, obtained more knowledge of her inward corruption and of the salvation in Christ. Her parents had associated themselves with the Herrnhuter, and desired to lead her on this way also. But she said she could receive no benefit from moving hither and thither, from one party to another. She knew on whom she believed, etc., etc., and would keep herself to his word, and not sell her faith and her birthright for a dish of lentils. She had no need to seek the Lord Jesus here or there in the wilderness, or in the chamber; for he was in his church, and with each believing member of it especially, every day until the end of the world. She had five English miles to church, and two streams to cross each time, but not like others the convenience of riding. Yet, without necessity, she neglected no sermon or opportunity for edification; and when there was no other way, rather waded through the water, as other poor people who had no horses were obliged to do. Our dear warden had by this time cared for it, that a long tree was laid over the one stream to clamber over, and a canoe provided for the other. This poor person had received much injury by wading through the cold water, and entirely lost her sight. Now, as she had to support herself by the labor of her hands, and was hindered in it by this accident, she took her mite, and other friends added thereto, that she might employ a physician in the city; but it availed her nothing. Afterwards her parents took her away, and traveled with her several hundred miles to a mineral spring in Virginia, which indeed has a great reputation, but produced little effect. She also returned from it again without improvement, and had to remain with her parents for a time. She was obliged to hear it often, that she lost her sight entirely in the Lutheran church. The Moravians endeavored to make her mistrustful of her faith, and according to their manner of speaking, to lead her to the Saviour. But she insisted that they could show her no better Saviour than he who is the corner-stone in the writing of the prophets and apostles, on whom she had believed. Among other things, a Moravian brother had said, that from a blind love to me she was unable to distinguish between the truths and falsehoods I preached. But she answered, the Scripture remained open to her for investigation, as it was to the Bereans. Now she has again returned to us, to her old place, and sings:

> Let Thy Word feed me all the way,
>   Therewith my soul to nourish,
> Me to defend that I may stay,
> When afflictions come this way.

During the time that she was with her parents, she labored diligently with her brothers and sisters, and so far convinced them, that they would willingly be instructed and confirmed by us if they could obtain the consent of their wavering parents. She esteems it as one of the greatest favors that the gracious God awakened our fathers and so many patrons in Europe, that they cared for the poor scattered sheep, and sent them shepherds and assistance. She also remembers them in her prayers before God.

The wife of the aforementioned warden spoke with me concerning the state of her soul, and said that from her youth she perceived in her heart an aversion to evil, and a desire after that which is good, and therefore also never could hold fellowship with vain young persons. She thought this resulted from the following causes: (1) In her tender youth, she had seen a good example in her parents, and received a deep impression by their admonitions from the word of God. (2) She early came among strangers, and was subjected to many afflictions, which taught her to attend to the word. After she came into the country here, and was deprived of hearing the word of God, and placed among sects of various sorts, she scarcely would or could be comforted. For it is quite too painful to be deprived at once of the beautiful worship of God, and as a weak child be weaned from the sincere pure milk. We cannot know how great the favor, when God's word dwells richly among a people, until the hunger for it occurs. She often thanked the Lord that he heard the prayer of the wretched, and raised his standard here among the dispersed. I noticed in the narration and other circumstances, that in the feeling of the good and evil, there was only an obscure and irregular apprehension of the evangelical power, and of the New Testament grace, or of the spirit of adoption, whereby we call Abba, Father. I therefore several times presented to her the Lord Jesus, as a shepherd, as one who pities, as a bridegroom and the like, who knows how to speak to the weary at the proper time, who does not extinguish the glimmering wick, nor break the feeble reed, who refreshes the weary and heavy-laden, who early fills the hungry and the thirsty, gives them to drink and satisfies them, etc. Now the more the loving, gracious and compassionate heart of the Lord Jesus was discovered to her through the gospel, the more her heart melted and became tender. She several times afterwards said to me, that her heart ever became more sick with a feeling of her misery, but that the Lord Jesus also continually became more necessary and important to her. At one time, there was in her a deep sorrow on account of her own and other people's sins and corruption, so that the world became almost too narrow for her. But when the consolations of the gospel came, she experienced such an inward joy, as if a birth had taken place. She shuns vain company, and delights to be where something good and edifying is spoken. She has a healthful relish for the word of God, and by her hunger almost draws the words out of the preacher's mouth. She has six sons, and an unwearied care for their salvation. She entreats and admonishes the children, day and night, yea, often with tears, and thinks that she must betimes portray the Saviour, so dear to her, before the eyes of the children, and plant him in their hearts, that he may be formed within them. Her husband is likewise a true Israelite, in whom there is no guile. He has now served the congregation and us preachers altogether about five years as warden, by prayer, word and deed, and by good conduct, and is still unwearied in serving, by day or by night. Yea, if it is for the glory of God, and the service of the congregation, and especially for the good souls in it, there is nothing to which his heart cleaves, nothing too dear, that he would not surrender from the mite of his means of living. But if we view such good souls from the side called man, who is yet in imperfection, dwelling in the sinful tabernacle, carrying the body of death, and surrounded by sins, which still adhere and would ever induce indolence, we might notice many faults, and pronounce an unkind verdict. It is sufficient, however, that there is *no condemnation to them which are in Christ Jesus, who walk not after the flesh, but after the Spirit.* As many of their faults as the good God discovers to them by his word and Spirit, so many they seek to put off in the daily renovation.

In New Hanover I had opportunity to speak with a sick married woman, concerning the state of her heart. The woman had scarcely reached her thirtieth year, but already suffered many afflictions and crosses. The afflictions consist in many different kinds of maladies and infirmities, so that she has scarcely had a well day in several years. The cross she was herself wont to describe by the verse: This is my pain, this me grieves, that I cannot sufficiently love as I should love thee (my Jesus). This is concerning the inward; of the outward she was accustomed to say: I must be called a fool because I confess Jesus and esteem all as loss, in comparison with the excellency of the knowledge of him. Apparently the woman has experienced a true change of heart, passed from darkness to light and from the power of Satan to God, and as a lost daughter returned to her covenant Father in Christ. From her heart she hates all ungodliness and worldly lusts, and gives diligence to live soberly, righteously, and godly in this present world. Her minor children she not only nourishes from her own breast, but seeks to infuse into them the sincere pure milk of the Gospel also. Therefore, we hear the minor tender lambs lisping of their Saviour, in a sweet little passage of the Gospel or an edifying verse of a hymn. She often bends her knees in secret and prays to him who sees in secret, gladly visits the sick, and also cares well for her outward business, as much as is possible for her in her infirmity. Her husband has not been satisfied with her for several years past; partly on account of her bodily weakness, as he is apprehensive that it might be a hindrance to him in their maintenance, and partly also, because he feared that she might pray too much and become quite melancholy. Foolish people advised him that he must keep her from praying and reading by force. Then, when the husband manifested his displeasure, she arose in the middle of the night, read some and prayed in silence whilst the man slept. False comforters also were not wanting, who said, she must not take so much to heart what Mühlenberg said, or she would become melancholy; whom she however answered: Dear people, I have to do with my God; if he wounds and causes me to mourn, he is able also at the proper time to heal and to comfort me. I am engaged in his work, and this you do not understand. At length, the dear God also permitted affliction and sickness to befall her husband, and is drawing at his soul. Now the man asks pardon, and says he did not understand her case before. He acknowledges and confesses that he is a poor sinner, who cannot stand before God; is sorry for his sins and begins to hunger and to thirst after the righteousness of Jesus Christ. This is a great comfort for the poor wife, that she can now, together with her husband, bow the knee and pour out her heart. God help furthermore, and lead the work begun to victory.

A young person, between twenty and thirty years of age, often came to me and edified himself with me and prayed. He said that he was awakened by the powerful evangelical hymns to seek his soul's salvation in Christ. I was accustomed now and then, after the sermon, to read a strong and edifying hymn which suited the sermon, and briefly to explain some of the expressions of the same, and to recommend such hymns to the hearers. This was not without a blessing; for the people wondered that such powerful expressions are found in the hymns which they sung many hundred times, and had not considered or understood.

An aged widow, who lives nine English miles from New Hanover, in the mountains, and is afflicted with a rheumatic lameness, had me called to her, and complained with tears that she had been for several months in great anguish of conscience and distress—that she could sleep scarcely any night on account of the exciting thought that she was lost and condemned. Her children had furnished her with various good books, among others with Arndt's True Christianity. But the more she read in it the greater became her anguish. In the conversation I led her to this: Did she perhaps commit some great sin? and inquired whether she did not receive other injuries to her health in addition to her rheumatism, whereby she became so depressed. But I could find no other cause than this, that the Spirit of God through his word was working in her. She said that she in her anguish prayed every text which treated of the blood of Christ. Such passages and blessed promises had somewhat quieted the anguish of her conscience, but she feared it might return again. I presented to her the beautiful and chosen examples of the New Testament, as of the prodigal son, the publican who smote upon his breast, and of the woman who was a sinner, Luke vii., and said that she must examine herself according to these. The mightier sin became in her, in the consciousness and feeling of it, the mightier also would grace become. For the greater strengthening of her rising but weak faith, and to attain to a closer communion with the Lord Jesus, she much wished to partake of the Holy Supper, which I administered to her, and which was received by her with a sincere humbling of her heart. She still remains under the operation of the good Spirit, continues in prayer day and night, and permits herself to be prepared for the blessed eternity. We have otherwise many sad examples of disobedient children in this country, especially when a widow is to raise a small number of them, as the youth are easily led astray and pride themselves on their liberty as against their parents. This widow also had a small number of children, and in addition, must for the most part depend upon them, as she became quite lame. But she reared her children in love and seriousness, and by earnest supplication obtained so much by prayer from her reconciled Father in Christ, that we must rejoice over their piety and blameless life.

A penitent married woman was oppressed in mind, and desired instruction and consolation. She complained in the first place of dejection and despondency, and was apprehensive whether she would remain faithful to the Lord Jesus, and not turn back again. In the second place, she was troubled about her husband, because he would not wholly give himself up to repentance and faith. She said the man was frequently affected, and at certain times acted as if he would wholly repent, but at other times he was altogether disorderly, and permitted his anger to rule, and also showed himself harsh towards her and towards his friends. In reference to the first point, I reminded her that the work of grace in repentance, and perseverance in that which is good, was not dependent on her natural powers, but upon the power of God. He who has given the will, will also grant the doing, Phil. ii. 13. He who has begun the good work in her will also perform it, until the day of Jesus Christ, Phil. i. 6, and our Saviour has

3*

given the assurance that no one shall pluck his sheep out of his and his Father's hand, John x. 23–28. But in the meanwhile she must not become slothful, as she still carried the body of this death, and must truly contend against the devil, the world, sin, and her own flesh and blood, if she would be crowned. Therefore she must watch and pray, and always be equipped with the armor of God. Conducting herself thus, she could rejoice, and still work out her own salvation with fear and trembling, Phil. ii. 12. In relation to the second point, she should follow the admonition of Peter, 1 Pet. iii. 1, and remain in Christian subjection to her husband, to speak a word in season in love and meekness, but chiefly seek to win the man without much speaking, by a pure life, in the fear of God, and evermore ask of God the precious adornment of womanhood, which consists in the imperishable decorum of a meek and quiet spirit. But in secret she should diligently pray to God, that he should more and more remove the hindrances out of the way of her husband, and aid him to a perfect repentance. Finally, she must have patience with her hus-

band, and reflect well, how long the gracious
God bore and still bears with her, herself, in
patience and with forbearance. She promised
to follow this advice, by the grace and help of
God, and requested that I might also admonish her husband in love.

A widow in New Hanover received an injury in her hand and arm, resulting from an
inflammation, so that it was feared that gangrene might ensue. She wept bitterly, because she still had several children about her,
not as yet grown. She regarded this accident
as a special punishment from God, because
she on a Sunday, mended her children's
clothes with the hand. I said to her, that the
hand was only an instrument, which worked
according to the determination of the understanding and will. She should therefore look
to the origin of her actions, and consider how
her heart was disposed towards God. She
cited many things, according to the first article of our faith, concerning the preservation
and protection of God, during her whole life;
on her voyage, in perils by water and by land,
and especially in her widowhood, and hence
concluded that she had a gracious God, ex-

cept the before-mentioned fault, when she worked on Sunday, and now received the punishment for it. But we pointed out to her that the gracious preservation, defence and protection happened for the sake of Jesus Christ, and were to lead her to repentance and faith. She thought that repentance and faith were pre-supposed from baptism onward, and knew how to cite beautiful passages in support of it. But when we inquired whether she had preserved the covenant of a good conscience, and the garment of righteousness in purity, she desired on her part to bring into the account an honest life. For this reason, we had to show her that the law of God is spiritual, and demands much more than outward obedience, and this brought her to silence and to poverty before God. The old tree was digged around by the Law of God, and is still manured by the gospel, to see whether the Lord may yet gather some good fruit. After the sickness, a man came who desired to marry her. When she asked him of what religion he was, he answered her by a short rhyme: Her parsons he deems as fools, them esteems, etc. She answered, he should go then and seek those like himself, and if he possessed the whole world full of perishable riches, she had found an imperishable treasure, which no thief could steal and no moth corrupt.

In Providence I was called to a lad of twelve years, who was sick. He is a fine child, in whom the grace of baptism is sensibly perceived. His memory is stored with choice passages and edifying hymns, as also with the principal parts of Luther's catechism; and on various occasions he is able to apply the truths properly. When, previous to his sickness, his mother had gone with him into the field where the winter grain was sown, and complained that the grain stood so thin, and could easily result in a failure of the crop, the son answered: Mother, do not grieve; behold the fowls of the air, they sow not, neither do they reap, etc. Reflect how much bread the Lord Jesus had when he fed the four and five thousand, etc. Thus is he in his intercourse, that he applies the divine truths unto edification. May God preserve this poor, tender shoot from the many temptations and from the wind of doctrine and offences in this country! I asked the father whether he would entrust the son to me, and I would keep him to study, that he might once, according to the will of God, serve our church or school. The father answered: The preachers here in this country were so despised by the sects and in the newspapers, must suffer so much, had no sure support, he would rather have him learn a trade, whereby he might also serve God and his neighbor, etc.

In Providence, a Reformed neighbor gave his daughter in marriage to a man belonging to our congregation. I had to marry them, and was therefore obliged to be present at the wedding. Now, when friends and neighbors meet on such occasions, we may count among the number very many different kinds of people, of various sorts of religions and opinions, as the several sects may call themselves, but mostly those born in Pennsylvania, and those who believe nothing. Therefore I would sometimes rather be in an offensive prison than in such company. There was also a mixed company present here, chiefly of self-invited guests, who scoff at churches and parsons. The parents of the bride placed me and my colleague, Brunnholtz, who was on a friendly visit to me at the time, together with several Lutherans and Reformed, in a room alone, and left the rest of the people in a side-room by themselves. We sought to edify each other with agreeable conversation, and also sang spiritual hymns. The scoffers in the side-room became as it were frantic, and disturbed us, and gave offence to several of our young people. We deplored this, and after we had in vain admonished them several times, we went home. Afterwards, the unruly people did not rest until they had seduced the young people into a dance. Several of the youth whom I had prepared for the Holy Supper withdrew from this vanity. Several others, however, were involved in it, of which the rest complained to me. The parents of the bride apologized, and said, that they were unable to resist, as the shameless people did not heed their words, and were afraid of neither God nor man. They had also not been invited to the wedding, but had come of their own accord. That such persons are somewhat tolerated and are not willingly offended, this reason may be assigned. The country people live separate, and not together. Their whole wealth consists in cattle and some grain. The grain they have either in barns or stacked in the open field. When such heads of families sometimes offend an audacious Irishman or intractable German, injury to their cattle or grain easily follows during the night, as everything is open and exposed to the revenge and fury of such obdurate people. For before one looks out of his house in the night, his barn and all his possessions may already be consumed, and before the nearest neighbor or the Justice of the Peace is called to help, a man may already have done the greatest damage, and retreated several miles into the forest. I will here relate what happened in my time to my present father-in-law, Mr. Conrad Weiser. As Justice of the Peace in his district, he had adjudged a punishment to a certain family for a crime committed. Some time after, his house was closed from without during the night, and a heap of straw taken into the vestibule under the roof of dry shingles, and set on fire. The smoke and crackling awakened several of the children, who awakened the rest. But as the door was bolted, they had to leap out of the windows and extinguish the

fire. If the dear God had not watched over
the house, in a short space of time ten persons,
viz: his whole family, except two children,
who were absent, would have been burned.
He had his suspicion as to who did this, but
could produce no proof according to the English
law. Now, although a believer does not fear
men, who only kill the body, and knows that
without the will of God not a hair can fall
from his head, and that the Lord and God of
Israel neither sleeps nor slumbers, but guards
the house; still weak human beings are fearful,
and are anxious about their life and sustenance,
because they do not rightly trust God.

A young woman, who at the before-mentioned wedding danced along with the rest,
afterwards avoided our divine service, until I
at length sought her and inquired wherefore
she separated herself. She answered, that she
was ashamed before God, because she had not
been more watchful, and had not contended
better against the temptation. I set forth before her how unfaithfully she had hitherto acted
towards the many gracious workings of the
Spirit of God, and against her own soul, etc.
She complained of much disquietude of con-

science since she resisted the operations of the good Spirit, but would ask of God in Christ pardon, and for a new heart, and that this injury should serve to make her circumspect. I called another young person to account, and asked him wherefore he acted thus at the wedding. He confessed with sadness, that they overcame him with much persuasion, and at length succeeded so far as to have him bring the musician. But when he had brought him, and looked upon the vain life, he became so afraid and alarmed that he left and went home. He assured me that he was heartily sorry, but would in the future follow the inward workings of the Spirit of God better, and walk more circumspectly.

A middle-aged married man lives in New Hanover, who, together with his wife, never as yet partook of the Holy Supper. He had in part depended on his earthly possessions, and therewith lead a life of excess. In part, he was also so ensnared by the counsel of the ungodly, walked on the broad road, and sat where the scoffers sit, that we had the least hope of his return. Now, when he some time ago uttered such things when drunk about another man's wife which he could not substantiate before court, and might easily thereby have lost his honest name, I interposed for the sake of his well-deserving father, and amicably settled the matter between the two parties, so that it did not get into the hands of the lawyers and before court. The man thereby obtained a love for me, and went to church diligently, although he still continued his bad life. Nevertheless, by-and-by a word remained, until he at length perceived that on the broad way he must go down to condemnation. As he had before been a crier and merry-andrew at every auction, he renounced his dishonorable occupation, freed himself from his wicked associates, took the Word of God in hand, joined himself to his wife, with whom he was at much variance before, and who was now not a little encouraged thereby. They were both instructed by me, manifested repentance and sorrow for their sins, and a hunger and a thirst after the righteousness of Jesus Christ; and although the wife was born of and raised by Reformed parents, she was gladly willing to be confirmed in our congregation. After I had bowed the knee with them in secret, they were both, according to their desire, publicly confirmed in the presence of the congregation, and admitted to the Holy Supper. The old associates think it impossible to do without so dear a comrade, and therefore daily try to persuade him to fall back into the ways of sin again. But the gracious God has hitherto not failed in the chastisements and admonitions of his spirit, although he is as yet very tender and weak, and still unable to bear much. If they scoff at him, he can well endure that, but it grieves him more when they ridicule his parsons and churches and religion.

It is almost incredible what hard and heart-knawing expressions some bold and dissolute persons utter in this free and licentious country. One of our churchmen came to a rich scoffer, and desired to borrow money. The rich asked the poor man: do you know where my God is? He answered: no. The rich man pointed to his manure pile before the door, and said: this is my God, he gives me wheat and all I need. The poor man was terrified, and rebuked him for such blasphemy. The rich man said: you must borrow of your God, to whom you pray and go to church, if

you are not satisfied with mine. The poor
man left, and would have nothing. Another
scoffer was admonished by a churchman, that
he should consider his end and the impending
judgment, and not do so wickedly. He answered that he had already for a long time
considered his end, and concluded, as respects
the soul, to enter into the swine, as he was
fond of swine's flesh. This man afterwards
hanged himself in his house. The before-mentioned dunghill worm had a valuable horse,
and also used blasphemous language in relation to it. The lightning struck the horse
dead, when the man was only a few steps off.
I said to my hearers, when they complained
of such, they must not be surprised at this,
but be excited to greater zeal, as this was the
language from the beginning of Satan, of the
old liar, who speaks of his own. The government had no time and wish to investigate such
matters; and if we seek to convince the poor
worms, they accept of no valid proof, but only
blurt out, with their inconsiderate talk. For
this reason, I had a conversation with a man
of some pretentions in Philadelphia. As he
admitted a Supreme Being, I sought to show

him that unassisted reason in its theory was without sufficient means for union with the Higher Power, and hence could not give permanent happiness and inward contentment; that a nearer revelation was desirable, and not only possible, but also, according to reason itself, must actually be present. But he immediately became rude in manner, spoke improperly of the sacred Scriptures, and said: the parsons must speak thus and so, that they may not lose their bread. As he would receive no argument, blasphemed still more grossly, and recommended to me the writings of Spinoza, Collins, Spinozer, Bayles, the independent Whig, and such like, I said that I had read such writings in part, and found that the authors, if they yet wrote anything that is true, stole it from the nearer revelation; but with their own perverted propositions, they had left no other impression of themselves with sensible people than that which was given of them long ago in the description contained in the 14th Psalm, 1 verse: The fool hath said in his heart, etc. But as for himself, he might reflect on what is written in Isaiah i. 3: The ox knoweth his owner etc.

An aged neighbor in Providence, who has children and grand-children, and never as yet partook of the Holy Supper, became attentive to his heart and to the Word of God, through a sickness of ten years duration. He certified that he had been baptized in Europe, and instructed in Christianity, but never yet became so heedful as during his protracted illness. As it seems, the Word of God attains in him more and more an appropriation and a power. As often as my worthy colleague, Mr. Brunnholtz, visited me, so often has he also had edifying conversation with this man, and refreshed himself with him. He confessed that he had for the most part forgotten the instruction of his youth, and in his sickness, as a pupil entered quite anew into the holy Scriptures. When he would promote his eternal well-being, he finds in it a plain, even, although narrow way. He knew of no other way for re-union with God than that he, with acknowledgment, confession, repentance and sorrow for his sins, return, and by asking, seeking and knocking, seek pardon and peace through Jesus Christ the Kinsman. He hoped that God would not reject, but graciously receive him. As he could do nothing by his own strength, God would more and more come to his aid by his Holy Spirit and his powerful word. In this frame of mind he is at present, and thinks that the Holy Supper would be a good means to strengthen his weak faith, and to aid him to a closer union with the most blessed God. I have seen what guide is found under such circumstances by an otherwise sensible person, who, by outward and inward affliction, is driven to the holy Word of God, if he reads and considers the holy Word of God without falseness. When I visited him at another time, he said the Lord Jesus appeared to him in a dream, and had commanded him to receive the Holy Supper. I answered him that he must be very cautious and circumspect with dreams. For although God in former times revealed one thing and another in an extraordinary manner by dreams, yet, in these times, he does not require us to wait for this, but has given us a sure word of prophecy, whereunto we should give heed, 2 Pet. i. 19. His dream was not to be condemned, because it accorded with the Word of God, and gave witness that his mind had been occupied during the day with such edifying matters. God did not need specially to reveal it to him in a dream, that he must partake of the Lord's Supper, because he had before already clearly commanded it in his Word. He might perhaps at another time dream something that ran counter to the Word of God, and be injurious to his soul. He should therefore always let God's Word be the foundation and only guide of his faith and life; thus should he continue on the right way. Afterwards, his illness increased, so that he thought his end was near. As he manifested a desire for the Holy Supper, I administered it to him. But he still lives, and still searches further into the Scriptures, because they give him spirit and life.

A man from the mountains above New Hanover, who professes the Evangelical Lutheran religion, but may as yet possess little living knowledge of the power of the gospel, came to me and complained that his wife was melancholy and pensive. The woman sometimes entered her chamber or the forest alone, and prayed on her knees. The neighbors in part had evil thoughts about his wife, as if she must have committed some gross crime or wickedness in Germany. When I questioned the woman herself, she acknowledged that she had a small number of unraised children around her, sat there in the wild thickets alone, as her husband must follow his trade round about, and earn his bread, but that she knew of no other melancholy than this: that God's Word, which she occasionally hears in church and reads at home, has become alive in her soul. She had indeed committed no gross offence according to the letter of the Ten Commandments, as the neighbors thought, but she knew that the law is spiritual, and that she according to it was a great sinner, and worthy of condemnation. In this condition, she knew of no better counsel and refuge than the sufficient propitiatory sacrifice of Jesus Christ. She therefore sought in silence, by prayer and supplication, grace and peace from God the Father, through our Lord Jesus Christ; and she was also concerned for her children. I gave her further instruction and prayed with her, and also said to her husband that he should treat his wife circumspectly, for it was no melancholy, but a godly sorrow, which worketh a repentance unto salvation, which no one repenteth of, and which he must also experience, if he would be saved.

A man who was born in this country, of Low Dutch parentage, lives three miles from me, and two years ago was instructed and baptized by me, together with five children, nearly all of adult age, earnestly desired that he also might come to the Holy Supper with his family. His wife is a preacher's daughter from Germany, and came into this country together with her mother, after she became a widow, and one sister. In Germany, this widow and her daughters, as they say, heard many good admonitions to a true Christianity; but here in this country, they strayed like lost sheep without a shepherd, and also had not partaken of the Holy Supper. Amid emotion and tears, mother, daughters, and son-in-law were prepared with exhortation and prayer, made a confession of their sins and of their faith in Jesus Christ, and received the Holy Supper to their and my special edification. They, and particularly the man, were sorry for the time spent in ignorance. The man confessed that in his former years he lived in a heathenish manner, and was given to drunkennesss and lusts. But now he leads a Christian life, and permits the Spirit of God to work in him, through his Word and means of grace. He is indeed weak as yet as a new-born child, and it grieves him when he is scoffed at and derided by some ignorant persons on account of his change, but he has still been faithful hitherto, and eager for the sincere milk of the gospel. Those people who submit to the arrangement of God, hold to the church, acknowledge and accept the Word of God and the Holy Sacraments as necessary means to repentance and salvation, are despised by others, who do not esteem these things, and yet live well by their temporal possessions. There are very many in this country who adapt themselves to the Quaker form, and contemn churches, preachers, sacraments, and the like, with the pretence that such things are inventions whereby the preachers obtain their bread. The poor people do not value and understand God's Word, and are confirmed in their sins by the perverted religious disputes and scoffings.

In the month of March I made a journey to the Northwestern mountains, fifty English miles from Providence. Many German people live there poorly and scantily, and have want in both spiritual and bodily nourishment. As several of our poor members moved to that place, and called to mind their divine service, they invited me to pay them a visit. Many grow wild, and no longer value churches and schools. Others employ such men who have set themselves up as preachers. Others still seek something edifying, and will have nothing to do with the self-constituted preachers, but fall on the other side, and attach themselves to the Herrnhuter of Bethlehem. My former hearers several times before sent men to me and asked for help. As I at this time had the assistant, Mr. Kurtz, with me, I sent him up several times, and through my father-in-law secured a little land from the proprietor for a church. On this land they were to build a wooden school-house or church. If in time they became able to keep a school-master, the children would thus first be assisted somewhat. The school-master was to read for them on Sundays, and I would visit them once or several times a year. It seemed as if they would for the most part agree, and approve of the proposal. They also began to build a wooden church. In the meantime, the Herrnhuter from Bethlehem diligently visited the place, drew those to them who were the richest, and persuaded them that they were the genuine Lutherans; also celebrated the Holy Supper with them according to the Lutheran mode, and sent a brother with his family to the families won over, who was to teach school. The other party seeing this, became exasperated, and employed reproachful expressions, and on this account the third party also withdrew. Now, though they had commenced to build the church, there has been no progress made, and the building begun stands there roofless until this day. Those inclined to the Herrnhuter are willing and able to finish the building, but on this condition, that it must be a Brethren church; but to this I did not consent, as the land is yet in my hand, and I have the hope in time to help the poor Lutherans with their building. At present I see no possibility of aiding such a ruined and distracted multitude, and of effecting an improvement, until the Lord provides me with means and ways, as yet unknown. On my present visit, I preached there, baptized several children, and exhorted my former members to a diligent reading of the Holy Scriptures and prayer; and on their suppliant entreaty and petition, I administered the Holy Supper to two aged people, whose children have associated themselves with the Herrnhuter, whereat they secretly wept, and received the Holy Supper in deepest reverence of heart, and promised to remain faithful to their only shepherd of souls, Jesus Christ, in life, in suffering, and in death.

The reasons we are invited to go to a distance, here and there, are the following: Our German Evangelical inhabitants, for the most part, came the latest into this province. The English and German Quakers, the Inspired, Mennonites, Separatists, and other such small sects, came in first, when the land was still very cheap. Those selected for themselves the best and richest tracts of land, and are now enriched. But in later years, after the poor Evangelicals also found the way, and numerously came into this country also, some perhaps here and there still found some of the good land. Most of them, however, had to serve for several years for their passage as manservants and maid-servants, and afterwards shift with the poor land, and eat their bread in the copious sweat of their brows. At length, also, not even poor land was any more to be had; therefore the poor rented the superfluous land from the rich. But the rich raised their rents so high that the poor were unable to bear it. Therefore they removed still further away, into the wild thickets. Those who still had somewhat of their own got other families, who were also obliged to remove further to move with them. Those who were in our congregations for a time, and from necessity had to go further, into the still uncultivated wilderness, sometimes wrote the most affecting letters, and bewailed their hunger after the Word of God. They also tell their neighbors how good it once was with them, and desire to hear once more words of life in the desert where there is no water. I have noticed that within the five years of my stay here, scarcely one-half of the first members in the country congregations are left. The other half is in part in eternity; most of them, however, moved away from forty to one hundred English miles, to the borders of Pennsylvania, to Maryland, and to Virginia.

In the meanwhile, the congregations did not decrease, but much more increased, as still more Germans arrived every year, and those remaining settled their children around them as far as they could find room and sustenance. But some too are perhaps wont to remove from our region, who have a disgust and are displeased with our churches and schools, and would rather live in darkness, where their works are not reproved by the light. In this manner we preachers far and near, must pass through honor and shame, through evil and good report; but rejoice in this, when the gospel is spread abroad and the name of the Lord is made known, and we long: "O that the evening came, when it shall be so light, and the bright lustre of the Spirit render us very compliant to thee. Yea, what more? That I might hear within, the night is past!"

In the months of April and May, besides my customary official labors, I was engaged with those in New Hanover and Providence who were being prepared for the Holy Supper. Among these, the following persons were remarkable beyond others in both congregations:

A woman whose father had been an exiled

Frenchman, of the so-called Huguenots. It is remarkable that such people, who were banished on account of the Protestant religion, and suffered much discomfort, so easily grow cold in this country, and permit their children and grand-children to grow up unbaptized, in darkness. The poor woman just mentioned had indeed been baptized in youth, but grew up without instruction and knowledge. After her marriage with a man who is a Lutheran, she diligently heard the Word of God, and at length obtained a longing desire for a nearer instruction for the Holy Supper. As much as she was able, with the consent of her husband, to leave her children and household work, she came diligently to instruction. She obtained an excellent knowledge of her ruined condition and of the grace of God in Christ Jesus; manifested repentance and sorrow for her sins, and a hunger and thirst after the righteousness and peace in Christ Jesus, and also promised with tears, that she would follow the guidance of the good Spirit, according to the Word of God, and by his aid remain faithful until death.

There was among the confirmants a young

person, who had been neglected in his youth as his parents were poor, and lived beyond the Schuylkill, where they had no school conveniences. The want of good schools is one of the saddest things, and one of the greatest obstacles in building up the kingdom of God. Quakers, Anabaptists and the like-minded are for the most part rich, and can keep schoolmasters at their own expense; but in their schools they will not permit the youth to be taught the catechism, or otherwise an order of salvation, but their children must merely learn to read, write and cipher with difficulty, so that they betimes engage in trade and commerce in the world. In relation to those of our religion, they are for the most part in want of good school teachers, as well as of the means to support them, and also of ability and willingness to labor with their children themselves. When such arrive, who had been half schoolmasters in Germany, they are apt to go far into the country, and report themselves as parsons. Others profess to be schoolmasters, and desire to earn their passage-money by keeping school, but have need that they should first go to school themselves. Our principal places have hitherto always had schools in winter. But it is highly inconvenient when the children must go to school in the rough winter season, from one to five English miles, especially as some of the parents are so poor that they cannot even provide their children with the necessary clothing thereto, much less make up the school money, and in addition the support of the preacher. The proprietor of the land, and other wealthy inhabitants draw the revenues and profits, but for the hurt of Joseph they are not grieved. If the dear God should once have helped us so far that we could have a free school in each principal church, a relief in many things would accrue to us. In summer it is also difficult to keep school, because on the one hand, the excessive heat and the painful torment of numberless flies render the children indolent and displeased; and on the other, the parents cannot do without their children who are able to work, and the schoolmasters cannot live from a few children. But to return to the before-mentioned youth; he had indeed been neglected, but was of a pliant and studious mind. On each occasion, he attentively listened to the instruction, and drank in the sincere milk of the Gospel, like a new-born child, and also renewed his baptismal covenant before God with many tears.

Among the number of those who were confirmed was a married woman, who was publicly baptized by me two years before. She wept bitterly, that she could not love the Lord Jesus so heartily since her baptism, as he loved her; and asked for more strength and faithfulness, that she might follow her soul's bridegroom, unmoved and undefiled in love and in sorrow, and, as a wise virgin, watch for his coming. As far as I know her, she leads a quiet and godly life, and prepares for eternity.

There was among them a widow's daughter of sixteen years, who desired to go to the Holy Supper with us, but who, not understanding the German language, was instructed in English by me. By the grace of God, I brought her on so far that she was enabled to make her confession of faith, and renew her baptismal covenant along with the rest, before the congregation. As much as I observed in her, she attained not only to a theoretical knowledge, but her heart also felt something of the power of a living faith in the great surety and mediator Jesus Christ, and also permitted the purpose to work in her, to deny herself, to take up his cross and follow him.

Likewise a young person of twenty-five years, who has friends living here, came over from Jersey, and desired instruction for the Holy Supper. But he was master neither of the German nor of the English language, and therefore I had to instruct and confirm him in Dutch. He improved very much in a short time. He had a pliant and hungry heart, and as I afterwards heard from his neighbors, he leads a blameless life, and walks in a manner worthy of his calling.

An unmarried woman of twenty-one years also announced herself, and desired instruction unto confirmation and for partaking of the Holy Supper. The gracious God led this person in an extraordinary way. From her youth, she remained at one place, where the greater number are scoffers. The father of this person was much grieved that his child fell among such people, but could not get her away, as, according to the English law, the parents cannot command their daughters when over eighteen years of age. She was also already engaged to an unbaptized Pennsylvanian, and desired to remain there. When she thought herself most secure, a terror suddenly seized her, as from an apparition, as she said, whereat she and another woman who was with her were both taken with epilepsy. The attack was very severe, and now her father was permitted to visit her. He asked me for medicine for this grievous disease, and as I had some, but very little, of a certain epileptic powder remaining, which was sent to me for poor people by a patroness of distinction, I gave it, and let him use it. This blessed powder helped the poor person, so that she obtained relief for half a year. Although she was very much prejudiced against me and the church, necessity obliged her to come to her father, and visit the church with him. She heard the Word of God with attention; still her heart and desire ever turned back to her former place. After half a year the epilepsy returned, and continues until this day. Affliction taught her to give heed to the word, and God's Word and his Spirit connected therewith also wrought repentance and faith in the Lord

Jesus Christ. She has attained to an excellent knowledge, knows also how to praise God, that he humbled her, and led her to repentance through severity and affliction. Her heart is broken, and faith, *inter terrores conscientiæ*, *i. e.*, amid the anguish of conscience, was born. Her mouth is full of praise and glorifying of God and her Saviour.

A married English woman made known her desire for confirmation and the Holy Supper. But as she lives about six English miles from the church, and has several young children around her, and also to overlook her housework, she could not come to instruction as often as she wished. She is of Quaker parentage, and in her youth was kept to reading, but knew little or nothing of God and the way of salvation. Now as she at a suitable age was married to a German, whose parents lived in Halle and in Voigtland, and still retained some feeling of piety, he sought to win his heathenish wife with love, and bought her an English New Testament. The woman read it diligently, and became still more eager for it. She had had but little direction, and yet, after diligent searching, soon found what the calamitous fall of man effected in her, and how necessary to her was a mediator, deliverer and Saviour; how God from infinite love ordained his Son for the salvation of fallen mankind, and through his sufferings and death found an eternal redemption; and how and in what order the Son of God would lead fallen man to the enjoyment and possession of the purchased redemption. When she in simplicity had comprehended the principal things concerning creation, preservation, the fall of man, redemption and sanctification, she desired through faith and holy baptism to be translated into the right and enjoyment of the blessings of salvation purchased by Christ, and to be made meet for a new life and behavior. Since she had attained to this several years ago, she now also desired to experience that which her Saviour from infinite tender love bequeathed to her and other fellow-Christians in his last Testament. From the Old Testament, she had read very little, but could give a reason for her faith and hope from the New Testament. During instruction, I prayed with her several times, and found her much affected, and sighing before God with tears.

Among other things, it was edifying to me that she said: that she indeed did not yet know how sensibly the Lord Jesus would reveal and impart himself to her in the Holy Supper, as she as yet had never received it, and felt indeed her great unworthiness and her nakedness before her Saviour, but would not enter into many speculations, but simply go and take, because the Lord Jesus commanded her. If her master had commanded that she should pass through fire from love to him, she must; yea, and would gladly do it, on his word and power. Wherefore then should she not come, when he has invited her to a banquet so blessed, in remembrance of him, and for her encouragement? She was confirmed, and partook of the Holy Supper with our small number of English in New Hanover, with reverence and devotion.

The son of a warden, 16 years of age, was remarkable among the persons confirmed. He was an uncommon youth, of whom we should almost suppose that he still stood in his baptismal grace. As much as I heard from his parents and neighbors during instruction, he had his pleasure in the Word of God, and according to his ability meditated on it very diligently. In case he found a suitable place in the house, there he portrayed a strong passage of the Bible with legible letters, which he had learnt without instruction. He is very quiet in his behavior, follows the guidance of the Holy Spirit, hates that which is evil, and loves that which is good. Towards his parents he shows himself respectful and obedient; towards his brothers and sisters kind, and exhorts them to that which is good. Towards his fellow-men he is discreet and humble. In the work of his calling he is faithful and industrious, and in special prayer, unwearied. When other young folks would entice him and draw him into their vain company, he reproves them from the Word of God. When his father occasionally gives him an hour for recreation, he exercises himself in mechanics, and makes various patterns and draughts of his own invention. May God preserve this excellent soul from the depths of Satan, and keep him in his grace!

A man from the New Hanover congregation had three children, viz., daughters, confirmed. They had been much neglected in their younger years ; partly because the father had not much regard for the Word of God, and partly because he, on account of poverty, had to permit the children to serve with other people, who were still less concerned about the salvation of the souls of the children. The man was the son of a landlord of distinction in Germany, and had married an old preacher's daughter in this country. They both fell into poverty and debt, as they were not much adapted to the hard work and housekeeping of this country. In these circumstances, as they had no living knowledge of God, and could not get along well in temporal things, they lived very discordantly and sinfully in wedlock, and thereby gave their children a bad example. But since I am here they have come diligently to hear the Word of God, and have also purchased a Bible for the family. By diligently reading in it, the man was brought to a saving knowledge and into better ways, and now begins to be a family preacher. They both assured me before God that they experience repentance and sorrow for their past sins and ignorance, and ask God the Father that he would for Jesus Christ's sake pardon all their sins, and give his Holy Spirit unto a better life! The wife said to me particularly, that she thanked her dear Heavenly Father many thousand times that he awakened our highly venerable fathers and patrons in Europe to care for the salvation of the souls of the poor, and that he also gave them a Bible in the house. For since they diligently heard and read the Word of God and with it prayed, they came as it were from darkness into the light, and from death unto life. The husband also said, that he could not sufficiently admire the mercy and patience of God, which with great long-suffering waited for him so long in the blindness and slavery of Satan, and in forbearance tolerated him. He now forgets all his poverty and affliction, because each day he becomes richer in Jesus Christ. Several scoffers have already at different times treated him with contumely, and said: he will now at once become rich and pay off all his debts, as he attached himself to the Lutheran Church and parsons. He answered them, that he loved his preachers, because they besought him, in Christ's stead, to be reconciled with God. In respect to his temporal poverty, since he with his family turned to God, he had already noticed much relief in his temporal affairs, and also more blessing, and already paid off many an old debt. God, who had given him his Son, would also in things temporal, neither forsake nor neglect him. The more he hitherto sought for the kingdom of God and his righteousness, the more blessedly the other things were added to him, according to his need. He labors diligently with his neglected children, who, by the grace of God, are beginning to rise up again like withered plants after a gentle rain. Oh Lord give thy increase!

In the month of June, I was invited to undertake a journey through Pennsylvania to Maryland, after I had with God's aid passed through Whitsuntide in good health, and abundant official labor in both congregations, amidst large assemblies of people.

On the 10th of June, I, in company with J. L., the schoolmaster in New Hanover, set out, and eight miles from the place stopped with an aged so-called Newborn, who some twenty and odd years ago, married a widow with whom he had five children whom the mother, as adults, against the father's will, in the first years, gave over to me for instruction and holy baptism, and for this reason had to suffer much from her husband. The old man alleges that he was born anew in the Palatinate. The tokens of this birth however extend no further, according to his oft-repeated assertion, than that he separated himself from the Reformed Church and the Sacraments, and was unwilling to take the oath of allegiance to the Elector who attained to the government at that time, for which he with others was called before the Consistory, imprisoned, and in his opinion persecuted for the sake of Christ and the truth. He accepts neither proof from reason, nor the higher revelation, according to all its parts and in its whole import. He also refuses to be instructed, as he is of weak understanding, of obstinate self-will, and violent passions, and abuses Pennsylvania liberty injuriously. After he came into this country he united himself with a sect which is called the Newborn. These professed a new birth, which they obtain suddenly, by a direct inspiration, visions from heaven, dreams, and such like. When they have gained the new birth in this manner, they are, according to their conceit, God and Christ, and also can sin and err no more. Therefore, they use the Holy Word of God no further than just that which seems to favor their false positions. The Holy Sacraments are to them ridiculous, and their expressions concerning these are in the highest degree vexatious. The woman, as she said, imprudently took the afore-mentioned man in marriage, and thereby prepared a rod for herself. When the five children were for the most part grown up, and the mother was again awakened to repentance and faith by a diligent hearing of the Word of God, she industriously instructed her children in secret and sent one after the other to our school, until at length they were baptized before the congregation in New Hanover. What they had to suffer on this account, was all for the best for them. The oldest daughter was grown, and was quiet and retired. This was observed by a young widower, A. E., who for several years had been a teacher among the Herrnhuter, who is also mentioned in the seven printed conferences of Count von Zinzendorf. Count von Zinzendorf had married him to the only daughter of an old separated friend, and as the father related to me, with the following brief negotiations, viz.: Benedict! I give your daughter to E., you and your wife I take along with me to Germany, and your estate belongs to the Saviour! He could not retain the daughter, as he with a good intention had already committed himself too far. But that the Count would even have the little estate in addition, which has cost the man his sweat and blood, was such a hard requirement, and made such a deep impression upon him, that he with his wife gradually returned again, and thought it was sufficient to give up his daughter. Now the important brother E. had to be preacher in the country, and then again in Philadelphia, and his young wife had to be a female elder. Their circumstances required large expense and their income was small, and for this reason the daughter came to the parents once and again, and had her pockets filled. At length the parents grew tired of this, and said to their son-in-law that he should lay aside his preaching and elder's office and follow his trade of shoe-making, so that he might properly support his wife and children.

Necessity also drove him thereto, and the parents were again helpful, so that the young people purchased a piece of land in the mountains, six miles from New Hanover. The old people were glad that their son-in-law was compelled from necessity to separate himself from his brethren for a time. They sold their land in New Hanover, and also built a house on the children's place, in the hope of establishing a little congregation of their own among themselves. Scarcely had they commenced building when the only daughter died, and soon after the mother also. Now both the old as well as the young widower, were obliged to look around for wives. The latter, as mentioned, applied to the daughter of the aforesaid Newborn and persuaded her with the promise that he would not disturb her in her religion, but rather be helpful to her, until she promised him marriage. The contract was closed with the consent of the parents. Now the question was, where should the couple be married? The bridegroom had already been disobedient to his brethren in many things, and was afraid he might increase his indebtedness with them, if he permitted me to join him in marriage. But as mother and daughter insisted that I should do it with the object of withdrawing him still more from the Herrnhuter party, they at length succeeded so far, that the young people were regularly published in our church, and to-day, June the 10th, they were married in the country. As much as I observed afterwards, he still lives in his retirement, but now and then permits his wife to come to church. The first father-in-law still lived with him in the country for a short time, but in his own house. At length he also took an aged widow in second marriage and finally left his house, again purchased a place for himself in New Hanover, and now occasionally comes to our church, as he well perceives that the separating of one's self from the Word of God, and the holy Sacraments is profitless. Otherwise he was of the Separatists who call themselves the silent in the land, but who for the most part, become so quiet, that they fall quite asleep.

In the afternoon of the aforementioned 10th of June, I traveled five English miles further, to an aged God-fearing widow, who, with her family and neighbors, longingly waited for us, and desired instruction. The widow had examined herself, and desired the Holy Supper, which was administered to her, together with two old men, after admonition and confession before God. Two aged married people, who lived far from the church, among many scoffers, and were very cold and dead, revived again by the word of him who will not wholly extinguish the glimmering wick. They promised with tears to use the means of grace, and to follow the good Spirit, working by those means. God be praised, who has given strength to their good purpose; as we see that they walk conformably thereto.

In the evening we rode nine miles further, and remained over night with an old inhabitant of our church communion. The man had long already rejoiced at our coming, and edified himself with us by prayer and spiritual conversation. God awakened this man in his old age, and he now seeks the one thing needful, and rejoices much when he finds opportunity to talk with us of the progress in Christianity. When his strength admits of it, the road to meeting of fifteen to twenty-four English miles to New Hanover or

Providence is not too fatiguing for him, because the delight in the worship of God outweighs all difficulties with him. He humbly thanks God, who has awakened so many dear children of God and patrons in Europe, to make and forward the arrangement, that salvation may be offered to the dispersed sinners in this land.

On the 11th of June we traveled eight miles further, to a place where the Lutherans and Reformed built a church together, and had already quarreled much with each other. Those of both religions are inter-married in this country. Now both parties have already made the attempt here and there, and built a union church. But as this place is far off, so that those of our faith there cannot well be cared for by us, and they also are unable to support regular preachers as in other places, they, as well as the Reformed, have made choice of those schoolmasters as preachers who came of their own accord, and say that they would rather have something than nothing at all, as otherwise, the people would become scattered among strange sects. Such preachers are generally unconverted and uneducated. They are ignorant of the fundamental truths of religion, and foolishly wrangle about external things and ceremonies. Thereby quarrels and hatreds arise among married people, neighbors, friends and relations. The other sects profit by this, and from such individual cases, form an opinion of the whole. This little church began in strife, and so ended, and as yet, there was no assignment made in writing, either of the church-land or of the building itself. Now as both parties requested me to prepare an assignment of the church-land and building, and I, thinking of the future, when perhaps regular teachers could be brought thither, arranged matters according to the laws of this country, and admonished both parties to true repentance, faith and godliness. Their preachers, however, have continued the quarrel, and the Reformed, especially, were instigated to demand their building expenses again, and let the Lutherans alone have the church, who afterwards accepted a certain preacher who lived near it. In the afternoon we rode sixteen miles further up the country, and in the evening came to my father-in-law, Mr. Conrad Weiser, at Tulpehocken.

On the 12th of June, I edified myself with my numerous relationship.

On the 13th of June, I traveled up six miles further, preached a sermon on repentance, and had confessional examination with the members of the congregation who wished to receive the Holy Supper on the day following.

On the 14th of June, on Trinity Sunday, I preached before a large assemblage of people on the regular gospel, baptized several children, and administered the Holy Supper to upwards of two hundred persons. In regard to the congregation generally, I find many awakened souls in it, who should be led further on, and set in better order. Some seem truly eager for the sincere milk of the Word. Such, also, are indeed not wanting, who merely depend on the *opus operatum*, or doing of the outward work, and intrench themselves in this against the nearer conviction of the Holy Spirit. In general, however, they can judge of the delivery of the Word of God, as in the course of years they heard many preachers of various sorts, and in them may have had many taskmasters, but few fathers. "Lord Jesus Christ, help thy people, and bless thine inheritance!"

In the afternoon I rode aside eight or nine miles, to another congregation, who were very attentive, as I preached the Word of God to them. In that place, I had to publish that in three weeks the Holy Supper would be administered, and several young people be confirmed. In view of this, they were heartily admonished to repentance, and to reconciliation with God. After the sermon, one soul and another said to me, that by the preaching of Mr. Kurtz, they were awakened from their sleep of sin to repentance and sorrow for sin, and to a hunger and thirst after righteousness, and are willing also not to rest until they had found the free open fountain for sin and uncleanness. In relation to the other external circumstances: the principal congregation there was just engaged in building. In the first place, a few years ago they built a fine stone church, chiefly by their own means. As yet they owed somewhat on it, and had no pews in it; but for this, Mr. Weiser advanced the money. Afterwards, they purchased nearly twenty acres of land at the church, that in time a preacher might keep a horse and cow. As they now had hope of getting Mr. Kurtz or some other preacher of our college, and retain him, they resolved to build a stone parsonage, which they had already actually commenced, and which cost the kind-hearted people much labor, and many mites taken from their means of support. In addition to this, they also provide for the support of the preacher as well as any congregation in the country, and, as they say, they do all joyfully, if they can only have a true pastor living among them. May the chief Shepherd Jesus Christ paternally care for them, and ordain a man for that place (Tulpehocken) according to his heart!

From the 15th to the 18th of June, I instructed several young persons who wished to be confirmed, as the assistant, Mr. Kurtz, during my absence, attended to my congregations in New Hanover and Providence.

On the 19th of June, we traveled from Tulpehocken towards the town of Lancaster, and arrived there in the evening. On the way, a landlord told us that a few days before, those people, both in town and its neighborhood, whom Mr. Nyberg had recruited for the Herrnhuter, had gone to Bethlehem, to be present at a solemnity.

On the 20th of June, I visited several wardens and elders, and inquired after the condition of their souls and the state of the congretion. In whole and in part, alas! things seemed sad and disordered. The otherwise numerous Evangelical Lutheran congregation was now wholly divided. The greater number maintained the Church and its rights, and from necessity with our consent, was attended to by the assistant, Mr. Kurtz, from Tulpehocken, as the Swedish preacher from Philadelphia would serve them no longer, and we could not visit them often without injury to, and neglect of our own congregations. About eight or ten of the richest families were led to the Herrnhuter sect by Mr. Nyberg. They separated themselves from the Church, as they were unable to get the mastery of it by force and fraud. These had in a short time and in great heat built a new Moravian stone church, in which, according to their rules, Mr. Nyberg and other impartial, *i. e.*, Herrnhuter teachers, but none of us, should have liberty to teach. In this church Mr. Nyberg preached the Herrnhuter principles more boldly than before, and yet pretended with all to be called a genuine Lutheran preacher. At that time a Reformed preacher, Jacob Lischy, preached alternately with him the very same doctrines. At length Bishop Kammerhof and others like him were there also, the better to regulate the new brethren. Mr. Kurtz preaches two Sundays for the Lutheran congregation, and two Sundays he must again be in Tulpehocken, when the congregation in Lancaster is without a sermon. Now, when no one is present on the two Sundays, some of our number go to the Moravian church, as they wish to hear something every Sunday, and also to be incited in every imaginable, manner. The Lutheran congregation keeps a schoolmaster, but he is incapable, and has but few pupils. The Herrnhuter have one or perhaps two schoolmasters from Bethlehem, and attract many children to them. Oh! God! how much strife, contention and uncharitable judging have not hitherto prevailed among both parties, so that true repentance, faith and godliness are wholly forgotten! If we speak of such important and most necessary articles, the Herrnhuter scoff and say, that is Halleish, and the wild and untaught Lutherans are immediately alarmed lest we become like the Herrnhuter, when we seek to turn them to God, and say that they must become silent, after the long noise and strife. The common people are becoming wholly wild and obstinate, as they are without a regular and constant teacher, and no discipline and order can be maintained. In a word, it seems as though all would go to destruction, notwithstanding our many troubles and afflictions which we must suffer in that place. My heart aches within me, when I must be here several days and see and hear the misery.

On the 21st of June, on the first Sunday after Trinity, I preached in the church in Lancaster, catechised the youth, baptized children, and permitted the congregation to elect one warden, as one had died. Some of the old wardens and elders wished to resign, as strife had arisen among them. But I did not find it expedient for them to do so, but exhorted them to remain for the present, until more favorable times, as I feared the already divided congregation might receive still more rents. In the afternoon I had to travel twenty-two English miles further, as I had promised to preach in

Maryland on the 24th of June. Ten miles from Lancaster we came to the broad river called Susquehanna. On this river, which is one mile and a half wide, a violent storm arose, which threatened danger. But God heard our prayer and helped us safely over. During the night we rode to the town recently located in Pennsylvania, called York. In part, the people yet ran together at midnight and rejoiced at my arrival, and expected that I would administer the Holy Supper to them on the following Sunday, as was already long promised. I was now in the district where the Lutheran congregations commissioned Mr. Nyberg, when they yet regarded him as a genuine Lutheran, to write in their behalf to Sweden for orthodox preachers. Mr. Nyberg had promised them to get such an one, who was still better than himself. Meanwhile, he diligently visited the congregations even into Maryland, and also awakened one soul and another by his lively discourse. Now, when he thought that his party was sufficiently strong, he attempted to introduce two of the brothers from Bethlehem here, as well as in Maryland. But the opposing party was unexpectedly too strong, resisted and said: That they desired Lutheran preachers from Sweden, and not Herrnhuter from Bethlehem;—whereupon a great division arose. Those people who were awakened according to his method, adhered strongly to him, desired to live with him and to die with him, and after his persuasion they said we were false teachers. The strongest party, notwithstanding, locked their churches against him, and said they would hold to our college. In the meanwhile, the Nyberg party was supported and strengthened by the before said Reformed preacher, Jacob Lischy, and others from Bethlehem. The former had already labored for some time in the Reformed congregations in this district. But after it became known that he thought like the Herrnhuter, his congregations here also became divided. On account of this state of affairs, I found myself in great difficulty at times. The awakened souls on both sides seemed to hunger, and also loved my discourse, except the words, law, repentance, prayer, combat and such like, which the Herrnhuter-minded could not bear, although I presented the matter clearly enough to them, from the Holy

Scriptures and from our books of faith; and when, from pressing necessity, I testified against Nyberg and other Herrnhuter, they regarded this almost as a sin against the Holy Spirit. In the largest party I found with pleasure, that by the contentions they were vigorously driven to the Bible and catechism, for opposition teaches attention to the Word. Their zeal for orthodoxy was also worthy of praise; if it had only always remained within the proper bounds of moderation, and the pure doctrine, accompanied by a holy life. In the mean time, I can give assurance, that some of our people, in the most dangerous disputes with the disguised Herrnhuter, have conducted themselves in a manner so steadfast, Christian, temperate and wise, that we must attribute it to the special grace of God, which preserves the simple.

On the 22d of June, we traveled twenty-one miles further, to the outermost place of Pennsylvania, where I also met with a congregation in a like pitiable disorder. Some wardens and elders adhered to Mr. Nyberg, and others were against him. I sought in love to unite them, and promised that they should be visited now and then when one of us came to York, and, if possible, I would, according to their desire, direct a schoolmaster to them, who could care for their poor youth, and read a sermon for the old. Some of Nyberg's adherents complained that for a time the others had to do with a certain imposter, Carl Rudolph, and had him for their preacher. The others said that in the beginning he seemed to be pious, and exhibited to them great seals and letters as testimonials of ordination. But when they perceived his godless life, they immediately drove him away.

On the 23d of June, I preached there in a large barn, because many people had assembled from far and near. Some requested the Holy Supper, but I said to them that they must before be better led to repentance, and to this end, be instructed in the Word of God. The little children whom they brought were baptized and the parents and sponsors heartily admonished in reference to their duties. I there found several acquaintances, who in the first years had been my members. They wept for joy, because they again heard the Word of God, and complained that they were wholly deprived of the means of grace. Two men from Maryland were also present here to fetch me, to show me the way and for company. In the afternoon at 2 o'clock, I rode away with them from this place, to go thirty-six miles further. It immediately began to rain violently. On account of the heavy rain and the deep roads we got no further by daylight than eighteen miles, and also found no house at which we could stop. Night overtook us in the wilderness. The rain became still more violent and the roads deeper, so that our poor horses had to wade in water and mud over their knees. Half-dead and wholly fatigued, we at length reached our quarters about 2 o'clock at night, and by the mercy of God we safely passed over the thirty-six miles without stopping, amid constant violent showers of rain, and through morass and stream. I now was in the region of the Monocacy, whereof the Herrnhuter have made so much boast in their relations. Here I found a wooden church, and two parties in the congregation. Some had associated themselves with the Herrnhuter, and were hitherto served by one of their teachers, Mr. Nicky, who when I came, had just traveled back to Bethlehem. The other party had the before-mentioned imposter, Carl Rudolph, as preacher, but had dismissed him again some time before. The latter party had just the same experiences with Mr. Nyberg, which those of York and Conewago had, and at length also locked the church against him, when he endeavored to introduce a Herrnhuter brother as a Lutheran preacher. They had now already for nearly a year anxiously petitioned that one of our Ministerium might come and administer the Holy Supper to them. We could not refuse their call, because since they left Mr. Nyberg and Carl Rudolph, they held to us, and from love also, contributed a mite to the church building in Germantown. My arrival was to them very delightful and joyful, but I was grieved in heart as I saw the injurious division, and found that those on both sides had dealt hard and uncharitably with each other.

On the 24th of June the violent rain still continued. We went to church, where most of our Lutherans were present. Three or four of the Herrnhuter-minded also appeared. Before beginning divine service, the church book, at my request was handed to me, and I wrote several propositions and articles in it, in the English language; among others, of the following import: That our German Lutherans acknowledge the Holy Word of God in the writings of the prophets and apostles, and also, the unaltered Augsburg Confession and the rest of the symbolical books; and when possible, have the Sacraments administered to them, according to these by regularly called and ordained preachers; and who, according to their rules, did not allow open, gross and wanton sinners against the holy ten commandments of God, and the laws of Christian governments to be regarded as members among them; and more of a similar import. This I publicly read to the congregation, and explained it to them in German, with this addition: whoever would be and remain such a Lutheran, should subscribe his name. Those Lutherans who were present subscribed readily. But when the turn of the Herrnhuter-minded came, they were unwilling to sign, but presented the following complaints: In general, they had observed all that before which I required in those articles written in the church-book.

For they had for several years past been deprived of regular teachers, and when, occasionally, a Swedish or German preacher from Pennsylvania visited them, he could not get money enough, and they also, on account of their poverty, could not raise enough, and thus at last the visits wholly ceased, and they, therefore, were obliged to call a Lutheran preacher from Bethlehem. Now they deem brother Nicky, whom they have hitherto had, a genuine teacher, according to the Word of God and the symbolical books; but when, some time ago, they wished to introduce him into the Lutheran church, the larger party resisted, and locked the church, and yet notwithstanding all this, permitted the before-mentioned imposter, Carl Rudolph, who was not ordained, false in doctrine and wicked in life, to officiate as preacher in the church. These circumstances, therefore, had obliged them to separate themselves from such a church, and to purchase a piece of land of their own, on which to build a church and a school. The others replied to this, and among other things said: that they knew of no Pennsylvania preachers who complained that they had not received money enough. I asked them altogether whether they meant me? Whether they had given me anything? Or whether I wished for anything from them? Both parties answered: no. In relation to other matters, I said to them they had erred on both sides, and given occasion to much calumny and scandal. The blessed Luther had given warning of a white and of a black devil, the emissaries of both did much harm. We afterwards sang a penitential hymn, and I preached on Luke xv., concerning the prodigal son. After the sermon, I asked the Herrnhuter-minded whether they desired to unite again with the rest, sign the articles in the church-book, and do better? They answered: yes, if I would remain there, and be preacher. I answered that this was not my calling, as they themselves well knew. But if they lived in harmony with each other, and had a true desire for an orthodox and pious teacher of our church, God would help and point out such an one as they needed. They answered that their brother Nicky from Bethlehem was such a man; that he preached just the same truths which I preached. The larger party rose, and asked permission to say a word, and with tolerable discretion, said: they had for the first time heard me preach to-day, and I had preached to them of repentance, faith and godliness. The Brethren, on the contrary, in their sermons, had nearly always scoffed at repentance, law, prayer, combat, and the like important truths. Avoiding all diffusiveness, I again asked whether they would separate themselves from the Herrnhuter party, and subscribe? They answered: not otherwise than before stated. After a short affecting address, and representation of the injurious consequences, I inquired of both parties whether they had personal hatred and enmity against each other, and would retain it? They yet charged each other with several hard expressions which they had formerly uttered in their dispute with each other, and forgave each other these, at least in word. Of the heart I cannot judge. The undersigned came together, elected wardens and elders among themselves, and promised according to said articles, to support the church and congregation according to their best knowledge and conscience. They afterwards once more affectingly entreated me for the Holy Supper, and said that they were almost forsaken, too far distant from the preachers, and as they had not partaken of the Holy Supper for a long time, they were hungering and thirsting for it. On my part, after much consideration, I could not find sufficient reasons wherefore I should wholly refuse the people. But, that I might not burden my conscience, I again publicly admonished them, in presence of the Herrnhuter, to true repentance and faith, touched their conscience as much as the Lord granted me grace, and directed them as weary and heavy laden to Jesus Christ and his righteousness and sanctification in following him. We humbled ourselves into the dust before the majesty of God, wrestled in prayer and supplication, knocked as we had ability, made confession, and then received the Holy Supper. My reasons for writing something in the church-book in this place, were the following: Wherever the Herrnhuter come to, they first seek to draw over to them the most honorable, the most pliant and the richest. As soon as they obtain a party in a place in this country, a strife of words, perhaps also of tumult and blows, begins about church and school buildings. Upon this follow the saddest divisions and quarrels between neighbors and relatives, parents and children, man and wife, brethren, brothers and sisters, whereto they misapply the beautiful passages, Matt. x. 34–37, but that which is written in Jer. xiv., 14, chap. xxiii. 21, Gal. v. 15, 2 Cor. xii. 20, they are unwilling to apply to themselves. The English authorities hear the tumult, strife and quarreling among the Germans everywhere, and do not rightly understand who is in fault. The Herrnhuter are able also so to calumniate and make offensive to the authorities the poor people who oppose their proceedings, and are unwilling to concede everything to them, as if they were the basest rebels against God and the laws of the country. Besides, the people have some laws and rules necessary among themselves, so that not every one according to his notion may pick up any vagrant as preacher, and thereby confuse and burden others. But alas! laws and articles and their signature are of little avail, if we cannot come to the help of the poor people with able and honest teachers. In the meanwhile it is very distressing, when we must see the sad state of affairs, and know not how to remedy them. I can testify in truth that I have as yet observed but little difference between the two parties. The party opposed to the Herrnhuter might perhaps with right be angry, but as they are as yet for the most part unconverted, so they, on their part also, are not without sin. They have, meanwhile, this benefit by it, that they are driven to the Bible and catechism, and we hope that the word may in time attain a happy vigor, if they should be served by able teachers of our church. The other party, which has united isself with the Herrnhuter, and the members of which esteem themselves far better and higher, are alas! just as well, base and corrupt enough. Although sins do not prevail with all in a gross form, they still love them, and they permit them to rule under the cloak of piety. The words and things of the law, repentance, faith, holiness, and conflict in prayer, are contemned both by beginners as well as by those who are advanced. Their faith rests for the most part on playful fancies and sensible feeling, and not upon the alone saving word of the prophets and apostles, of which Christ Jesus is the corner-stone. Their love is very partial. In a word, I found on my journey that they need true repentance and amendment, just as much as the eighteen on whom the tower of Siloam fell, Luke xiii. 4.

On the 25th of June, we rode up ten miles further, to a newly-located town, where several Lutherans are living who belong to the congregation, and who on the preceding day were unable to come on account of the heavy rain. The greater part of these signed the articles in the church-book, and elected several from among themselves as wardens and elders. Three or four persons had joined themselves to another man, who formerly represented himself as a preacher in New Hanover, who moved from there to Virginia, and now back again to Maryland. There was a large assemblage of English and German people in that place. At their earnest desire, and after preparation and prayer, I administered the Holy Supper to several Lutherans, baptized children, and joined two couples in marriage. Both those in the town and in the country entreated that I might consider their dispersion, poverty, and need of a teacher, and present their case to our highly venerable fathers. They would keep together as long as it was possible. In the evening, we rode back again the ten miles, to our former quarters, where several had assembled, with whom I edified myself with prayer and singing. They all much desired that God might grant them a true teacher.

On the 26th of June we returned. After we had proceeded several miles, an English gentleman met us, who was a patron and counselor of the small number of Herrnhuter. He invited me to his house, desired to converse with me, as many things may have been related to him concerning me. He gave us some refreshments, and inquired of me how I found the condition of the German church people in Maryland. I answered, that altogether they had need of experiencing and practicing more true repentance, living faith, and godliness. He said: The large party is still very wicked, and must experience this; but the small party loves the Saviour. I answered: We people are apt to see and judge by the appearance. God sees and judges at the same time, according to that which is within and without. He said: I love the Saviour, and all those who love him. I answered: If you love the true Saviour, you must keep his word, believe and live according to it; first have a universal love for friends and foes, and then a special love for the true followers of Christ. He presumed the Moravian brethren were followers of the Saviour. I answered: You must first receive more enlightenment, so that you may be able to understand the pure doctrine of the Saviour, in the whole and in every part; that you may be able to compare the system of doctrine of the Moravians closely with it, judging their faith and walk according to the doctrine of Christ; and after that, as a man who may err, decide cautiously. The Englishman said: The Moravian brethren are the only people who believe and live according to the articles of our English high church. I answered: When the chief of the Moravian brethren, viz., Count von Zinzendorf, and his people are in Russia, they believe and live just like the Greek Church. When they are in Catholic countries, they believe and teach that which the pope and the councils taught to their advantage. When they are in Switzerland, they live and believe according to the Synod of Berne. When they are in Sweden, they conceal themselves behind the Augsburg Confession; and when they have to do with the English, they just adapt themselves to the English articles. How can we say of such hypocrites, that they are the true followers of Christ? The Englishman hastily said: You are an enemy of the good people! I answered: I am no enemy of their persons, but of right I hate their crooked ways and methods. That which I said before, I can prove, partly by my own experience and partly by the writings of approved men. The Englishman replied: I have as yet found no people in my whole life who were so like the Saviour, in love, humility, gentleness, friendliness, and ardent desire to win souls. In our English church at home (*i. e.*, in old England) preachers and hearers are dead. Carl Rudolph, whom the Germans had here, was an adulterer, a striker, and a drunkard. I answered: To judge of a whole church so lightly is very dangerous. To draw a conclusion of the whole from individual cases, is not allowable; and in relation to Carl Rudolph, he is no regular preacher, but a vagrant and a cheat. And if you have known him and others as open sinners, still you must be cautious about the rest. There are three kinds of messengers. Those preachers who in their office live in open sin and vice, are gross servants of sin and embassadors of Satan; against these, an honest man in his natural state, not to say an enlightened man, may guard himself, so as not to follow their evil conduct. But Satan may also transform himself into an angel of light, and have messengers who, in the humility and spirituality of angels, go forth in hypocrisy and lies, and take men captive with excellent and sweet words, as you see in the apostolical letters; and these are the most dangerous for awakened, weak, and as yet unestablished children in Christianity. The third kind are the mediate messengers of Jesus Christ, who keep themselves close to the revealed will of God, believe it, teach pure doctrine, walk conformably to their calling, and also willingly suffer for it. Such, however, are not plentiful, because they do not run whither they are not sent; and that is the reason perhaps wherefore you have seen so few of them as yet. The

Englishman said: I hold the Moravian brethren to be the true messengers and servants of Christ, until I see the contrary. I answered: You have liberty to do so, on my account. Only thus much I desire, that you may seek the right way to heaven, through repentance, faith, and godliness, according to the infallible word of God; aye, and not permit yourself to be seduced into by-ways. The good Spirit of God has for this reason faithfully warned us, that we might learn wisdom from the loss of the misled Christians of that time. If we trust ourselves too much, and permit ourselves to be led upon all kinds of by-ways, we meanwhile neglect the precious season of grace, remain perhaps wholly in the years of apprenticeship, ever learning and never attaining to a true knowledge. The Englishman said: That is true. My only request and desire is this, that I may find the nearest and the safest way to the temporal and eternal welfare of myself and of my family, and to walk in it— not only begin, but also continue and persevere. I love all mankind, and especially those who with me seek the Lord Jesus, as the way, the truth, and the life. I also have sincere respect for those preachers who are faithful in their office, and seek to lead souls upon the true rock and foundation. I replied: This way you can most surely find, if you in simplicity permit yourself to be led by the Spirit of God through his word, and judge all human systems of doctrine and opinions you meet with by this holy rule. The Englishman inquired: But do you mean that the Moravian brethren have a system of doctrine contrary to the Word of God? I answered: They never as yet came forward so sincerely and honestly with a full confession of faith like our fathers in the Augsburg Confession, and your ancestors in their Articles, but have here and there set their sails according to the wind existing at the time, and published a part of their pretended doctrines; and if we take all the published parts together, there results a self-contradicting giving and taking, turning and twisting against the Word of God. But the last piece, viz., the twelfth appendix, to their collection of hymns, turned out the most impious of all. The Englishman asked: Can and will you show me this book? I answered: It is written in the German language, and must first be translated by an impartial man; when this is done, I will impart it to you. The Englishman said: Yet one thing would I request. When you have the opportunity to recommend a preacher for this place, seek and appoint a man who is impartial, and honestly teaches the principal doctrines of repentance and faith, and who also himself walks accordingly. I answered: I will present the matter to God and to my superiors. The Lord will order it aright. Farewell! We hereupon rode away from there, and towards evening again reached Conewago, where I had preached on the 23d of June.

On the 27th of June we continued our journey, and arrived in the town of York at about twelve o'clock, where the members of the congregation had assembled, and desired to have themselves recorded for the Lord's Supper. I went into the house of a warden, took those men and elders with me who had hitherto cared, and had been diligent that the church and congregation might not fall into the hands of the Herrnhuter. I requested that they should dismiss all scattering and contentious thoughts, and turn their hearts to God, and seek with him, through Jesus Christ, grace and the forgiveness of sin, and also impartially tell me, according to their best knowledge and consciousness, how each one had hitherto conducted himself who would now apply and come to the Holy Supper. Their aged schoolmaster, who had hitherto been diligent with the children, and also read sermons for them on Sundays, and thereby kept the congregation together, was also present, and was questioned concerning some complaints against him. On account of his faithfulness and firmness, he was a thorn in the eyes of the other party, who charged him with many gross sins and vices. On investigation, however, we found that in most cases he was blamed too much, and things said of him through hatred, although he himself confessed that he had once or twice offended. He promised to ask the dear God for a wholly new heart, and for his Holy Spirit, and to walk more circumspectly. One or more of the wardens had also been too passionate and loud in the Herrnhuter quarrel, for which they were reprimanded in love and gentleness, and their attention directed to the motive of the heart.

Now when those present, one after the other, gave in their names, there were found three sorts of persons. Of some it was testified that they hitherto diligently heard the Word of God, and had conducted themselves orderly and quietly. Of others it was said that they had hitherto lived in strife with their neighbors, and did not diligently hear the Word of God. Of such it was desired that they should come with their opponents and be reconciled. Some were reconciled, and promised to give room in their hearts to the Spirit of God and his Word, and to resist no longer. The Justice of the Peace was himself present, and complained of a quarrelsome neighbor; he, however, was rude and unruly, and was unwilling to show himself, and therefore was refused until amendment. The third kind were some who were somewhat awakened by the sermons of Mr. Nyberg and his adherents. The warden complained that they did not diligently come to the prelection on Sundays, but rather followed Nyberg and others. They answered: that the before-mentioned preachers moved their hearts. They were awakened from their sleep of sin by their discourse, acknowledged themselves as poor sinners before God, and desired nothing more than that they might become free from their sins, and receive strength unto a new life. They moreover certified that they had a desire for the Holy Supper, and not to turn away from the Evangelical religion, but that they were more established therein, as the Word of God and the catechism of Luther had now, for the first time, become truly tasteful to them. The wardens desired that they should promise that they would in future hold to their church better, and be present at the reading, and no more run after Mr. Nyberg. They replied that we should not bind them up so closely, and rob them of their liberty. But this they would promise, if a true teacher of our college came there and preached, it would be a joy to them to hear the same, and to follow them, in so far as they were the followers of Christ. In the reading of sermons, they found no power and no edification. Among these few persons, were two daughters of a widow, whose mother was present, and was asked how her daughters conducted themselves. She said that since the awakening, they diligently read in the Bible and catechism, also prayed in silence, and conducted themselves in a Christian-like manner. I well saw how matters stood on both sides, and therefore desired to speak with the wardens alone, and afterwards with these persons specially also. The wardens said they rejoiced when souls were awakened and led to better thoughts, but they had to be somewhat strict, else the congregation might become scattered; on the one hand, led to the Herrnhuter; and on the other hand, be driven to the ungodly preachers, such as Carl Rudolph and those like him who were in the neighborhood; and if this happened, the little harvest might be prevented, which we otherwise had hope for, if, in the course of time, a teacher from our board were sent to them. They had no enmity against Mr. Nyberg and other persons, and also loved their gifts. But as they were attached to the Herrnhuter sect, the awakened souls would not continue in their first simplicity, but would gradually be misled. I approved of this, and said they must nevertheless be somewhat circumspect, and spoil nothing on either side, as we generally find a clinging love in the first awakening between teachers and such hearers, which in the further growth is gradually corrected. In the meanwhile their intention and conduct were proper, as they did not act from personal hatred and enmity, but had for their object the true welfare of their congregation. I afterwards also spoke with the before-mentioned persons, admonished them to persevere in the good work, yea, diligently to prove all things by the Word of God and the catechism, and to build their house, not upon the sand and the opinions of men, but upon the true rock, Jesus Christ. From three to four of these people came to the Holy Supper, and several remained away. In the afternoon at 4 o'clock, we went to church, and had a blessed preparation on Matt. xi. 28, etc. The people were all very attentive and hungry, and drank or drew in the Word as the dry earth does a warm rain. After the preparatory service and confession, I took in hand the small number of young persons, whom the schoolmaster hitherto instructed with considerable diligence, for confirmation. I examined them in the Order of Salvation, and exhorted them to true repentance and a living faith, and to a renewal of their baptismal covenant, which was now publicly to take place. After divine service, I conversed particularly with several persons, who spoke of what had been chiefly edifying to them in the discourse, and inquired further concerning that which they did not understand. In the evening, I edified and refreshed myself in the house with the wardens and elders.

On the 28th of June, on Sunday morning early, several as yet applied for the Holy Supper who lived far away, and could not be present the day previous. Some few of Mr. Nyberg's adherents also yet announced themselves; but when we desired to give them an admonition, as the others, they showed themselves unruly, and remained away of their own accord. The church was too small for us on this occasion, and nearly one-half of the hearers had to stand on the outside, because a great multitude had come together from ten to twenty English miles. I first as yet had preparatory service and confession with those persons who last announced themselves, preached on the gospel of the Great Supper, baptized a considerable number of children after the sermon, examined and confirmed about fifteen young people amid many tears, administered the Holy Supper to two hundred communicants, and closed therewith the public Sunday labors, after the whole congregation had bowed the knee, and given thanks to the Father in Jesus Christ for all unmerited grace. In the evening, I was invited as guest by the Justice of Peace.

Early on the 29th of June, I held a prayer-meeting in the church, with the people of town present, and took an affecting leave of them. He that standeth may well take heed lest he fall, in such confused and critical times. We again crossed the Susquehanna safely, and ten miles from Lancaster were received by several wardens from that place, and escorted thither.

On the 30th of June, I had all the wardens and elders in Lancaster before me once more, and sought with much trouble to prevent and to remedy their seemingly dangerous rupture. Oh! Jesus, trample Satan under thy feet! About 12 o'clock at noon, we rode out of Lancaster, traveled thirty English miles, and in the evening arrived safely in Tulpehocken.

The 1st to the 3d of July I employed in the further instruction of several young persons who were to be confirmed on the next Sunday, and admitted to the Holy Supper. They were so far advanced, that of the most necessary articles of faith they could give a reason, and were not without some ability.

On the 4th of July, I traveled to a congregation belonging to Tulpehocken at Northkill, and had preparatory service and confession. Those present were tolerably attentive and affected. In the evening I rode back again.

In the forenoon of the 5th of July, I preached at Northkill on the Gospel Luke xv., of the sheep lost and found again, baptized several children, examined and confirmed the young people amid an extraordinary awakening of the congregation, administered the Holy Supper, and afterwards hastened eight miles further to the larger congregation, which had an appointment in the afternoon at 3 o'clock. I preached there, and took leave of the dear congregation, as I had now to return again to my regular congregations. When, after divine service, I returned to the house again, with my father-in-law, we met a little

king or chief of one of the savage nations.
He had with him on horseback a grown son
and son-in-law, and desired to confer with Mr.
Weiser concerning some land and military
affairs. A retinue of women and children on
foot had already gone before. When we look
at the poor people, we must deplore their
blindness and darkness in things spiritual;
and when they see us, they think we are to be
pitied, which is in so far true, as we have the
light, and yet for the most part love darkness
more than the light. The French papists, already
many years ago, made an attempt at
conversion among the northern savages of
Canada, but accomplished nothing, because one
and another of their missionaries offended
against the Sixth Commandment, whereof
they still recount the history and transmit it to
their posterity. According to the description
of Mr. Weiser, our savages are very wise and
sagacious in natural things, and although they
have no manner of writing among themselves,
yet they are enabled to know and to preserve
many historical facts which transpired long
ago, because they are diligently transmitted
and kept by oral tradition. Against white

people they generally have an inveterate prejudice and mistrust, and say the whites sprang out of the earth on the other side of the great sea, but they on this side. The white people should have remained on their ground from which they were taken, supported themselves there, and let them be unvisited on this side of the sea. They had come over here to them for no other object than to take away their land, diminish their chase and catch of fish and birds, and to make their livelihood more difficult. They also claim that their nations were much diminished by various kinds of death since they received strong drink from the whites. If we desired to present to them something of our revealed Word of God, the proper phrases are wanting in their language wherewith to express and make spiritual and heavenly truths understood. A natural theology, and the historical truths out of the Word of God, might with difficulty be effected with their language. Mr. Weiser once and again endeavored to tell them something out of the books of Moses. They answered: That may all be true which the Supreme Being revealed to the white people on the other side of the sea, but this does not concern us. Our God has revealed other things to us on this side. Attend to your, and we will attend to our affairs. When the English and French nations wage war against each other, they do not readily join themselves to one side, unless moved thereto by very large presents from the one party. They would rather remain neutral, take presents from both, and say: The white nations are never satisfied in this strange land on this side of the sea. Let them destroy each other, lest being once united among themselves, they wholly destroy the savages. Still they would rather see the English nation triumph and keep the upper hand, because they get their wares cheaper from them than from the French. Their history of times of peace and war, of alliances and treaties with the white nations, are transmitted by some aged, wise persons who can no longer support themselves. The young people occasionally meet together and let such an ancient professor of history sing the history for them, and in return for it they bring something from the chase for his support. They have certain tunes or kinds of melodies. According as the matter is joyful or sad or moderate, so is also the tone and the posture of the body; so that we find true natural orators among them. Mr. Weiser thinks that if we desired to make an attempt for their conversion, among many other rules we should have to observe the following: 1. One or several missionaries would have to live among them, seek to become master of their language, adopt as much of their customs, dress, and manner of living, as could be without sin; and as for the rest, rebuke their national vices by a holy walk. 2. They would have to translate the revealed truths into their language, and make things as plain as possible. 3. They would have to learn the Indian tunes and melodies, and present to them the law and the gospel in such tunes, so that it made an impression, and then, under God's blessing and aid, wait for the fruit in patience.

On the 7th of July, I again traveled with my companions to Providence, to my home, and found my worthy colleague, Mr. Brunnholtz, and pastor Hartwick, on a visit in my house. After a few days, my colleague, Mr. Brunnholtz, complained of an excitement in his blood, whereupon the measles showed themselves a few days after. We also ceased not publicly and privately to pray for his recovery, and employed such remedies as we had at hand. The gracious God granted a favorable termination, so that he soon recovered again, although he had been very sick. Otherwise, at this time, not a few young and strong people died with this malady. God, however, gave us the dear brother once more again, as we still need him so much. His holy name be praised for this! The assistant, Mr. Schaum, meanwhile attended to his official duties in Philadelphia and Germantown, and pastor Hartwick was also helpful. Nevertheless, the congregation longed soon again to see and to hear their regular shepherd.

Our assistant, Mr. Kurtz, had served the congregation in Tulpehocken from December, 1746, until now, as catechist, and had his residence and entertainment in the house of my father-in-law. The Swedish preacher in Philadelphia visited the rent congregation in Lancaster once every month. In the meantime, a long Rescript from the Archbishop of Sweden and from the chief consistory had arrived from Sweden, as an answer to the report which Mr. Peter Kock had sent to Sweden concerning the conduct of Mr. Nyberg. The doctrine of the Herrnhuter was declared erroneous in the same, and the acts of Mr. Nyberg much condemned. Our dear pastor Brunnholtz and the Swedish preacher translated said Rescript into German, and the latter read it publicly to the congregation in Lancaster. But as the German language was too inconvenient for the Swedish preacher, he resigned again after the lapse of several months. Now the poor congregation was again without a preacher. Mr. Weiser had to go to Lancaster at certain times, to hold court there with other magistrates. Now, as he knew of the sad condition of the Lutheran congregation in that place, he inquired of us whether he would be allowed to take Mr. Kurtz along with him for once, and permit him to preach there. We were agreed to this, and he took him along in the month of February, 1747. When Mr. Kurtz had preached there once, the wardens and elders gave us no rest until we finally consented that he might occasionally preach there. When this happened, the congregation was again drawn together, and the Herrnhuter-minded came diligently into the Lutheran church. The wardens and elders concluded, from the entrance of Mr. Kurtz, that their congregation might again get into a good condition if they had him as their preacher all alone. But we could not permit this for many reasons, although we had to yield so far that Mr. Kurtz should preach two Sundays in Tulpehocken and two Sundays in Lancaster. This was very burdensome for Mr. Kurtz, as the two places are thirty miles apart; still he continued it from May until into winter.

Many years ago, several Lutherans, among whom was Mr. Weiser, took up a small tract of land in Tulpehocken, and built thereon a wooden church, and by its side a schoolhouse. In the church they were wont to have reading on Sundays, and now and then permitted a traveling preacher to preach in it. After some time, a man named Caspar Lentbecker, a tailor by profession, came to Tulpehocken, continued the reading in the church, kept school also, and catechised. The united members of the congregation prepared a call for a preacher, and desired that Mr. Lentbecker should send it to the court preacher Ziegenhagen in London, and through him to forward it to Halle. In this they petitioned for an educated and pious preacher, whom they would support. When in the meanwhile some time had elapsed, Lentbecker himself began to preach, and alleged that a preacher named Bagenkopf, had been sent by way of Hamburg and London, but had died on sea. This, among other things, gave rise to the separation of Mr. Weiser and several others from Mr. Lentbecker's congregation, as they suspected some dishonesty with reference to the call, and the man began to exalt himself and to undertake something beyond his ability. Some ten or twelve families remained with Mr. Lentbecker and acknowledged him as their regular preacher, as he even alleged that he was ordained. Others still had to do with another known preacher, C. St. The former with his adherents, and the latter with his party, were almost always in strife with each other about the church, although the Lentbecker party retained the superiority. At length Count von Zinzendorf came into the country and also to

Tulpenocken, and stopped with Mr. Weiser, who, among other things related to him the condition and course of church affairs, and at the same time inquired whether the Count had a correspondence with the theologians in Halle. The Count said: Yes, he had himself studied in Halle, and stood in close connection with the theologians there; promised also to write for a preacher from there for Tulpehocken, and meanwhile to have the congregation served gratuitously by several brethren from Bethlehem, and also immediately sent one after the other there, but still only ad interim. Lentbecker had already died before, and his adherents immediately went with the Herrnhuter. The other party which had Mr. St., and at last V. K. as leaders, increased meanwhile, and when they saw that the Herrnhuter had the old church and school-house in possession, they sought another place three miles from the old, and began to lay the foundation for a stone church at their own expense. When I came into the country V. K. went to Lancaster and St. conducted himself badly, so that he was partly compelled to resign of his own accord, and partly removed by his wardens. Under these circumstances I was called to Tulpehocken for the first time in 1743, and found three parties there. Ten or twelve families had the old church in possession, and Herrnhuter brethren as teachers. Another small number still adhered to Mr. St. The third party held to the church newly begun, but were without a teacher. These last desired help from my superiors and from me. But I could as yet promise them nothing, as I was entirely alone, and Tulpehocken was too far distant from my congregations. Whereupon the party of the new church with my consent called, but only ad interim, another preacher, Mr. W., who had but recently arrived in the country. He was unable to unite the two other parties; consequently, his third party was too weak to support him with his large family. Meanwhile, they continually held on to me, that I should aid them in getting one of our newly arrived preachers, who was without a family. When Mr. W.'s, the last mentioned preacher's second year agreed upon was up, he resigned the congregation, and moved further down to other congregations. By this means, we were obliged to place Mr. Kurtz up there, as he had already been there several times on a visit, and was desired by all that he should move to that place, as above mentioned. In December, 1746, with proper instructions, we permitted the two congregations to have him as assistant, to preach and to catechise. He was received in great love, and esteemed by all the three parties. The congregation increased daily and was encouraged by Mr. Weiser to finish the church entirely, and to build a new parsonage near it. In the first winter, 1747, a man of the small number of the Herrnhuter died suddenly, *i. e.*, he owned a mill, and unawares got under the cog-wheel and was crushed. His grown sons were not as yet wholly Herrnhuter-minded, but mostly held to Mr. Kurtz, and wished to have him buried on the Herrnhuter church-yard. The Herrnhuter teacher, however, would not bury him, although the deceased had contributed much to the new church building during his life. Now when he refused, the sons asked Mr. Kurtz to bury their father on the Herrnhuter church-yard, and preach the funeral sermon in the church. Mr. Kurtz consented thereto, and went to the house of the deceased to attend to the funeral. The sons sent some one to the Herrnhuter preacher, and asked for the key to the church. He answered: Mr. Kurtz should first come to him in his house. Mr. Kurtz said: That he might come to him, to the house of the deceased, if he had aught to say; which however was not done. They went to the grave with the corpse, and sent once more for the church key, but none came. Now when they had buried the body, Mr. Kurtz had to preach in the snow at the grave, This conduct offended not only the sons of the deceased, but also some others; and on this account the whole little company of the Herrnhuter-minded fell into a bitter quarrel and dissension among themselves. The congregation at Bethlehem recalled their brother, the teacher from Tulpehocken, in haste, and Mr. Spangenberg, Kammerhof, and others, came themselves to extinguish the fire. But when they could not agree, and the one party asked Mr. Weiser for counsel and assistance, he advised that the church council of Mr. Kurtz's congregation should again take possession of the schoolhouse and place a lock on the new Zinzendorfer church, because the land was at first taken up for a Lutheran church and school-house, and was hitherto illegally held by the Herrnhuter. The advice was followed, and our congregation took possession. Many letters and embassies took place about this matter between the heads at Bethlehem and Mr. Weiser, until the former at length disavowed all friendship for Mr. Weiser. In the ensuing autumn of this year, 1747, my worthy colleague Mr. Brunnholtz, after he had regained the strength lost by sickness, undertook a congregational visitation to Lancaster, York, and Tulpehocken, and when they opened the Herrnhuter church for him, he reconsecrated it, and dedicated it as an Evangelical Lutheran church, according to the foundation of the prophets and apostles, and our symbolical books. Since then Mr. Kurtz occasionally preaches in it, in the afternoon, as several of the members of the congregation live in that vicinity. What may yet be the issue we know not. Three or four families partially hold to Mr. Kurtz's congregation, and the other five or six families still adhere to the Herrnhuter, as their children are still in part living in Bethlehem, and in part are married to the Brethren.

In the month of August, I traveled up and visited the hill congregations in Upper Milford and Saccum, chose judicious men for church councils in both congregations, for the sake of better order and administration, as I could but seldom visit the congregations. I afterwards examined the people in reference to their external and internal condition, as much as I was able, and settled some little differences, and hereupon had confession and the Holy Supper with them. Like children, both the old and the young willingly permitted themselves to be examined by me; but they also readily quarrel like children, and keep everything until the parson comes, so that he may have somewhat to arrange. I therefore appointed the church council, that they, among other things, might settle their trifles themselves, and preserve better order. There are such little *cœtus miserabilium*, who easily touch each other where it gives pain; still, we also find among them some excellent, awakened and simple souls, who seem to be concerned for their salvation. It is only a pity that we cannot have them nearer at hand, and cultivate them more. Still the hands of God are not shortened, and his Spirit is able also to improve such souls. A man in the congregation lying in the last extremity desired the Holy Supper, which I could not refuse him, as he before made a beautiful confession of repentance and of faith in his Redeemer, so that all present wondered and were moved to tears. The day following he died. For three or four days on this journey, I became thoroughly wet by a cold rain, got a fever thereupon, and was obliged in this condition, and in more rain and wind, to travel back thirty miles to my home. On the way, I had to administer the Holy Supper to a young person, who was very sick in body, but well prepared in mind.

As soon as I came home, I was taken with an inflammatory fever, and lay three or four days before I could properly collect myself. But when I collected myself, and the fever still continued, I experienced an uncommon gnawing pain in my head. My English friends of New Hanover immediately visited me, traveled to Philadelphia, and brought medicine for me from the English doctor. My dear colleague, Mr. Brunnholtz, also came up to me, aided me with prayer and consolation, and suffered much discomfort by me. The Lord reward him for his faithfulness! External circumstances and my family were a little disquieting to me; still I committed these unto the Lord. In relation to my soul's condition, I saw on the one hand nothing but sin, deficiency and want, in office and station; but on the other, I inwrapped myself in the grace and mercy of my dear Lord and Redeemer Jesus Christ, and lived in the sure hope that my God would not reject me for the sake of Jesus Christ, but receive, and through grace, yea, alone through grace, grant me a little room among the least and meanest in heaven. About my office I was not so much disturbed, because I surely believe and know that God is able to do all without me, accomplish his work, and set others to the labor who are far more faithful, earnest, better and wiser than I am. Meanwhile, if I should still live, I will pray the gracious God for an increase of faith, of love, patience and faithfulness, and call upon him that, for the sake of Christ, he may not enter into judgment with me on account of the sins of my office and station, and also preserve in life my beloved brethren in office, and send more faithful laborers into the harvest, if he should call me into eternity. When I had passed about two weeks with the inflammatory fever, and had to go out on account of necessary official duties, I was thereupon taken with the tertian fever and ague, and labored under it for two weeks more.

During the past year, I lost four Sundays on account of my sickness. Otherwise, when at home, I have, by the grace of God, preached according to arrangement, every Sunday forenoon in the principal church, and catechised the old and young, but in the afternoon I preached English, according to opportunity, in both congregations. In the week days, I here and there cultivated the scattered out-parishes on the Skippack, beyond the Schuylkill, in the Oley mountains, with the Word of God, and administered the Holy Supper twice in each congregation, baptized about one hundred and nineteen children, and confirmed thirty-six young people. May the merciful Father in Christ, according to his promise, not let his word return wholly empty, but accomplish the purpose whereunto he has sent it! When I look at the circle of my congregations and out-parishes, it embraces more than thirty miles, wherein the scattered members of the congregations live. That which grieves me most is this: that quite too little time, strength and opportunity remains for the *cura speciali* (special care). In the winter months, we are often glad if we can only attend to the common official duties in the churches and out-parishes. In summer, the household is too much overburdened with work, so that we do not readily find any one else in the house, except little children who are shut in. The rest must work, or else they will have no bread. I find scarcely any other time and opportunity than when, on Sundays, I catechise the old during, and the young after the sermon, and when the communicants announce themselves for the Lord's Supper a week before, in sickness, deaths, baptism of children, and the like. On Saturdays and Sundays, there is constant work and traveling, without exception. During the week, I can seldom be at home several days in succession. On week days there is a private baptism to-day, to-morrow a sick person, the day after a funeral, and so on in succession ; and each act requires nearly a day, because the dwellings are so remote. Where is there time for study? If there is still a day left, we gladly go in quest of such souls as are under the workings of the Spirit. But where is there time remaining for the correspondence due the highly venerable fathers and patrons in Europe?

THE YEAR 1748.

In this year God visited our country with a grievous pectoral disease, which at certain times quickly snatched away many people. God has hitherto as yet graciously spared our country congregations, when all around us many were removed. On the other side of the Schuylkill, in a distance of sixteen miles, about fifty women became widows. Several houses and families wholly died out, especially among the English. This chastisement creates an alarm among many, and teaches them to give heed to the Word, when at another time they live in security and think of nothing but their belly. In our congregations, the effect of the Word of God moves in one and in another towards repentance and faith, when otherwise they are indolent when they are without trial and affliction. This has given me courage again, so that I think we should always confidently sow in hope, and commit the blessing to the Lord. He has all manner of disciplinary means at hand, and by severity and goodness ceases not to call us human beings to repentance. The deceased Professor Francke, who is now resting in God, sometimes prayed in his sermons that God might lock up some little word in the heart of the hearers, and preserve it, so that it in its time might bear fruit.

In the month of January, a member of our congregation beyond the Schuylkill died. He was already considerably advanced in life, born in Alsace, heard the Word of God diligently, and made use of the Holy Supper. He told me before, that he in his life endured much poverty and affliction, which, however, did not give him as much pain as when he, here in this country, had to suffer scoffings and reproach on account of his religion from all kinds of sects, before God and our worthy superiors sent in the preachers. He thanked the Heavenly Father that he gave him the opportunity to enjoy his Word and Holy Sacraments, for the edification and life of his soul. In simplicity, he knew and believed what, according to his catechism and the Holy Bible, was necessary to his salvation; and manifested, especially in the last years, by his conduct, that the gracious God had wrought the beginning of repentance and of faith in his soul by his Holy Spirit, by means of his Word, and died with a fully assured heart.

Another, a young man of the same place, was sick for several weeks. I visited him, and examined him with reference to the state of his soul. He had an excellent literal knowledge of the order of salvation, knew also how to speak and give answer concerning practical truths, was a faithful member of the congregation, and neglected no meeting for edification without necessity, and led a quiet life, as the neighbors testified. He recovered from his sickness again, but had scarcely been well for a few days when a relapse ensued, and took him out of time into eternity within twelve hours, from his poor wife and minor children.

A man of the Reformed church, in the same neighborhood, on the other side of the Schuylkill, attended our preaching diligently, and found pleasure in the Word of God. Having been in our meeting a few days before, he heard with emotion, and also answered when I repeated the discourse by question and answer. He was attacked by pneumonia in such a manner that he quickly died. He desired to speak with me, but as it was about sixteen miles from my house, and I was away from home, it was impossible for me to reach him. Before his death, he bade them greet me, and ask that I should bury him. There were many Germans, English, and Irish, at the funeral, of various opinions, and manifested an eagerness to hear something, because they were placed in fear and terror by the prevailing disease, as there were still on that day from six to seven corpses unburied in that neighborhood. The English and the Irish entreated that I should give them instruction in their language, because they were in need of it in these sad and dangerous times. I preached for them for half an hour at the grave on Job xiii., how we must repent, believe, and live, if we would drive away the bitterness of death and be saved. Afterwards I preached for the Germans on 1 Timothy vi. 6, 7. The people were all very attentive and affected. May the Lord care for the poor dispersed and wandering sheep!

One of our wardens was visited with affliction, inasmuch as his whole family, consisting of six sons, were lying sick at the same time with the measles. He conducted himself in a Christian manner under these circumstances. He often went in secret, bowed his knees, and wrestled in prayer with his Saviour; committed himself and his children for life and for death, and in calmness and submission to the will of God, obtained much consolation and joy in believing. By his prayer and faith, the children were all preserved, and recovered without medicine.

In the month of February the pectoral malady raged still more violently, and carried away many old and young people into eternity. An Irishman, who also understands German, of the Reformed religion, and who comes diligently to our meeting, desired to speak with me. When I came to him, he was again convalescent. He related to me what the gracious God had done for his soul in his illness. All the sins which he had committed from his youth up were placed before him. The more he considered these, the greater and the more innumerable they became. In this representation he had a deep impression of the holiness and justice of God, of death, of the last judgment and eternal damnation, and esteemed himself worthy of all this. In this condition he had passed two days and two nights without the least sleep, with a cold death-sweat, and could not find the least comfort, until at length the most important passages of the sufferings and death of Jesus Christ, and of his sufficient righteousness and atonement occurred to him, and impelled him to prayer and supplication. Great strength was imparted to him by these passages. When his wife and children observed this, they assisted him by prayer and reading of the New Testament. As sinful, yea, so exceedingly sinful and worthy of condemnation as before he saw himself in his blood, so gloriously was the free grace in Christ Jesus, his Kinsman, disclosed to him in prayer and striving. Through the living consolation and assurance of grace, the sickness of body and soul was so lost, that he no more felt any anguish of soul, nor pains of body, and rose from that hour. As far as I could understand, the sickness may perhaps have been at its most dangerous height. Now when such a poor soul perceives that the bond between it and the body is to be broken, it might well seek out the truths heard which had long lain buried, and by the workings of the Spirit connected with the word, experience such a process. Still, I said to him that this perhaps might only have been a draught of the building itself. As God had lengthened out his life, so he should now seek to experience this still better in the proper order, whereof he had an impression before. The law of God, if he properly considers it, will reveal to him his deep ruin, viz: the inclination to evil and the aversion to the truly good on his part, and the essential, and to sinners terrible, holiness and justice on the side of God. Yea, if he would yet somewhat nearer view the holiness and justice of the Most High, and his own deep and unsearchable ruin and guilt, he should earnestly follow the Son of the Highest as his surety in the evangelists, and consider how holiness and justice oppressed him from Gethsemane to Calvary for our sins; and from the green tree draw a conclusion with reference to the dry. If he attained to such a fundamental knowledge of his deep ruin, to a true hatred, disgust, and aversion to it, and recognize sin as sin before the most holy Majesty, so would the gospel be to him a truly joyful message; yea, a power of God unto salvation and to a truly new life. Then would Jesus Christ be his righteousness, his peace, his joy, and his one and all, as he could further read in the second chapter of the second book of the late Arndt's True Christianity. But now, if he was not faithful, and did not build his house on the true Rock, Satan, the world, and his own flesh and blood might again get the mastery, and take his soul captive anew, and finally suggest to him that he only had a conceit or a melancholy incident in his sickness. Therefore it is said: Thou wast sick and art well, see that something worse does not befall thee. He thought that it was impossible to forget such an impression, and promised to follow the workings and the guidance of the good Spirit by means of his Word.

A woman in New Hanover, of our congregation, lay sick, and desired to be strengthened in faith by the Holy Supper. When I arrived there in the evening, several persons were assembled. Before she received the Holy Supper, I inquired of her what was the ground of her faith, on which she would live and die. She gave a reason for the hope that was in her, and spoke so clearly of penitence of heart, of living faith, and especially of the justification of a poor sinner before God, which she, as a poor sinner, had experienced through faith in Jesus Christ, that I thought I heard the blessed Dr. Luther speak; whereat I most heartily rejoiced, and all present were moved to tears. She thereupon confessed in true poverty of spirit, and received the Holy Supper, as a pardoned Mary Magdalene, beneath the cross of her Master. She still lives and profits by her talent among her acquaintances, and gives me also great encouragement. Among others, an Englishman was present, who had been an elder in the English church in Philadelphia, and now had moved into the country, on whom the confession of this woman made a deep impression. He spoke with me, and wished that he might have such an experience of living repentance, faith and justification.

Some days afterwards, this same woman requested me to go with her to the house of a distinguished and rich Quaker, where a penitent person was lying sick, and desired consolation of me. When I came there with her, I found a young man of twenty-five years, who had recently arrived here from New England, lying sick of the pectoral malady. The woman had already spoken with him several times before, concerning the condition of his soul, and found that the Lord had begun his work of grace in him. I asked him how it was with his heart? He said that he was baptized in the English church, brought up in it, and taught to read and write. But in all his life, he had not so experienced what actual Christianity signifies, as in this sickness. For he feels himself as the greatest sinner between heaven and earth, who from his head to the soles of his feet found no soundness in himself, but only sores and abscesses; yea, who has merited God's wrath and condemnation, and is not worthy to lift up his eyes toward heaven. He felt and perceived more of the deep ruin of his soul than he was able to express in words. But he could not help himself, nor recall the time lost, much less blot out his sins and transgressions, and reconcile God. I answered him that if he sensibly felt that which he said before, and believed it without hypocrisy, he must now look around for a sufficient righteousness, which is able to cover the guilt of his sins, intercede for him before the most holy judgment of God, cleanse him from all sin, and place him in a state of blessedness. He answered: this was just now his contemplation; with this he was occupied. I asked whether he had a conception of the great and only Saviour of the world, and of the work of reconciliation? He answered that he in his life had heard much of him, in sermons and in instruction, but his heart was never so affected as during this illness. He felt a hunger and a thirst after his righteousness, and cast himself at his feet, in the hope that he will not cast him out, but issue grace instead of righteousness. As I then observed a penitent heart, and a beginning of faith in him (as far as man can judge by outward signs), I inquired of him how he would conduct himself if God should

lengthen out his life. He answered: that by
the grace and help of God, he would abide
with his crucified Lord Jesus and his word,
follow the workings of the good Spirit, strive
against the devil, the world and his corrupt
flesh, with the armor of God, and be and continue his Redeemer's own, body and soul. I
asked: whether he so loved his Lord Jesus,
that he was willing to do and to suffer the before-mentioned for his sake? He answered:
that he indeed still found himself weak in the
faith, but still he already felt a sincere love to
Jesus, and would pray: Lord, strengthen my
weak faith. I thereupon gave him several
consoling passages. After this was done, he
desired the Holy Supper, and said that he had
not as yet taken it. He always had a secret
dread of it, and thought he might perhaps receive it unworthily; and perhaps even after its
reception again presumptuously sin, and therewith add to his judgment and condemnation.
Now as he was very weak, and in danger of losing his life, I asked him in the shortest possible
manner the most necessary parts concerning the
Lord's Supper, which he answered clearly. I
presented his circumstances to the dear God

in prayer, and inquired of the man whether the state of his heart was such as I had prayed. He said that which I had prayed he had sighed. Thereupon I absolved and confirmed him with the laying on of hands, and administered to him the Holy Supper, which he received with humiliation of heart, and also recovered soon after from his illness. May God preserve the poor soul, amid so many thousand allurements in the world, and especially in Pennsylvania.

In said month of February, I was obliged to visit Upper Milford and Saccum. We had very deep snow, and therefore concluded that there was still deeper snow lying between the mountains. I thought there was already a beaten path to that place, but found no path further than within ten English miles, and so bad, that the ten miles were more than a five hours' ride. When I came into a particularly deep valley between the mountains, it was night. Now I had no path at all any more, and very deep bogs and holes to pass. Back I could not well get, and forward I had still six miles to my quarters; and as I had no path whatever, I also was unable to see the snow-covered holes. First I rode about two miles out of the right way, got too far to the left, and had laboriously to work my way back again. Afterwards I hit upon the road pretty well, but several times I unexpectedly fell with the poor horse, through the snow and soft ice, into the sloughs; but, by the help of God, worked myself out again. The horse became tired going forward in the untrodden, deep snowy roads; therefore I was obliged to go before on foot, and make a path for the horse, which fatigued me very much, as I had as yet three miles to go. I would gladly have remained sitting, on account of weariness; but as it was fiercely cold, and I was in a copious perspiration, I dared not rest, but in the name of the Lord I gathered my remaining strength together once more, and in the same night safely arrived in my quarters. I was specially refreshed in the congregations this time, as I observed one and another good motion of the Spirit of God through his word. We would indeed sometimes gladly remain at home when such bad roads and weather occur; but as our coming must generally be announced several weeks beforehand, and the people also come together from a considerable distance, the sects profit by it if we fail to put in an appearance, and say to our people: such are your parsons, they promise much and keep little.

In the month of March, I was again nigh unto death, which God however graciously averted. I visited a sick person several miles away, and had to ride on a narrow road, along a precipice, which was still icy. I fell with my horse, which luckily, however, turned over with me towards the high side of the hill, and remained lying so long, until I could loosen myself, and hold on to the bushes. Had the horse fallen on the other side with me, he would have had to roll over about seven times into the valley, and life have been lost. In how many dangers has not the gracious God spread wings over me?

In this month the oft-mentioned Swiss preacher, Mr. Jacob Lyschi, came to me, and related the following: Since his awakening from his fourteenth year, he in his fatherland became acquainted with some awakened souls, and finally with the Herrnhuter, and by reason of the sweet doctrine of the atonement, and their seeming lovely harmony, he thought that the latter must be the best people in the world. He had visited their principal places, such as Herrnhut, Marienborn and the like, in Germany, and also came to Pennsylvania in connection with them. He was commissioned by the Herrnhuter as a Reformed preacher, and used for their plans, still he was never properly deemed a full brother. Now, when he had preached among the Reformed for several years, around about in the country, and awakened some souls by the word and by his intercourse, and also was present at the conferences of the brothers, a part of his hearers insisted on it that he should honestly confess whether he was a Herrnhuter brother. These, on the contrary, several times demanded that he should say whether he was willing to work by their whole plan? In this manner, he for a time hung between the two, until at length three written questions for answer were laid before him from Bethlehem, viz: (1) whether he was a natural brother of the congregation, or (2) a friend, or (3) whether he intended to be an enemy of the congregation in the future? This induced him to set a time, and to go to

Bethlehem, so that he might for once consider their matters in proper connection, with impartial mind, and come to a decision. Now when he had been there several weeks, and impartially reflected upon their affairs; and having heard very blasphemous expressions from Bishop Kammerhof in public sermons, and in private conversation purely offensive things, he took leave, and recalled the fellowship which he before had with them. The chief heads, especially Mr. Spangenberg, tried their utmost to retain him; but he could not do otherwise than to preserve a general commiserating love towards them, but was forced in the first place to have a declaration printed in mild terms, and to show wherefore he must set himself free from their community. Should they reply in their usual manner, with abuse and lies, he has still much in store whereby he is able to uncover their shame and nakedness. I reminded him in love how greatly he sinned in holding secret communion with these people, and several times assuring his poor Reformed hearers in his sermons that he was no Herrnhuter or Moravian brother. He did not deny that he thereby occasioned much sin and harm, but would ask of God grace and pardon, and a pure heart, and a new and right spirit, etc. He further said that now he stood alone, and it was easy to imagine that the Herrnhuter would invent and publish all manner of reasons and motives concerning his separation; and he therefore requested that we should include him in our prayer, that the Lord might manifest in him the abundance of his grace and mercy, preserve him from falling, and give him strength to contend against the devil and his artful assaults. For should he now commit the least fault, the Herrnhuter would trumpet it forth to all the world, and say: There you see the reasons wherefore Jacob Lyschi could not remain with us! Afterwards he published his declarations, and united himself to the Reformed preachers sent by the Classis of Holland. He lives on the borders of Pennsylvania, beyond the Susquehanna, where he purchased a piece of land, and serves several congregations.

In this same month, Mr. Kurtz had to visit the congregations on the Raritan once more, according to our promise. The reasons of our sending him there were the following: In the month of November last, the notorious Carl Rudolph came to Raritan, after he had traversed Georgia, Carolina, Virginia, Maryland, and finally Pennsylvania also, and given us much offence, being dispatched to that place by a certain preacher by a letter of recommendation. This he had showed to several in Raritan, who may perhaps have had prejudices against us; but to the rest he brought a friendly greeting from us, and inquired how they were disposed. Before the latter could receive intelligence from us, he had already attached to himself a number of credulous people, and made a written agreement with them concerning the preacher's office. The more prudent inquired of us concerning his circumstances. On the contrary, with cunning and fraud, he represented to the poor people how dangerous their fellowship with us was. Sensible persons, who had powerfully experienced our work in their souls through the Word of God, immediately saw that it was a gross failure, opposed the other party, and locked their two small churches against him, and overran us with letters and embassies and entreaties that we should not withdraw our hand from them, on account of this precipitation, of which the imprudent were chiefly the cause. They could not deny that they themselves had at first thought that the man had been sent by us, as he had brought greeting from us and spoken in a Christian manner. We gave them a necessary reproof, lamented their condition, and promised to send Mr. Kurtz once more in four weeks. Perhaps we would soon receive intelligence from Europe, and see further what was to be done. In the meanwhile, Carl Rudolph still thought himself established, as the English about there united with his German party, and promised him a moderate salary. But when they read our report, and also saw that the man began to practice lewdness publicly, and to steal, they quickly removed him. He wore a black clerical dress which he had stolen from old Valentine Kraft. From Raritan, he betook himself to the other part of Jersey, where there were Germans also, but did not remain there long, but came to Philadelphia again and enlisted as a soldier for New England, and where he now is we know not. Grossly as Satan this time raged against us at Raritan with his slanders, still he gained but little advantage, and honest souls were only the more manifest thereby. Under these circumstances, we found it necessary to send Mr. Kurtz to that place once more, as neither I nor my colleague, Mr. Brunnholtz, had time or strength to go there.

In the beginning of this month, a young Swede came to me, complained with weeping eyes, that the breast complaint prevailed with them, and they had no preacher to comfort them. The poor youth grew up in ignorance and vanity. I was urged to come unto them, and preach repentance. Two weeks afterwards this man died, and I was brought to bury him. The place lies between two streams, called the Schuylkill and Manatawny, sixteen miles from my dwelling. As the land is rich in that tract, the Swedes first settled there, and afterwards the English and others. For several years, the Swedes were occasionally visited by their national preachers from Philadelphia, and had the holy sacraments administered to them. The English neighbors, who professed to belong to the church, on such occasions had the Swedish preachers preach for them in the English language and administer the sacraments, as they also studied this language. At length, a Swedish preacher, who had resigned in Philadelphia, settled in this place, and succeeded so far that they built a small church in which divine service was held in the Swedish and in the English language. He was indeed a man of good intention, but was unable to harmonize properly with the people. Now, as the Herrnhuter were in full wooing, so there was also a Swedish student, Prizelius, sent to that place by them. This student and others like him had already stolen some hearts of the Swedish, English, Irish, and German people, and began to occupy the church with them. Now, when he had appointed church services on a certain day, and the old Swedish preacher heard of it, he proceeded to the church somewhat earlier, and awaited the new recruiting-officer, who also came after the people were assembled. The old man went out from his desk toward him, and said to the young man: Thou comest into the sheep-fold as a thief and a murderer; and with great gravity struck him hard on the mouth. But before the fight proceeded any further, the members of the congregation came and sepa-

13*

rated them. The Swedish preacher did not always remain in the place, and also could not steal the hearts of the people like Absalom; consequently, the Herrnhuter obtained a footing there. Soon there came from them a Swede, then a Scotchman, and soon a German, and preached in their church. In the second year after my arrival, several Swedes who were disgusted with the Herrnhuter requested me to come up for once and preach in the English language. I did this, and they entreated that I should still, now and then, come up during the week and hold divine service, as they gladly heard a discourse of repentance, faith, and godliness. When a new Swedish preacher arrived in Philadelphia, he traveled up, and offered to come there himself occasionally, and to serve them with the Word of God and the sacraments, as his predecessors had done. This pleased me, as without this I had burden and labor enough. But he remained away, and the above-mentioned aged Swedish preacher went to Europe; consequently the door stood fully open to the Herrnhuter, who sent one preacher there after the other, and had also concerted with

Mr. Nyberg, of Lancaster, that he should occasionally visit the congregation and help draw the net. The Swedes and the English were very well satisfied that the Herrnhuter preachers demanded no support, but labored in hope. But these expected to lift the principal at the same time with the interest, and bring them into their Saviour-treasury, which, however, beyond expectation proved too difficult. The Herrnhuter piped songs of Bethlehem quite too sweet for the Swedes and others, and ever said: Come and see! But the people would not. They had so far converted a rich Irishman in the same region, that he placed two of his older children in their school establishment in New Hanover. But he desired too much to remain master over his children, and especially over his property, and when his other children at home were taken with a mild type of measles, and easily passed through them, so he also wished to have the children home from the Herrnhuter, that they also might take the same kind of measles and recover. But these, *i. e.* the Herrnhuter, noticed it very well that they could not get control of his property in the future; therefore they gave up the children and became angry, left him, and concerned themselves as little for his soul as they did before. So far the Herrnhuter had cultivated the field, when they left and went away. Now when the sickness and the disturbance would have taught the people to give heed to the word, there was no word sowed by the Herrnhuter, which remained in the trial, but they were in ignorance, darkness, and in a disconsolate condition. I was invited to bury the above-mentioned young Swede, and at the same time also an Englishman. After the funeral sermon, several aged Swedes, the above-mentioned Irishman, and an awakened Englishman, who had moved up from Philadelphia, came together, and entreated with tears that I should take their condition to heart, and decide occasionally to come up on Sunday and preach for them. As gladly as I would have rid myself of such heavy work, as much as I besides alleged the too heavy labor of my extensive office, so unceasingly they persevered, until they prevailed over me to promise them only something after a while. I thereupon soon commenced and preached there, once every two weeks on a working-day, and once every two weeks on Sunday afternoon. This place is distant fourteen miles from New Hanover, over a good road, and only ten miles over a rough, stony mountain, and beyond a stream. When I had finished the divine service on Sunday in New Hanover, and was through, about twelve or one o'clock in the afternoon, I mounted my horse and rode to the place in haste in the great heat of the sun, so that I could be there about two or three o'clock. I first preached an English sermon, and afterwards made an exhortation in German, as various poor German servants and others of the Lutheran and Reformed religion live in that vicinity, and are also eager to hear something. The Swedes and the Irish understand English as well as their mother tongue, because they are born and raised here in this country among the English. In the first sermons, I explained to them the plainest passages of the New Testament concerning repentance and faith. Afterwards, I expounded for them the examples of holy baptism, from the Acts of the Apostles. In the week-days, when I had more time, I commenced catechising with old and young. It is almost incredible how much ignorance is found among old and young. Still they are attentive and in fear, as various sudden deaths took place among them.

On the 30th of March, God granted unto me the special joy to see and to entertain in my house the newly-arrived pastor Handschuch, together with my worthy colleague, Mr. Brunnholtz. According to all the circumstances, which we have accurately noticed from the valuable letters of our fathers, we believe that it was the gracious and perfect will of the Lord to set this man, as a witness of the truth, among the perverse generations of Pennsylvania. God be praised forever, through our Lord Jesus Christ, and recompense our highly venerable fathers, and all benefactors, in time and in eternity, for their almost innumerable efforts and benefactions, which they from pure pity and compassion, showed from the beginning until now, unto their poor, dispersed and intractable co-religionists. As we have understood, the beloved pastor Handschuch had a hard and sorrowful voyage, which fatigued him very much. Now as the gracious God has made known his gracious will unto us hitherto, from the past, by circumstances, so will we in his name begin a new era, call upon him diligently, let the pillar of cloud go before, and gradually follow, and see where the way is opened for us, and we are permitted or commanded to enter in. To this end we purpose to visit all our congregations shortly. Pastor Handschuch first began to scatter the seed of the divine word in Philadelphia and Germantown. I intended to administer the Holy Supper in my congregations on the approaching Easter festival. In recording and examining those who desired to come, I found one and another good evidence of the grace of God working in them, which delighted me.

On the 7th of April, on Maundy-Thursday, I had pastor Handschuch brought out to Providence.

On the 8th of April, the quiet Friday, we kept the holiday. I preached on the fourth word of Christ on the cross, and held preparatory service and confession with the communicants. He testified that the day had been to him important to his soul.

On the 9th of April, I was up with him in

New Hanover, and had preparatory service and confession with the communicants of that place.

On the tenth of April, the first day of Easter, I heard the beloved brother preach for the first time to a numerous congregation. God be praised for the gift bestowed unto him. After the sermon we administered the Holy Supper, baptized a child in the neighborhood, and traveled over again to Providence late in the evening.

On the 11th of April, pastor Handschuch edified our congregation in Providence with a sermon, and afterwards assisted in administering the Holy Supper. Mr. Kurtz arrived in Philadelphia from Raritan on the 5th of April, saw Mr. Handschuch there for the first time, came up to me, and traveled on to Tulpehocken, so that he might have divine service there on the quiet Friday, and publish our coming, as we had resolved to celebrate the Holy Supper in that place on the first Sunday after Easter.

On the 12th of April, I went with pastor Handschuch seven miles to my out-parish on the Skippack, and let him preach, and returned home again with him in the evening, where we found our beloved colleague, Mr. Brunnholtz, in good condition, although much fatigued by the festival labors.

On the 13th of April we commenced our journey to Tulpehocken, and took our friend Mr. Vigera with us, as he gave us some relief in external matters. About 11 o'clock a. m., we reached the Swedish-English congregation, where I delivered an English, and Mr. Brunnholtz a German sermon, and performed several baptismal acts, whereupon time passed almost too quickly. There was a promise to preach ten miles further on, in a small German church. Pastor Handschuch with Mr. Vigera now indeed rode on before, but came too late, as the people for the most part were scattered again. With those who remained he held a meeting for edification.

On the 14th of April, we set out early, passed the Schuylkill safely, and in the afternoon arrived in good condition in the house of Mr. Weiser, in Tulpehocken, where we were received with much joy.

On the 15th of April, we rested, and before God, remembered the gracious guidance and the highly venerable fathers, together with all dear patrons in Christ whom we left in Europe.

On the 16th of April, we went five miles further to the church, and held preparatory service and confession with the communicants, not without noticable emotion; visited Mr. Kurtz in his dwelling, and in the evening returned again to our quarters.

On the 17th of April, we all went to church together, and each one of us had his part to do. The one served before the altar, the other baptized, the third held a short preparatory service and confession, pastor Handschuch preached, and afterward, with pastor Brunnholtz, administered the Holy Supper to upwards of two hundred communicants. Everything was done in an orderly manner and unto edification. In the afternoon, at about 4 o'clock, we proceeded to the contested Moravian, or the now so-called old Lutheran church, and heard Mr. Kurtz preach. Several wardens from the town of Lancaster were also present. In the evening we again returned to our quarters, and edified ourselves with each other by Christian conversation. We sat until

12 o'clock at night. Scarcely had we gone to bed, when Mr. Weiser was attacked with a colic so violent that it seemed as if he might instantly die. This incident was among other things very sensibly felt by me, because the Herrnhuter had shortly before, in a shameless manner, given him to understand, not indistinctly, that they would as it were pray him to death. They would certainly have made an improper use of his death, and said it resulted from their power, because he opposed them. In reference to his salvation, I had good hope; because he, so far as we can judge by the fruits, is in the faith which worketh by love, and seeks to lay aside his infirmities and faults by a daily repentance. We had no medicine with us, and there was no doctor at hand. I entreated my colleagues that they should agree before God in Christ, in reference to his life and true welfare. This they heartily did, and when at break of day, a doctor from a distant place was called in, and ordered some medicine, it had a good effect. But the prayer likely availed the most.

At daytime, April the 18th, Mr. Kurtz also came, and we humbled ourselves together in our chamber before God in Christ, and asked for grace and compassion. After a prayer, we went to the patient, and among other things, I asked him, in the presence of my colleagues as witnesses, on what foundation he would live and die? When he had answered thereupon, in a few but strong words, to the satisfaction of us all, I inquired once more whether his conscience reproved him, that he proceeded thus, and not otherwise, in reference to the Herrnhuter. He answered, that he had acted in the matter before God, according to his best knowledge and conscience, and was conscious of no correction on that account. As he had not partaken of the Holy Supper the day before, he asked that we might administer it to him, and also at the same time partake of it with him. We made preparation thereto, made confession together before God, and acknowledged our sins with true humility of heart. He permitted himself to be assisted, so that he could bend his knees in the dust before God, offered up a penitent and believing prayer with tears, and partook of the Holy Supper with us.

On the 19th of April, we rested, and edified

ourselves with each other at home; and as our beloved brother Brunnholtz and Mr. Kurtz also complained somewhat of indisposition, they were bled.

On the 20th of April, I had to bury the wife of a warden from New Hanover. The woman had gone to Tulpehocken eight days before, to visit her children living in that place, and died. She had chosen the 42d Psalm for her funeral text, and for her death-hymn: "Alas! God and Lord, how great and heavy are my committed sins," etc., to show thereby what had been her meditation in life and in death. She lived with an aged man in wedlock, with whom she had nine children, of whom eight are still living, and all are of good hope, because the mother had used all possible diligence with them. Outwardly, she was much afflicted by infirmity, and had otherwise also not a little sorrow. Such tribulation drove the woman to prayer, and attention to the Word of God, and the faithful God let this conduce to her faith and godliness. I several times asked her specially concerning the state of her heart, and she replied: that she was indeed a poor sinner, worthy of death and condemnation, but the Lord Jesus had blotted out her sins for his name's sake. She knew on whom she believed. She thanked the Lord that he led her to repentance, through severity and goodness, and brought her by his means of grace to a fellowship in the suffering and joy of the beloved Lord Jesus. She was indeed thereby crucified unto the world, but the world was, on the contrary, also an abomination to her. I tried her with various objections, to ascertain whether she had a true foundation for her faith. But she answered with joyful lips: "If I look upon myself, I am a lost daughter, a Mary Magdalene; but the Lord has clothed me with the garments of salvation, and with the cloak of righteousness, so that I must sing to his praise: 'Now beloved of my heart, I am no longer mine, for what I am is altogether thine! My love and hatred I have left to thee,'" etc. Two weeks previous she was with me in Providence, and among other things, manifested a desire soon to depart and be with Christ, which the Lord also heard, and took her home.

On the 22d of April we took leave of our

friends, traveled to Lancaster, and also took our assistant, Mr. Kurtz, along with us. When we were yet nine miles from Lancaster, all the wardens of the congregation met us, as they had received intelligence of our coming, and with whom we arrived in town towards evening.

On the 23d of April, we had many things to discuss with the wardens and elders, and told them that the object of our visit was not to force upon them Mr. Handschuch or any other preacher, but only to see whether they would again unite themselves in love, and once more enter into such order, that we might advise and promote their best welfare. We could make them no definite promise, as our highly venerable fathers had sent only one preacher, and the congregations at Tulpehocken and Raritan were vacant. My colleague, Mr. Brunnholtz, and myself were much pressed and embarrassed, as to how we could meet the will of God, in relation to the best interests of the poor congregations. Now as we were for once forced by necessity to offer our hand to the congregation, and as the forsaking of it would have caused its entire destruction, we could not decide otherwise than this, that pastor Handschuch must labor in it for a time on trial, until we might know the will of God more clearly.

On the 24th of April, pastor Handschuch preached an edifying sermon on the gospel of the Good Shepherd, before a very numerous congregation. After the sermon, my colleague, Mr. Brunnholtz, and myself, together with all the members of the congregation, remained in the church, and inquired whether they would give us liberty to appoint a preacher for them, according to our best knowledge and conscience, who was best adapted to their circumstances and to their edification? They all answered: yes. We further asked, whether they, according to the manner of the other congregations entrusted to us, were willing to elect a college of twelve persons, and acknowledge them as superiors, according to certain articles? They answered: yes, so shall it be. We appointed the six men for election who had hitherto been wardens, because they were the most respectable and judicious, and added six others to those, as good as we could find them. I hereupon permitted six and six of the members of the congregation to enter into the sacristy, to whom my colleague, Mr. Brunnholtz, presented the names of the men set up for election, and allowed them to vote. After the twelve men, consisting of the six old wardens and six new ones, were chosen, they were admitted by the congregation by giving of the hand, and had to subscribe to their instruction. Thus there was joy in all good-meaning souls, and fear in the Herrnhuter, because they were apprehensive lest some order should be effected.

On the 25th of April, my colleague, Mr. Brunnholtz, and myself, passed our time in anxious prayer and solicitude, that the beloved Father in heaven would grant unto us to know his gracious will more clearly. Dear pastor Handschuch had anxiety of mind, because he noticed that we intended to lay on him the burden and the heat of the day in this desolated vineyard. At length we permitted the previously elected church council to meet, and told them beforehand, that we, after much reflection and prayer, knew of nothing better than to appoint pastor Handschuch as their pastor. We submitted this to their consideration, and desired a brief answer; but told them that if one only among them was restless and dissatisfied with our counsel and arrangement, we would turn to the other still vacant congregations, and were unable at present to aid them in any other manner. After consideration, they were all agreed, and asked for pastor Handschuch. But thinking of the matter, we concluded only to appoint him to that place at first on trial for half a year, because he was altogether unwilling on his part to accept the call for life, but only on trial; and we also desired to retain our liberty, that we might always still more deeply understand the will of God afterwards. We accordingly prepared a writing, with the consent of pastor Handschuch, and promised to give him on trial as their preacher to the congregation in Lancaster for half or at most for one whole year, with this proviso, that if one of us should die in the meantime, then our first united congregations should have the next claim to him.

On the 26th of April, we again departed from Lancaster. We let Mr. Kurtz return to Tulpehocken, and held divine service in Earltown, which lies twelve miles from Lancaster. The people had petitioned that they might have a part in the new parson, which was conceded to them, on condition that they would unite themselves better, and give room in their hearts to the Spirit of God by means of his Word. But whether this was done, and whether pastor Handschuch could endure the laborious journeys, we have not as yet been informed. After the divine service, we traveled still seven miles further down, and in cold and wet weather reached the house of a doctor, who received and kindly entertained us.

On the 29th of April, the beloved brethren, Messrs. Brunnholtz and Handschuch, traveled down again together to Philadelphia, where the latter as yet remained for a few weeks, desiring to set in order the affairs of his voyage, and then enter upon his calling in Lancaster.

On the 2d of May, I also went to Philadelphia, and remained there a few days. The congregation in York beyond the Susquehanna had long and earnestly petitioned us that we should aid them in their forsaken circumstances. We therefore resolved to send Mr. Schaum (as assistant, on trial to that place), who had hitherto taught school in pastor Brunnholtz's house, and occasionally preached for him. The dear pastor Brunnholtz was willing alone to take the burden of the two congregations in Philadelphia and Germantown upon his sickly shoulders.

When I again reached home on the 5th of May, I found my wife and two children down, very sick with the measles. The wife was not properly cared for in my absence, and the wrong medicine was administered, by which the measles were checked. This resulted in a suffocating catarrhal affection on the next day. It had proceeded so far that she had lost her speech, and had assumed a brown color. I employed in haste that which I had at hand. She beckoned that I should pray for her. When this was done, she forced herself to pray, commended herself as a poor sinner to the reconciled Father in Christ, exhorted me to be faithful in my office and station, to fight the good fight, and finish my course, and also take care of the children, etc. By this earnest praying and speaking, the choking rheum passed away, her speech still became stronger, and before we thought of it, the measles again appeared, and were fully cured in time, so that she and the children recovered by the help of God. Under these circumstances, her earnest and vehement prayer was crowned with health of body and soul.

In this month, I also prepared several young persons for the Holy Supper. Among these were twins, a certain man's son and daughter of eighteen years. The two young people manifested various signs, from which we were enabled to judge that the Holy Spirit, through the Word, worked and was active to create in them a new heart. The son of a warden, who was brought up for the Lord by his parents in discipline and admonition, showed himself very pliant in the workings of the Spirit, and gave good hope and joy to both me and to his parents. The daughter of a man of the Reformed church came diligently to our church, and as her mother, after her father's death, gave her liberty to receive instruction and partake of the Lord's Supper with us, or according to her father's denomination, she chose the former, and during instruction, one and another gracious drawing of the Holy Spirit were noticeable in her. The rest were cultivated and watered as plants along with these, and according to their own and their parents' desire, consecrated to the Lord who bought them, by prayer and the laying on of hands, after they had made their confession of faith with tears before the congregation. In the instruction and confirmation, we always inculcated the importance of these things as impressively as the Lord Jesus gave us grace, and we trust to the living God and the Chief Shepherd Jesus Christ, that he will himself care for the work of his hands, and his dearly ransomed souls. After confirmation, we seldom see the poor youth together again, because in this extensive country the one must go here and the other there. It is not as in many places in Germany, when afterwards we have them present in the instruction of the children, and are enabled to give them further information.

In the middle of the month of May, our colleague, Mr. Handschuch, with Mr. Schaum, departed from Philadelphia with many tears, and entered upon his office in Lancaster, and also traveled from there to York with Mr. Schaum, and introduced him as assistant in that place, after he had been provided with the necessary instruction. The reasons wherefore we did not place pastor Handschuch in Raritan or Tulpehocken, but in Lancaster, besides that which can already be gathered from that which has been related, and what the direction of God placed in our hands by circumstances, are, among others, the following: Both I and my colleague, Mr. Brunnholtz, are infirm and, not without reason, anticipate a speedy end or a bodily inability in such hardships as we must suffer. Consequently there must be some one near to take our united congregations if it should please God to take us away, if his Word and Sacraments, as a table and candle-stick, are to be preserved here after us for the benefit of the little company of returning sinners. Pennsylvania is particularly assigned to us, therefore it is right that we first make a trial in it with the gospel before we accept of other more distant congregations. Lancaster is particularly an important station. We also could not advise pastor Handschuch to Raritan, because circumstances there are still more complicated and laborious than in Lancaster.

A young German married the daughter of a Mennonite who was unbaptized, and after he had lived with her in wedlock for a few years, he fell into some kind of craziness, whereby he was able nevertheless to go about and do his work. In this condition they notwithstanding already have six children. The poor woman thereby suffers much affliction and trouble, and may perhaps also have disquietude of conscience, because she has as yet not made the covenant of a good conscience with God by holy baptism. Her mother and brothers and sisters are still living, and would perhaps gladly see her baptized by the Mennonites and not by us. She herself always thought still to wait until her husband was better again, for she was of the opinion that in the confused state of things, when her life was scarcely safe, she could not be a true follower of Christ. But we told her that under these circumstances it was the more necessary to have a true, durable foundation and comfort, whereon she could stay herself in life, in suffering, and in death, etc. Now, as in the past months so many were removed by the pneumonia, and also several of her brothers and sisters had died, and she herself was in delicate health, and her life in danger, she besought her mother for permission to be baptized by us. Her mother left it to her free choice. She prepared herself by prayer and by a diligent contemplation of the Word of God, for holy baptism, and although she was unable to repeat from memory the words of our catechism, yet she had nevertheless obtained a solid knowledge of all necessary articles of faith from the New Testament, so that I was surprised and most heartily rejoiced when I examined her. After examination, she was baptized amid much emotion of heart, and promised with tears to be faithful to her beloved, reconciled Father in Christ, to submit quietly to the workings of the good Spirit, and to follow his guidance. May the merciful Saviour not permit the poor soul to be wrested from his hands, turn her cross and tribulation to her advantage, and preserve her, that she may obtain the end of faith, the salvation of her soul.

On the 31st of May, I preached in the recently accepted Swedish-English congregation, concerning the repentance and baptism of the centurion Cornelius, Acts x. After the sermon, a young English woman came forward and desired holy baptism. Her parents had died early, and left her unbaptized, although they had been of the English church. She was nineteen years old, could read English, and had diligently read in the New Testament, learnt the catechism in the English common prayer-book, and otherwise read edifying books, and also took well to heart the sermons preached here before, and especially the last. She lamented with tears that she had in the years passed wandered about like a lost sheep in the wilderness, without a knowledge of and fellowship with the Lord Jesus, but testified that she had a heartfelt longing to be visibly baptized with water, according to the command of the Lord Jesus, and to be cleansed invisibly, in heart and conscience, from inherited and actual sin by his precious blood, and to be received into communion with him for time and eternity. Now, as I had before spoken with her on several occasions, and inquired after her circumstances, and also received good testimonials of her Christian conduct, I could not refuse her holy baptism. I examined her publicly before the congregation, and when she had answered all questions clearly and properly, she prayed the articles of faith and renounced the devil. I encouraged the congregation to intercession, and commended her in prayer to the Triune God. She kneeled with reverence, and received holy baptism. All present, otherwise immovable souls, wept almost aloud, and prayed with us. Several aged Swedes, born in this country, said they had now obtained a lively idea how it was in primitive Christendom.

In the month of June, a married woman announced· herself, and said that she long already had a desire for holy baptism. Her parents and ancestors were Hollanders, who came into this country almost with the first settlers. She was twenty-four years old, could read, and had obtained an excellent knowledge from the New Testament. I examined her after some time, and found that she could give a reason concerning the articles of faith from the Word of God, and also heard that she led a quiet, orderly life. Consequently, I could not withhold baptism from her, but buried her by it into the death of Jesus Christ, and exhorted her, that she should walk in a new life with him, by virtue of his death and resurrection, which she promised to do, by the aid of the Holy Spirit. Her child, which was born to her in wedlock, was baptized at the same time.

In the same month of June, I again held divine service in the Swedish-English congregation. After the sermon, two adult daughters of an English Quaker were invited forward, who desired holy baptism. The father first had a Swedish wife, and had two daughters with her. The children desired holy baptism, but could not attain to it with the father's consent, and therefore waited until they attained their majority, according to the laws of this country. When the sons are twenty-one and the daughters eighteen years old, they can leave their parents and begin for themselves. But before these years, they are subjected to their parents, almost as vassals. Now, after the daughters had attained their majority, the father could no more prevent them, and I also could not refuse them the water, because they had prepared themselves for it. They, with emotion, made their confession of faith publicly before the congregation, and gave themselves to him for a possession who redeemed, gained, and won them, not with silver and gold, but with his holy, precious blood, and by his innocent, bitter sufferings and death, that they should be his own, and live under him in his kingdom. They were faithfully admonished, that weary and heavy laden, they should come to Christ, obtain rest, learn meekness and lowliness of him, deny themselves, willingly take up the cross, and follow him as faithful disciples; because we well saw, beforehand, that derision and scorn would not be wanting to them, and that they would have to hear many an irritating slander on account of holy baptism. Several years ago, I baptized an aged Englishman, who on account of age had a gray head, and on the top of his head a baldness, which many old people get. A few days after receiving baptism by virtue of his calling, he came to an old rich Quaker, who ridiculed him for it in the most irritating manner for permitting the preacher to sprinkle water on his old bald head. Whereby he employed such language as we hesitate to cite, it being quite too offensive. At the present baptism, there were few in church who were

M

unaffected and were not encouraged to pray with us for those who were baptized. The Lord be their shepherd so they shall not want.

Still in this same month of June, I was obliged to visit one and another scattered sheep, in the so-called Blue mountains, from forty to fifty English miles from my home. When I came there, a great multitude of people, Lutherans and Reformed, assembled. I preached to them of the sheep lost and again found, and of the piece of silver, Luke xv. They were very attentive. After preaching, a small number followed me into my quarters, and desired to hear something more. I entered into an edifying conversation with them. I perceived among them several Lutherans and Reformed who five years ago lived in Providence as proprietors. They were still able to tell me the chief contents of my sermons in Providence, and assured me that many a night they had pondered these truths upon their beds. That which I have learnt by experience often gives rise to reflection. When people have the Word of God abundantly and in superfluousness, they readily become satiated and wearied, and when they for a time must suffer want and hunger, they become so voracious as if they would eat up the preacher together with the Word. In the meanwhile, I rejoice that a word remains with one and with another, because it is an imperishable seed from which regeneration shall take its rise.

In the beginning of July, I visited the hill congregations in Upper Milford and Saccum, examined a small number of young persons in the same, whom the schoolmaster had instructed with special diligence and faithfulness, and prepared for confirmation according to our directions. After I had yet myself instructed the young people for a few days, I confirmed them, and celebrated the Holy Supper with the old and young, whereby I observed one blessing and another, which encouraged me still to retain the congregations, if God grants life and strength.

The congregations on the Raritan in Jersey had long already petitioned that one of us should visit them once more, and administer to them the Word and the Holy Sacraments. As the promise was made, the lot fell to me, although I had some fear about going there, because our highly venerable fathers were unable to find a pastor for them. I therefore consulted with my worthy colleague, Mr. Brunnholtz, whether and how far we could in future care for these congregations, or whether we should separate ourselves from them? We had as yet no sufficient reasons to forsake them altogether, because we yet found some good-meaning souls among them, and because the Herrnhuter lurked on the border, and other adversely disposed persons might find matter for scoffing and calumny by our leaving them. On the other hand, we saw no possibility of sufficiently aiding them. But as Mr. Schaum had some unpleasantness in York, the thought presented itself, whether we should remove him from there, and again place him at Raritan for a time. Thus matters stood when I set out from Providence on the 25th of July. I took the schoolmaster, J. L., along with me for company, traveled thirty-five English miles the first day, and arrived at the great river Delaware in the evening, which divides Pennsylvania and Jersey. At the river I met pastor Hartwick from New York, and two wardens from Raritan. The latter intended to fetch me. The former traveled further on to Philadelphia, for the purpose of conferring with pastor Brunnholtz.

On the 26th of July, I traveled further on to Raritan, in company with the two wardens. One of these had served on sea in his youth; left his fatherland early in life, and did not take much knowledge of the Evangelical religion along with him. At length he abandoned the sea-faring life, and settled at Raritan, and afterwards also began to concern himself more about his religion, and to this end read the holy Bible diligently, and also again learned the catechism in the Dutch language, and attained to a well-grounded knowledge and exercise of faith and life in Christ. He had a son of twenty years, whom I confirmed with other young people some years before. This son had died, and according to his observation, had died an edifying and happy death. Before his end, he presented to his father various passages and hymns concerning faith, life and the resurrection, and said, thereupon he would die with confidence, because he knew that, through his Word, Christ was in him, and he in Christ, etc. All this and more he related to me on the way with tears. This man is also very much esteemed by pastor Brunnholtz, on account of his unfeigned and solid piety.

When we reached Raritan, we put up with the most respectable man and warden in the congregation, who is very well versed in the Bible, and is affable.

The 27th of July I passed for the most part in edifying conversation with several well-meaning members of the congregation.

On the 28th of July, I traveled to the congregation on Leslysland, held a catechetical preparatory service, confession and the Holy Supper with sundry members of the congregation. Those who had been on the side of Carl Rudolph, and otherwise offensive in conduct, remained away from the Holy Supper of their own accord, because we told them that they must first be still better cultivated, and led to repentance.

The 29th of July I abode with the hill congregations, and was obliged to settle one dispute and another among neighbors, married people and others. One family had fallen into a bitter strife on account of the last will of their deceased father, and would scarcely yield, and gave us so much trouble, that we had to labor with them until 12 o'clock at night before they were reconciled, and were willing heartily to forgive each other. On the 30th of July, I had preparatory service and confession in that place. On the 31st of July, I preached, baptized several children, performed a marriage, and also preached afterwards in their language to the English people living around there, and buried one aged man of the congregation.

On the 1st and 2d of August, I visited the sick, and prayed with them according to their circumstances.

On the 3d of August, I had preparatory service, confession, Sacrament, baptism and instruction of children in the third small congregation on Fosseberg.

On the 6th and 7th of August, I had preparatory service, preaching, the Holy Supper and baptism, in the fourth small congregation, on Racheway, so called. After the German service, I delivered an English sermon, because the English and the Dutch living around there made much entreaty for it. The people were much aroused and delighted, and said that they would all unite with the congregation if some one of our college came there, and preached English also.

In the intervening days, I visited the sick, and otherwise had many useful conferences, concerning the improvement of the internal and external condition of the congregation.

On the last day, I had all the small congregations come together once more. I repeated before them by what circumstances we were drawn into connection with them, how we had dealt with them from the beginning until now, what means we employed to improve their inward and outward condition, what difficulties presented themselves when no preacher could be sent for them, and what is further to be done, on their and on our part. Several among them wept, set forth their forsaken condition, their widows, their orphans and awakened souls, used the most feeling expressions, and thought that we had no sufficient grounds for leaving them wholly. But I could promise them nothing more than present circumstances seemed to justify. I accordingly promised them, after the agreement with my colleague, Mr. Brunnholtz, to let them have Mr. Schaum on trial for one year. In the meanwhile, we would have time to report the circumstances anew to Europe. They were all satisfied, and were willing to accept Mr. Schaum for one year thankfully. Moreover, the question was, how should they do about their necessary church-building, and whether they could expect any aid from our benefactors? My answer was, that they should arrange the building itself, according to their own ability, and could expect no help from Europe, because the congregation in Philadelphia was far more needy than they. Several of the elders offered to give fifty pounds of the money of this country as their part, if a stone church was built in the midst of the four congregations, so that they could have divine service every Sunday. Three of the congregations were well satisfied with such a building, but the fourth from the hills would not consent, with the pretext that they lived too far away; but which others also might have said, who reside from ten to twelve miles distant. The three congregations agreed to stand together, and gave time for consideration to the fourth. In consequence of this, I permitted each congregation to choose three men out of their midst, who together should constitute a church council or board, to attend to external order and arrangement. Besides this, each congregation had also to elect two wardens, to whom the superintendency was entrusted at divine service.

On the 8th and 9th of August, I traveled home again, and from the very great heat and exertion, I had a violent attack of fever, which was prevalent, by the way. But as I immediately made use of some remedy against it, there were no further consequences. When I reached home, I found my worthy colleague, Brunnholtz, and pastor Hartwick there, with whom I conferred about the consecration of the church in Philadelphia, and the ordination of Mr. Kurtz; and on the 12th of August, I traveled with them down to Philadelphia.

On the 13th of August, pastors Brunnholtz, Handschuch, Hartwick, and I were together, and examined Mr. Kurtz, and let the wardens and elders from Tulpehocken, who were present, sign the call for him, and also let Mr. Kurtz give a religious reciprocal obligation.

On the 14th of August, the tenth Sunday after Trinity, the invited preachers and deputed elders from our united congregations assembled in and before the residence of pastor Brunnholtz, and went to the church in procession. The Swedish provost, Mr. Sandin, and pastor Hartwick, took the lead. These were followed by pastor Brunnholtz and myself, with the church councils from Philadelphia and Germantown, and the deputies of the congregations from Providence, New Hanover, Upper Milford, and Saccum. After these came pastor Handschuch, with the deputies from the town of Lancaster, and from Earltown. Finally, Mr. Kurtz, with the deputies from Tulpehocken and Northkill, followed. Mr. Schaum could not very conveniently be present with his deputies, because York lies at the greatest distance, and the invitation, on account of the short time, had not arrived sufficiently early. In the beginning of the divine service, the hymn, Come, Holy Spirit, Lord God fill, etc., was sung chorally and harmoniously. All the preachers present stood around the altar, and all the deputies from all the congregations made a semi-circle around these and the choir. After the hymn, one of us read a congratulatory letter, which the oldest Swedish preacher had sent, in the English language, as he himself could not be present. Thereupon one of us delivered a short address, and called to mind that the foundation-stones of this church were laid with the object that in it should be taught the Evangelical Lutheran doctrine, according to the foundation of the prophets and apostles, and according to the unaltered Augsburg Confession, and all other symbolical books; and also under what sorrowful circumstances, temptations, and trials God, and so many faithful patrons for the sake of God, nevertheless kept a generous hand beneath us, so that the building has been erected thus far with difficulty. Further, the whole church, and all the parts of it, the pulpit, the baptismal font and altar, were once more consecrated for the use of the alone saving Word and the Holy Sacraments, according to our symbolical books; and the Church Board of Philadelphia had to promise publicly and verbally, that as long as God would preserve it from fire, water, and other casualties, they, with the help of God, would endeavor to maintain the church for the before-named object, from generation to generation. Finally, it was called to mind that the church was only an outward scaffolding raised for this purpose, that thereby the hearts of all hearers should be prepared for consecrated temples of the living God. After this address, several verses were sung of the hymn: Praise and glory be unto the highest good, etc. Thereupon the preachers and deputies kneeled down, and with heartfelt and fervent prayer, commended the now-called Michael's church to the omnipresent God. The Provost, Mr. Sandin, and Master Näsman, prayed in the Swedish language; pastors Brunnholtz, Hartwick, Handschuch, and Kurtz prayed in German, and the import of their prayers was, that the name of the most high God might be hallowed in this house by pure doctrine and holiness of life, his kingdom be promoted therein, and his will be done, and thereby the blessed design of all the worthy patrons and benefactors be attained. After this, we again sung, and performed a baptismal act, when a truly edifying and powerful sermon was delivered by pastor Handschuch. After the sermon, we preachers, and several of the members of the congregation, partook of the Holy Supper, and closed therewith.

In the afternoon, we again went to the church in procession. Pastor Hartwick delivered an edifying sermon on the words of Ezek. xxxiii. 8: *But his blood will I require at thine hand.* After the sermon, the Provost, Mr. Sandin, the pastors, Brunnholtz, Hartwick, Handschuch, and myself, together with the candidate, Mr. Kurtz, who was to be ordained, surrounded the altar. The Reformed preachers were spectators. The deputies from all the congregations again formed a semi-circle. One of us read the ordination formulary, prayed in conclusion, and together with the rest of the preachers, laid hands on the candidate, and therewith consecrated him to ministerial office.

On the 15th of August, we preachers and deputies met in the church, and held the first general conference, or synod as we may call it, whose import however still for the most part only related to the outward preparation.

In the month of September, I had to prepare several adults for baptism in the Swedish

English church. An English woman, who has a Swedish husband, manifested a desire for holy baptism. She had given diligent attention to the Word of God, and could also answer very well when I catechised her. Her mother is a Quaker, as yet living. As much as I have heard from judicious people, she leads a Christian life. The second person was her sister, a grown-up maiden, who likewise desired holy baptism, and who enjoyed instruction with her. The third was an unmarried man of twenty-eight years, whose parents indeed belonged to the English church, but who had died early. He lives among the Quakers, and must bear many an insolent speech from them. But as he can read, and uses the Bible diligently, and is very attentive to preaching, this establishes his heart the more firmly in the truth. He asked me to furnish him with edifying books to read, but I had none but a small book, which was composed for the instruction of the Indians, and the books of Thomas á Kempis, translated into English, concerning the following of Christ, and a small book on the Holy Supper. These I lent him, and also noted the passages of our hymn of faith. The fourth was an English woman, whose husband led a dissolute life. She said, that as she was at any rate forsaken in the world, and without true consolation, she would seek an abiding comfort in her Lord Jesus, conform herself to his holy rule, and become a member of his body through faith and holy baptism. As is my custom always, I among other things ask the persons to be baptized, before the congregation, whether they perhaps had secondary aims or worldly motives in asking to be baptized. But they answered, that they had no other motives to holy baptism than the command and promise of their Master and Redeemer. They knew of no temporal interest to be gained thereby, but much more they must suffer therefor derision and contempt, which, according to the state of affairs in this country, we can readily believe.

During this month, I received the newly-arrived student of theology, Mr. Weygand, into my house. When the congregation in York heard that we intended again to remove Mr. Schaum, and to send him to Raritan, they again united, and obviated it in time. We therefore gradually arrived at the thought whether Mr. Weygand would not do for the congregation at Raritan, as was already reported.

In the month of October, I was called down to Philadelphia, as my beloved colleague, Mr. Brunnholtz, lay very sick with inflammatory fever. He had already labored under the disease during the month previous, but now it was fully developed, and to human eyes the end seemed to be approaching. I much feared his departure, because on the whole he is still so necessary, and I have become dull and useless; yea, almost disabled from managing my country congregations: much less could I provide for the town congregation along with these, even for a time only. Before pastor Handschuch, in his enfeebled condition, could travel sixty miles from Lancaster, and Messrs. Schaum and Kurtz eighty miles from York and Tulpehocken, and act as vicars, everything might perhaps be in ruins. Hence the burden came nearest to me, and it is for me absolutely impossible. May the Lord graciously have mercy upon us, do more than we ask and understand, and preserve the beloved pastor Brunnholtz yet for a long time, for his name's sake! It cannot be denied, that the station is too difficult for him alone; for there are more inward and outward troubles, burdens, and labors than we can describe. His spirit, his faith, and his love are large enough for the station, but the feeble bodily tabernacle cannot keep pace. The English doctors have again spared no diligence and skill in his case, and it seems as if God would again give him unto us once more. For this, his holy name shall be praised.

In the said month of October, I was called to a member of the congregation beyond the Schuylkill, who was sick. The man complained of a violent contest in his soul. I asked him, whether he then was so afraid of death, and still gladly wished to live. He answered: no; but the contest was on account of sin. When he would think of his Lord Jesus, comfort himself with his sufferings and death, and through him obtain peace and rest, all manner of wicked thoughts occurred to him, which disturbed him in his good intention. I said to him, that he was engaged in a good work. The evil which occurred to him was a proof of his inward horrible sinfulness. As to where the thoughts come from, he should only search deeper, and he would soon discover the foul source whence proceed evil thoughts, murders, adulteries, etc., Matt. xv. 19. But that he also should not cease from earnestly seeking the free and open fountain for sin and for uncleanness, and so he would find rest for his soul. He promised to lay his whole evil heart before the Lord Jesus in prayer, and to ask of him grace, peace and pardon. He also desired that I should pray with him, and help him to wrestle, which I did, and thereupon inquired, whether he had more strength? He answered: yes, the prayer was to him a perceptible help, and strengthened his faith in the Lord Jesus Christ. He had one of his friends brought to him, who was by trade a tailor, and charged him in my presence that he had once seen him purloin something in cutting; that he should indeed leave off from such and all other sins, and heartily repent, for the last hours were very serious, when conscience waked up. Many things occurred to him lately, which he otherwise had not regarded as sins. He had to strive much before he attained grace, peace and pardon with his Lord

Jesus. As for the rest, he made good use of one and another strong passage and promise, continued in prayer and supplication, until his removal two weeks afterwards.

A widow in New Hanover lay sick for several weeks, and desired the Holy Supper. I had noticed sundry faults in her, which I represented to her in love and seriousness, and thereby led her to the examination of her heart. She confessed with tears, that she, during several years past, was often awakened to repentance and faith by the Word of God and by his Spirit, but did not properly do violence to the kingdom of heaven, and permitted herself to be prevented by many hindrances which occurred. She now regretted it, that she did not manifest more earnestness. She was a great sinner, who, on account of her intentional and unintentional sins, merited eternal death and condemnation; but that she knew also, that the Lord Jesus would cast none out who penitently comes to him. She had not merited heaven, and to all eternity could not merit it; but like the Canaanitish woman, she would ask only for the crumbs beneath the table, and be saved through grace.

I said to her, that it is certainly to be regretted, that we so squander the irrevocable time of grace, and do not redeem it for the beginning and advancement of true repentance and faith, inasmuch as the gracious Father in Christ has bequeathed and served up for his baptized covenant people not a dog's, but a child's portion, and fullness of bread in his holy Word and Sacraments. If, however, we waste the child's inheritance with the prodigal son, we must then indeed seek the crumbs under the table, if we would not be utterly destroyed and perish. She confessed, and repaired to the great grace and compassion of the reconciled Father in Christ, and partook of the Holy Supper with sincere humbling of the heart, and also, in a few days thereafter, passed away amidst prayer.

In the months of October and November, Mr. Weygand and I alternately instructed twenty young people in New Hanover, who purposed communing the first time. Among these was a young married man, whose father, about eighteen years before, here in this country, had gone over from the Evangelical religion to the Anabaptists, but who was now dead. The father had permitted the son to be taught to read and write, but he was not allowed to learn the catechism, because the father and those like him said, that it was a book of the devil, wherewith the Lutheran parsons bewitched the children. The father would gladly have taken the son along with him to those like-minded with himself, but he could not; as he secretly made use of our hymn-book and catechism, and also diligently went to our church. He was baptized in his infancy, before his father's deviation, and with the Holy Supper he intended to wait until he was of age. But his father died at the same time when he attained his majority, and consequently he had his full liberty. He had gathered an excellent knowledge of salvation, and with it he had a docile and upright heart, as far as I could judge from his intercourse and behavior. Another young person, whose father is called Reformed, but who leads a disorderly life, came to instruction, and wept at different times. When I asked for the reason, she said: that nearly every time, when she would go to my instruction, her father uttered horrid imprecations against her and the parson. I said: that in silence at home she should ask of God a penitent heart for herself and for her father, and otherwise show herself filial and respectful towards her father in all things. This she observed, and not without advantage; for her father himself was present at the confirmation, and was not a little affected. A young person of eighteen and a girl of fifteen years, two children of a Reformed mother who lives ten miles from New Hanover, requested permission of their mother to unite with our denomination and congregation, and to be allowed to be confirmed on our doctrine. The mother gave her consent, and the children showed themselves very attentive and wakened in the instruction. A young man of fifteen years, who had to serve with a Moravian brother until of age, but whose mistress holds firmly to our congregation, came to instruction, and manifested a docile heart, so that we cherish the hope of abiding fruit. The rest were all children of our denomination, and were cultivated by planting and watering, according to the grace which God bestowed. The Lord alone can give the increase.

In the night of the 5th of November, I was

taken to the father of a family in New Hanover. The man had five children, whom in part I had previously baptized. This father, however, had been a foolhardy man; he passed his time here as a Separatist, and lived of his own confused opinions. He also on one occasion expressed his opinions in a long letter against me and against Mr. Kurtz, because Mr. Kurtz in my absence buried one of his neighbors, and may have proclaimed him happy in the funeral discourse. This was repugnant to the old man, as he would not have his neighbor in heaven. The son in the meanwhile did not wish to walk in the footsteps of his father, but came to our church diligently, and also read the Bible and Arndt's True Christianity at home, which led him to better thoughts, and upon the plain way upon which those do not err who had been fools before. When I came to him, he lay upon his bed sick, and had seemingly the beginning of a hectic fever. I inquired: How is it with you? Patient: It is as bad with me as it can be with a human being in this world. I: What should be wanting to you? You are a man who has enough to live on, and a good testimonial from all your neighbors. Patient: I perceive indeed that you would prove me, whether I trust in the witnessing of man, and cherish a pharisaical righteousness. If men give me the best testimonial for outward honesty, this cannot in the least justify me before the most holy God, for I am the greatest and most abominable sinner on earth. I: Have you then committed great sins and crimes against the holy Ten Commandments? Patient: I have the germs of all sins against the holy Ten Commandments in my heart, but outward circumstances were in my way, that such inward evil inclinations did not always break out into open sin. I: Do you also reckon the inward evil propensities among the sins, although not accomplished? Patient: Yes; the meditation and the seekings of the human heart are evil from youth up; *behold I was begotten of a sinful seed*, etc. I: Have you only propensities to evil? Patient: Alas! I also find at the bottom an aversion to that which is truly good. *For the flesh lusteth against the spirit, etc.* I: Now tell me honestly, how do you at present know and feel yourself to be before God? Patient: I know and feel myself full of *wounds and abscesses: my wounds stink and are corrupt, because of my foolishness; my sins, as a heavy burden, are too heavy for me.* I: Do you not think that God created you so wicked, and for condemnation? Oh, no! God is faithful, and there is no evil in him; he is righteous and merciful; but I am begotten of a sinful seed, and therefore lust conceived in me, and brought forth sin, and when it was finished, it brought forth death for me. I: But in your infancy you were born again of water and of the Spirit, to a new life, by holy baptism. Patient: yes, I cordially believe this; but, on my part, I did not keep the covenant of a good conscience, but, with the prodigal son, I have squandered my inheritance. I: Are you then heartily sorry for this? Patient: Yes, I feel on this account heartfelt repentance and sorrow in my soul. I: Then how will you help yourself? Patient: Here I lie, between heaven and earth, and can expect nothing else than death and damnation. I have well merited the righteous wrath of God, and punishment into eternity. Still I would not willingly perish. I: Have you any knowledge of the Mediator and Reconciler between God and man? Patient: Yes, I know and believe from the Word of God that God so loved the world that he gave his Only-begotten Son, that whosoever believeth in him should not perish, but have everlasting life. I know that this Son is true God, born of the Father in eternity, and in the fulness of time became man, that as God and man he might redeem all men from sin, death, the devil and hell, by his perfect obedience and bitter sufferings and death, and that he appointed the order of repentance and faith, wherein we may become partakers of his redemption and of salvation; but very believingly and certainly, I cannot as yet appropriate this to myself, because I am quite too sinful. That which makes me most afraid and timid is this: Some time ago I was once already powerfully affected and awakened. I felt my load of sin, and prayed in secret. Weary and heavy laden I went to the Lord Jesus, and also found some comfort and rest for my soul. But when I afterwards began to build my mill, I was gradually entangled in the cares for a livelihood and the disquietude resulting therefrom, and was thus drawn away from my first love. Although I always retained a drawing and a chastening, still the proper seriousness and wrestling on my part were wanting, as it is wont to happen in mills and other public places, where much vain talk takes place. I, indeed, did not wish to follow the example of others, but I also did not earnestly testify against it, but rather, from a fear of man, remained quiet. Should the merciful God, for the sake of Christ, once more, out of pure grace, forgive me all my sins and debts, give me his peace, and seal it in me by his good Spirit, and also lengthen out my life, I would, through his strength, lead a wholly different life, deny myself, take the yoke of my Lord Jesus upon me, and faithfully follow him. I: If your repentance is genuine, as you have confessed to me, then you are with the prodigal son, in the act of going back to the father. In that example, then, take to heart that which can give you courage. The son walked, and the father ran to meet him. *Like as a father pitieth his children*, etc. *With him there is much forgiveness. Though your sins be as scarlet, they shall be white as snow. The weary and heavy laden shall find rest*, etc. *But where sin abounded, grace did much more abound.* Venture it and come, *and you shall not be cast out.* Can you believe this? Patient: Lord, I believe: help mine unbelief! I: Will you pray with me? Patient: Oh, yes! He desired to force himself upon his knees in bed, but could not on account of weakness. I said to him that he should bow the knees of his heart, and pray after me, or sigh. After prayer, I inquired of him whether the state of his heart had been as I prayed. He answered with joyful countenance: I perceive more faith, and can hold myself to the promises of God, and I feel grace and pardon. He raised himself up in bed, and was strengthened in soul and body. Now, said he, one thing is yet wanting to me, viz., the Holy Supper. Now, as he had never partaken of it, and, according to his ancestry, was of the Reformed persuasion, I inquired of him whether he also had the right understanding of it. In his reply, he gave to me entire satisfaction from the word of God, and assured me that he would receive it simply according to the plain command and promise of our Lord Jesus. And when I again asked whether he had any scruple to receive the same according to Christ's command and promise in our evangelical Lutheran persuasion, he said that he had had sufficient time to examine in his measure various persuasions in this country, and found the greatest consolation in the Evangelical Lutheran Church, because we simply remain in the Word, and in its power. By the grace of God he also wished to live on it, and to die on it. After confession, I laid my hand upon him, administered to him the Holy Supper, and praised the Lord with him. He said in conclusion, that if he should live, I should come unto him, and still edify myself more with him continually. But two weeks afterwards, he fell asleep with confidence in the Lord, and passed from faith to sight.

During the night in the said month of November, I was called from New Hanover fifteen miles, to an Englishman. He lay very sick. He asked me, whether I thought that he might again recover? I answered: with God there is nothing impossible, but according to present appearances, he might perhaps soon die. He said, that his soul's condition was bad, because he was not reconciled to God. I inquired in what persuasion he was brought up? He answered: in the English church. For long years he had been present at the divine service, and also diligently prayed along with them the common prayers. I: Have you also experienced what true repentance is, and a living faith, which worketh by love? Patient: I have never as yet been to the Holy Supper, and have also not experienced repentance and faith. I: Do you then now feel somewhat of regret and sorrow, on account of your sins? Patient: I feel a heavy load of sin, and the righteous wrath and displeasure of God, because of my sins. I cannot represent God to myself, otherwise than as a stern Judge. I: You are right. If you as yet stood in your baptismal grace, and kept the covenant of a good conscience, or if you had again turned to God through faith and repentance—been reconciled to him through Christ Jesus, and had walked according to his Word in the Spirit, you could represent God to yourself as a beloved reconciled Father, and rejoice in your departure. Patient: What shall I do, that I may not perish? I: It is high time that you, with the malefactor on the cross, turn to the great Saviour of the world, to his atoning blood, and to his righteousness. It is time that you, with the poor publican, smite upon your breast, and ask that God, for the sake of Jesus Christ, may forgive all your sins. The faces of those who look upon him, and run unto him, shall not blush with shame. Patient: I cannot help myself; my sins are too many, and my anguish is too great. I: Shall I pray with you? Patient: Yes, pray for me; I will sigh after you. After I had offered a penitential prayer with him, I inquired how he was? Patient: I am somewhat more easy, and am also able to believe somewhat, and I hope that the Lord Jesus will not cast me out. I: How do you stand with your fellow-men? Patient: So far as I know, I have lived in civil peace with my fellow-creatures; but I cannot justify myself. I hope that my neighbors, whom I have offended, will forgive me for God's sake, and if any one has offended me, I also will willingly forgive him. I: You must unceasingly turn in your thoughts and desires to the Saviour of the world, and sigh: *Father I have sinned against heaven and before thee, and am no more worthy to be called thy son!*

Lord, enter not into judgment with me! Oh! Lord, remember *me in thy kingdom!* Oh! Lord let grace be accounted for righteousness, and mercy for Judgment! Oh! Lord, let the atonement be valid for me, the great sinner! Patient: Oh! that I could receive the Sacrament of the body and blood of my Lord Jesus, for the strengthening of my weak and trembling faith! I: You have had sufficient time in your days of health; wherefore was it neglected? Patient: It was not properly enjoined in our church. Still, I must admit on my part, that I had often intended to partake of it, because Christ had commanded it. But when I had formed this purpose, a secret fear and awe came over me, with the thoughts that after having partaken of it, I might again offend my Lord Jesus by sinning, and thereby increase my condemnation. I: This malady I find with many. Some have no proper sense of the nature and object of the Sacraments, and are unwilling to use the remedy before they are well, and do not consider what Christ said: the *whole need not a physician, but the sick.* Others would indeed receive it, if only they need not experience repentance of heart and faith, but might be permitted to continue in their accustomed sinful course. You must seriously examine yourself, whether there is a true beginning of repentance and faith in you, and an earnest purpose to forsake sin, through the power of the holy Spirit, and to follow after the Lord Jesus. Patient: I am sorry for my sins. I believe on my Redeemer, Jesus Christ, as well as he gives me strength to believe, and I am also willing, by the help of the Holy Spirit, to amend my life. Because he petitioned for it so much, and his illness increased, I presented the saying of our sainted Luther to him: *He is truly worthy and well prepared, who has faith in these words, Given and shed for you for the remission of sins, etc.,* and administered it unto him. He said that he was comforted and strengthened. Four hours afterwards he died.

At the close of the month of November, when I visited the Swedish-English congregation to take leave of them, as the deep roads and high water in winter would not admit of our attending them, I had an edifying conversation with a genteel English widow. The husband had been naturally kind, hospitable, and benevolent towards the poor, and had died about nine months before. The Herrnhuter had wooed him much, but about his baptism they had not been much concerned, but let him die without it. The widow also was as yet unbaptized, because her parents, and especially her mother, held to the English Anabaptists. She said that she had been at our English meeting on each occasion, and was graciously visited by the Lord. As for Lydia, so the Lord had opened her heart that she gave heed to his Word. She was also convinced that she, according to the command of Christ, must believe and be baptized if she would be a friend and a follower of him. Since her widowhood, the faithful Saviour had led her to repentance through pure goodness. Whatever she recognized as sin and corruption in her, she had with prayer presented before her reconciled Father in Christ, and through the Word of God obtained the assurance that she should have life and salvation, and be comforted, because she believed. At present she could have joy and consolation in nothing in the world, but the faithful Saviour was her all. Much as she was afraid when God placed her in the state of widowhood, having not only a number of small children, but also the sole management of an extensive household, yet she found therein great alleviation, because she perceived a special gracious providence, even in the smallest affairs, and experienced that the Lord would not forsake her in any manner, nor yet neglect her. The Word of God was her daily food and nourishment. Still she must acknowledge when she read in the Bible, and came to the places where something is said concerning holy baptism, she was disquieted, because she had not as yet observed the command of the beloved Saviour concerning baptism, and yet he had expressly said: *Ye are my friends, if ye do whatsoever I command you.* She heard my farewell sermon with great attention, on Matt. xxv., of the ten virgins, and after the sermon invited me to come to her house, seven miles distant from the church. I took several witnesses along with me, and spoke various things with her relating to the command, the institution, the necessity and promise, of holy baptism. In the evening she requested that I should deliver an exhortation in English to her domestics, negroes and white people. After this was complied with, I yet prayed specially with her and the two witnesses present, and then retired. On the following day, she said that she had meditated and prayed during the whole night, and had been still more fully convinced of the necessity of baptism, only she still had some doubt about our mode of sprinkling, as she found in the Acts of the Apostles that most of the baptismal acts, were by immersion, and various apostolic phrases, as: *Buried with him by baptism into death*, and the like, pointed to immersion. I assured her that I would by no means obtrude myself upon any one, and also did not seek to get adherents, but to advance the kingdom of Jesus Christ; but if she would receive an enlightened sense from God, she must discriminate well between the essence and the incidental circumstances in baptism. The chief thing in baptism was the covenant of a good conscience with God, in virtue of the resurrection of Christ. There belongs to it on the part of God the whole sufficient atonement by the blood of Jesus Christ, his Holy Spirit, and the water connected with his command and promise. But on our side there is required faith, which is wrought in children by the baptismal act, but in adults through the Word of God and his Spirit, and confirmed by holy baptism. Now if the essential or necessary parts are present, much or little water could add nothing to it, but water would only be and remain a visible means whereby the covenant between the Triune God and the person baptized was executed. When God, after the deluge, made a covenant with eight souls, he ordained the bow, resulting from natural causes, as the token of the covenant executed. Now should the bow appear whole, half, or the one-fourth part of it, it could take nothing from the Noachian covenant, nor yet add anything to it, and it would still remain a sign of the covenant. Some of our distinguished divines have themselves wished that immersion had been retained, because baptism had its foundation in the death and resurrection of Jesus Christ, and in immersion the death of sin and the resurrection to a new life would have been better represented to the senses. But according to Christian liberty we dare not be punctilious about such incidental and not absolutely necessary circumstances, but may be satisfied if the main point is right. *For it is not the putting off of the filthiness of the flesh*, etc. Simon the sorcerer had been immersed, but as on his part a principal thing was wanting, viz., true faith, much water did not help him. At the washing of feet, Peter desired to be washed all over, but his Master set him right; it was sufficient for this time if his feet were washed. Whether the jailer was immersed is uncertain, still the essentials were present in his baptism. Whether Cornelius and his friends were immersed is not clearly announced. In the time of the apostles, and in the first three centuries, many a believer on a sick and death-bed may have been baptized without entire immersion. If we used no water at all, as the Quakers affect, we would do too little. If we should stubbornly hold on to immersion, and cherish besides false doctrines, like the Baptists, we should lose the substance, and remain hanging by the shadow. As respects the sensible representations in immersion, or in our mode of sprinkling, both modes counterbalance each other; because the Greek word βαπτίζειν signifies to sprinkle as well as to immerse, and in sprinkling we can represent to ourselves, for edification, as many glorious passages concerning the outpouring of the Holy Spirit, as others can be applied in immersion. She at length said that she had found spirit and life in our doctrine, and now also had no more doubt remaining concerning sprinkling, and desired to be baptized. We prayed fervently with each other, and she confessed the Christian faith, renounced the spiritual enemies, and received holy baptism, amid many tears and emotions of heart. Calumny and derision will also not be wanting to her.

In the evening, I rode on towards New Hanover on a new horse. The roads were very deep, and when I had scarcely come into the rough stony hills, dark night overtook me. My horse lost the way, and got with me between morass and rocks. I dismounted, and wished to find the way myself, but now and then I fell into the bogs up to my waist. By laboring so much, I became so heated, that the sweat came through my double winter clothes. I could not stand still, because perspiring, I was afraid of being injured by the cold. I was unable also to build up a fire, otherwise I would have remained in the forest until day. After wandering about for two hours, I at length came to a hedge, and found a house, where I rested a little, and reached the New Hanover school house about 10 o'clock. Several days afterwards I became sick, as I have already mentioned elsewhere.

In New Hanover an aged widow was sick. She had sent for me, but as I was not at hand by reason of official labors, and first came to her on the third day, she wept, and was of the opinion that I did not wish to visit her, because she was a poor person, and a despised widow before the world. I informed her in love, that in surroundings so extensive, I, as a man, could not be omnipresent, but with great effort must plague myself in the bad roads, in passing from one to another. As much as I understood in the conversation with her, she had already been a widow for long years, had lived among Catholics in Germany, and suffered much oppression, because she was unwilling to let her children become Catholics, but instructed them in the Protestant doctrine. In this country she diligently heard the Word of God, brought up her children well, and governed them in a godly manner, and to all appearance she had been a true widow, who remained solitary, placed her hope in God, and continued in prayer day and night. She contributed her mite to the building of the church, and esteemed it a great favor and kindness that the Lord sent teachers hither. I prayed with her, and edified her with consoling passages, and administered the Holy Supper to her. She wished me long life, grace and blessing in my difficult office, and said she hoped to see me again, in yonder life, at the right hand of the Lord Jesus. A few days afterwards I buried her, and understood from those of her family that she continued in prayer unto death, and also affectionately admonished her children, that they should abide in the Word of God and in the Protestant doctrine, and live aright.

In this past sixth year of my Pennsylvania pilgrimage, I administered the Holy Supper twice in my regular congregations and out-parishes, and only discontinued the public worship of God on two Sundays, because during the rest of the time, in my necessary absence, the congregations were provided for by my dear brethren in office. The number of children whom I baptized was about one hundred and eighteen. I confirmed thirty-eight young people, and buried twenty-nine persons. The gracious Father in Christ be most heartily praised, that he has borne with us in such great patience and forbearance, kept my beloved official brethren in life, and preserved our limbs in our journeys. May this same essentially good God and Father be gracious and merciful unto me poor sinner, for the sake of Jesus Christ, on account of my manifold sins of office and station, errors and faults; not enter into judgment with me, but blot them out as a cloud, and cast them into the depths of the sea, grant me his Holy Spirit in my difficult office, and through grace soon take me out of this vale of misery unto himself, and send laborers into his desolated vineyard, who possess more faithfulness, strength, courage, wisdom, experience, and gifts of office than I. Especially may the Lord permit the beloved Messrs. Brunnholtz and Handschuch to live yet a long time, and increase and strengthen their bodily vigor.

HENRY MELCHIOR MÜHLENBERG.

CHAPTER II.

CONTINUATION OF THE REPORT OF SEVERAL EVANGELICAL LUTHERAN CONGREGATIONS IN AMERICA, ESPECIALLY IN PENNSYLVANIA.

I. Intelligence concerning the most recent circumstances.

As may be seen in the previous article to the the praise of God, among other things, how the Lord had previously granted his blessing on the labor of his servants in the congregations in Pennsylvania, wherein that of which pastor Mühlenberg has written more at large, is to be so regarded, that a conclusion may be drawn from it also in reference to the work of the other preachers, so in this second section, therefore, intelligence is to be communicated of that which transpired since the publication of the preceding fourth continuation, in relation to the congregations in Pennsylvania, and of the changes which have taken place in the situation, according to the more recent letters hitherto received.

§ 2. As was already stated in the said former continuation, two new fellow laborers were again sent, Messrs. Heintzelmann and Schulze, who in July, 1751, began their journey from Halle, by way of London, to Pennsylvania. Now, as it was thought necessary that they should be ordained in Europe, that on their arrival they, according to circumstances and necessity, might be immediately employed in official acts, they took their way by Wernigerode, and after previous due examination of their fitness, they were ordained there on the 11th of July, by the High County Consistory, and besides also enjoyed many favors and much kindness from the High County authorities, and were abundantly refreshed by other good friends.

§ 3. They thereupon continued their journey by way of Magdeburg, Stendal, and Saltzwedel, in which two latter places they tarried several days with the relatives of Mr. Heintzelmann, and not without special blessing, being strengthened by them in the Lord and encouraged. Arriving in Hamburg on the 4th of

August, they again went aboard on the 11th, and arrived in London on the 2d of September. After a short stay there, which they sought to make use of for their further preparation and encouragement for their future circumstances, under the direction of the Royal Court preacher of London, Mr. Ziegenhagen, they again embarked at Gravesend, on the 17th of October, and after a short voyage of eight weeks, reached Philadelphia, safely and well, on the 12th of December, where they were received first by pastor Brunnholtz, and afterwards also by the rest of the preachers, with great joy and amid much praise to God.

§ 4. Among the many proofs of the providence of God on their voyage, they especially recognized this as a great favor, that a merchant from London traveled in company with them from Hamburg to England, who on their arrival directed them properly and kindly cared for them, whereas otherwise, on account of their ignorance of the English language, they could not so easily have gotten along in this strange and extensive city. And as they moreover, in the short time they remained there, could not acquire much of the said language, so it was in like manner to their advantage that on their further voyage to America, a son of a very kind friend of the preachers in Pennsylvania, from Philadelphia, was on the vessel with them, who manifested much love to them, and who was very useful to them among the rest of the company, consisting wholly of Englishmen, inasmuch as he spoke both English and German.

§ 5. Now, when all the preachers had come together and maturely considered all the circumstances, they esteemed it best that these two new fellow-laborers first remain, at least for a time, with the oldest two preachers, pastors Mühlenberg and Brunnholtz, as these needed help in their congregations in their already considerably wasted strength in the service of the Lord, by accumulated labors. Accordingly, Mr. Heintzelmann became the fellow laborer of pastor Brunnholtz in Philadelphia, lives in his house, and enjoys from him a free dwelling and table, because at present the congregation is as yet unable to decide upon a particular salary for him. Until another capable schoolmaster is found, he superintends the school three hours each day, whereof he obtains the remaining necessaries; and assists pastor Brunnholtz in preaching, catechising, and other public and private official acts. Now, as this arrangement conduces to a perceptible alleviation, and his upright intention and faithful assistance to a great comfort for pastor Brunnholtz, so also has the school (in which the organist does the remaining work) not only hereby attained to perfect order and good acceptance, but the most certain blessing is also to be hoped for, when the children enjoy solid instruction in Christianity from their tender youth, and are led to Christ, whereas labor with the old is often labor lost. As respects Mr. Schulze, pastor Mühlenberg took him as fellow laborer in church and school, and even from his only moderate salary, he allowed him the one-half for his support for a time. Afterwards, the congregation at New Goschenhoppen made the request that he should preach for them every two weeks, which, with the consent of his colleague, was also granted by pastor Mühlenberg, and accepted by Mr. Schulze, who in return for this receives aid from this congregation.

§ 6. In that which relates to the other congregations, it is to be observed in the first place, that a change has occurred in the congregation at Lancaster. Pastor Handschuch had accepted of the office of preacher in the same in May, 1748, for a time only on trial, and exercised it there during three years with indefatigable diligence and faithfulness. But as the congregations in Philadelphia and Germantown became much too extensive on the one hand, to be sufficiently cared for by one preacher, and as the Theological candidate, whom pastor Brunnholtz had taken for a time, with the intent that each congregation should at least have one regular sermon on each Sunday, had meanwhile been sent to several other congregations; and as, on the other hand, various circumstances counseled and required that a change be made with pastor Handschuch, all the preachers, after mutual consideration, thought it good that he should take leave of the congregation in Lancaster, and accept of the call as preacher in the congregation in Germantown, that he might labor in common with pastor Brunnholtz, in both the congregations in Philadelphia and Germantown; and as necessity required, the one assist the other in his official transactions.

§ 7. Now after this resolution was made known by a letter of all the preachers, which the schoolmaster read to the congregation at the close of the divine service, many good-meaning persons, who in part had been awakened to a greater concern for their souls by the services of pastor Handschuch, manifested their grief at his approaching departure with tears, and entreated him that he should remain with them longer, and also repeated this request through several wardens. But he could so much the less consent, as experience had latterly taught him, that by most of the congregation, his office was made burdensome to him. He thereupon, on Sunday Cantate, 1751, preached his farewell sermon in Lancaster, amid much emotion on the part of the hearers, and removed to Germantown soon after Whitsuntide, where he has hitherto administered his office with a blessing.

§ 8. To gain more room in the church in Philadelphia, several galleries not only had to be built, but also various other things for strengthening the building, and therefore nothing of the debt amounting to over 2,800 Rix dollars could be paid; yet it was also not increased, because the faithful God, by his kind blessing, presented the greater part to defray these new building expenses. Now, however, we hope that no further expenses will be required. But the room obtained by the galleries is not superfluous, inasmuch as the whole church is for the most part so filled, that there are no vacancies, whence the great increase of this congregation is perceived (consisting, however, mostly of poor members); and it is very well understood, that whilst Mr. Heintzelmann remains in Philadelphia as the fellowlaborer of pastor Brunnholtz, and the congregation in Germantown also has a preacher of its own, that this is not more than is needed, but that there is work enough for all the three preachers in these congregations. According to a more recent report, the church debt in Germantown amounts to nearly 750 Rix dollars. May the faithful God still further permit the fountain of his blessing to flow, that first of all more aid be extended to both these congregations, for the payment of the said debts.

§ 9. In relation to the fruit of the Word of God in the congregation in Philadelphia, pastor Brunnholtz, under date of March 16th, 1752, reports briefly concerning it as follows: "As respects my Philadelphia congregation of this place, of the most of them, and of the outward great mass, I cannot exactly boast much, as very much corruption is still among them. But the Lord has granted me a small gleaning in those who were awakened by the Word to seek the path of peace, and who permit themselves to be prepared for the rest of God with seriousness in silence. Among young married people, adult single persons, servants, and children, I still always have the most hope of seeing something accomplished. I ever find at my instruction of the young (Kinderlehre) (which I held in the church from the beginning, and continued in these later years with much pleasure and great earnestness, and also since the close of the year 1750, began still another special instruction for the youth, in my house on Friday evenings) occasions such an attraction, not only among the young, but also among others, as I perhaps would not have obtained by mere preaching, because the people comprehend and understand a discourse in question and answer much better than a connected sermon which sometimes is allowed to pass listlessly. On Sunday afternoon, therefore, when I have instruction for the young in the church, there are almost as many people present as in the forenoon, during the sermon. Many young men provide themselves with small Bibles, take them along to preaching and instruction, look for the passages, and also indeed answer when necessary. The most of them heretofore had no small Bibles, but now, when they are put to the blush by the youth. they become eager to follow them. Very many have their small Bibles before them, and use them diligently during the sermon and instruction; so that I am myself often encouraged, because I see that by these means they are kept more attentive; and they also have this advantage, that they are the better enabled to repeat the sermon at home, and to call to mind again the truths delivered by the passages looked for. A considerable number of the Halle Bibles, therefore, have already been sold, and those sent for this purpose are of great advantage to us. Yes, the servants, or bought domestics, indeed save something of the gratuities which they occasionally receive, until they are enabled to purchase a Bible with it. If they are altogether too poor, I indeed present them with one-third of the price, so the object is only attained. The young continually attain to more ability and pleasure in answering, in looking up the passages, and to show and to draw the answers therefrom. This is indeed not a real blessing, but still it is the beginning thereto. The one soweth and the other reapeth, John iv. 36. May the Lord then not let it be in vain that his Word is so abundantly proclaimed here in this wilderness, and also heard with much eagerness by both young and old, and preserve this seed scattered, together with all the powerful emotions of heart which are wrought thereby, that in time and eternity an abundant and superabundant fruit may accrue therefrom, to the praise of his glorious name.

§ 10. By reason of the faithfulness which the preachers exhibit in their congregations in Pennsylvania, and the blessing which the Lord bestows upon their labor, it is not to be wondered at, that other congregations continually manifest a desire to be so happy also, as in like manner to enjoy such faithful pastors. At least in such other congregations, there are always found some souls, hungry and eager for the Word of God, who not only wish to be fed therewith themselves by faithful teachers, but also when they see with what indescribable trouble and indefatigable diligence the Pennsylvania preachers gathered their congregations, and brought them into good order, they obtain the hope, that if their congregations could share in such honest teachers, these would be regulated in like manner also, and thus the entire ruin of the pure doctrine be avoided in the case of the children and descendants.

§ 11. It was this, also, which induced the Lutheran congregation in New York, which consists in part of people from the Netherlands, or who at least understand the Netherlandish language, afterwards to call pastor Mühlenberg as their regular preacher, when he in a journey to that region also came to that place, and at the desire of the wardens preached in their church. As they were at the time without a regular preacher, and an injurious division had arisen among them, they very earnestly petitioned him that he should not decline accepting this call, as they hoped that the division would be healed, and everything be fully brought into good order again by his diligence and faithfulness. Although he could not as yet determine to leave his congregations in Pennsylvania, so also he could not persuade himself to let the earnest entreaty of the New York congregation be entirely fruitless, without at least caring for them meanwhile in some manner.

§ 12. For this purpose, he permitted himself to be induced, not only to remain in New York, in the year 1751, from the 18th of May until the 26th of August, conducted divine service there, and fed both old and young with the Word of God, but he was also willing to go there again during the present year, 1752, for several months, when meanwhile Mr. Weygand also, after the departure of pastor Mühlenberg, had to remain in New York for a time, and provide for this congregation. In New Providence and New Hanover, during the absence of pastor Mühlenberg, the sermons and other official acts were provided for by his colleagues, of all of which more appears in the future articles of the report of pastor Mühlenberg's official transactions. It cannot be denied, that the worthy pastor Mühlenberg, in his journeys to New York, and his stay there, had to accept of many an inconvenience and denial, as he left his family in New Providence, and passed through many a peril on his travels. But the desire of various hungry souls found there, and the necessities of the congregation so strongly moved him, that he permitted nothing to prevent him from serving them. Thus much may suffice for the present, as a preliminary report of the most recent circumstances, as in the future continuations, the reports and letters of the preachers themselves are to be communicated, from which these and all other circumstances and changes will appear with additions.

§ 13. It can meanwhile not be otherwise, but that the heart of the faithful servant of God must bleed, who is truly concerned for the advancement of his kingdom, when he perceives the hunger for the pure publication of the Word of God in so many forsaken souls, and still has not the means in hand to care for them effectually, and therefore must let slip so many opportunities, when the work of God might be advanced. The greatest fault indeed consists herein, that so few of the large number who have outwardly devoted themselves to the ecclesiastical order, truly have the glory of God for their object, nor yet permit a hunger for winning souls to influence them; and that among the few who have a true desire in their hearts to carry forward the work of God with zeal, there are still fewer who are willing to deny their native land and relationship, and to follow the call of God abroad, not to say that there are many also who have real hindrances in their way to keep them back on account of their health, or their parents and other obligations. Indeed, if this lack of able and faithful laborers, so very much to be deplored, did not prevail in our time, such congregations, eager for the Word of God, could sooner be helped, and God would also impart the required outward means by his liberal blessing.

§ 14. Nevertheless, it is also not to be denied (as the Lord still has his true disciples and followers everywhere, and among the rest, also among the candidates for the preacher's office) that by the divine blessing, the necessary laborers for the vineyard in Pennsylvania may also indeed yet be gradually found. But from the want of the necessary expenses thereto, more cannot be undertaken for the present to promote the salvation of these souls. The congregations are unable to meet such expenses, and so much has also not been received by liberal benefactions, that even the traveling expenses of one or the other fellow laborer, to be sent, could be defrayed, or that any further aid could be extended to the congregations in Philadelphia and Germantown, for the payment of their debts, We justly commit to the faithful God (whom these souls cost the blood of his Son) the care for their deliverance, and for the extension of his kingdom, who will also in due time hear the most earnest prayer of his servants and children, and himself send faithful laborers into his harvest, and consequently also whatever of temporal blessings he recognizes as necessary for the advancement of his work, he will graciously bestow.

§ 15. This is the fixed purpose of the court preacher, Ziegenhagen, and of Dr. Francke (who have hitherto faithfully cared for these congregations, and to which they have been accustomed for a long time) in all good institutions, having in view the glory of God and the extension of his kingdom, to look only to God, and to follow the tokens of his gracious providence and guidance. Therefore, in order to proceed in this most safe of all ways, they also hitherto had no pleasure on their part, in availing themselves of other means, although in themselves unobjectionable.

§ 16. Thus it was proposed some time ago to the preachers of Pennsylvania, by a certain theologian earnestly concerned for the glory of God, and especially for the salvation of the congregations of Pennsylvania, to seek a general collection in the evangelical states of the Roman Empire; and also for the gathering of it, to send one to Europe by their own means. But although there is nothing objectionable in the thing itself, yet on account of the many abuses which are otherwise wont to occur with such collections, the above-mentioned servants of God hesitated to give their counsel and consent to the employment of this means. They rather committed it to the only heart-directing power of God, in what manner he would further awaken the hearts to a voluntary contribution, and how many means he would place in their hands, in whose faithful application, they on their part would let nothing be wanting.

§ 17. But some prejudices should be met on this occasion, because Christian benefactors might be hindered thereby from promoting these good institutions. Some may think that it is unreasonable to care for these people, as the most of them went into this distant part of the globe from their own irregular impulse, and without necessity or calling, because it no longer suited them to comply with good order in their native land, and to support themselves by the labor of their hands. Now, this conduct of these people is by no means to be approved, who as yet to this hour by hundreds, yea, and by thousands, give up their regular calling in which they already stand in Germany, and by many deceivers coming from America, permit themselves to be seduced to go to Pennsylvania, but thereby plunge themselves into indescribable spiritual and temporal distress. And that they should have any participation in the irregularities of these people, or approve of them and promote them, is a thing far from the court preacher Ziegenhagen and from Dr. Francke.

§ 18. But as regards those Germans already living in Pennsylvania, it is quite a different case. A great number of them have now already been born and raised there, and even if their parents did wrong, and acted contrary to the call of God when they removed to that place, still their children cannot now atone for that. But in relation to the old German immigrants who are yet living, or those who only arrived in later times, they are now there for once, and are unable to return again, and also have so little calling, and as respects the most of them, still less means for returning. Now, if these acknowledge and repent of their fault, and obtain a desire for the Word of God, shall we on this account let them starve with this hunger, not for bread, but for the Word of God, because they placed themselves in these circumstances? Or shall we not now rather seek to save their souls and to preserve true religion among them and among their children? If God should never permit himself to feel pity for the spiritual or temporal distress of those who plunged themselves into it, we should all perish.

§ 19. Others think that the good institutions established for these congregations are of no permanence. Let such however consider on the one hand what God has already wrought hitherto, and how he has granted his blessing. Shall he begin something, and not finish it? Or did he not hitherto prove that that which is begun in his name, he is also able to keep and to perfect? On the other hand, the servants of God have to this time gone no further, and in future also will go no further, than the footsteps of the divine guidance go before them, and the tokens of his providence manifest themselves. Now, as they do not outrun God, or undertake anything from their own impulse, so they also trust, and indeed with all right to his gracious aid, and confide in him in strong faith, that he will still further show his blessing.

§ 20. Others still are of the opinion indeed that the institutions are already so far advanced that no further assistance is required for them; and they might well be strengthened in such opinion, when they among other things read in the preface of the twelfth part of the Senior Doctor Fresenius' Pastoral Collection: " How pastor Schlatter assures him that the Evangelical Lutheran preachers had already brought their congregations into a far better condition than could have been done in the case of the Reformed congregations; which resulted herefrom, that they began sooner, and were bravely seconded by our fellow believers in Germany." This testimony of the man (parson Schlatter) zealously exerting himself for the glory of God among the Reformed congregations in Pennsylvania, may serve as a proof of that which was adduced in these reports, as already actually attained. But the highly esteemed Senior Fresenius did not intend by this that the institutions for the congregations of Pennsylvania needed no further aid; inasmuch as he himself explained his opinion in this behalf wholly otherwise in the supplement which he subjoins to the communicated true narrative of the shepherdless (Reformed) congregations in Pennsylvania in the said twelfth part of his Pastoral Collection ; as he there, after the foregoing citation, adds what was already done by the divine blessing for the best interests of the Lutheran congregations also: "Still I must here announce that more honest teachers, as well as further respectable pecuniary means, are necessary, if the great need is to be thoroughly remedied, and the American vineyard is to be so planted and cultivated that its fruits may be perennial."

§ 21. As for the rest, we cannot read without emotion that which said Reformed preacher in Philadelphia, Mr. Schlatter, reports of the condition of such Reformed congregations in his published letter of the pastorless congregations in Pennsylvania, which is inserted as noticed in the frequently-mentioned 12th part of the Pastoral Collection of Doctor Fresenius. It cheers us, but also at the same time justly shames us, when we see therefrom with what zeal the highly-esteemed Synod of Holland took to heart the distress of these shepherdless congregations, and laid it to the hearts of the rest of the brethren of their faith, and which God also thus blessed, that Doctor Fresenius could write in the preface: "There is no doubt that Mr. Schlatter and his assistants are now also better enabled to attain their object, after such respectable aid is put forth in Holland."

§ 22. All that which Mr. Schlatter truly relates concerning the lamentable condition of the Reformed congregations, may likewise be applied to the Lutheran congregation. He reckons the number of Reformed Germans in Pennsylvania at 30,000, who are dispersed in 46 congregations, out of which 16 parishes might be formed, and served by an equal number of preachers. He reports that the congregations united, and mentions what each one is able to raise for the support of their preachers. But he supposes, nevertheless, that for their support, and for the maintenance of a schoolmaster in each place, besides that which the congregations give, an annual contribution of 2,000 Hollandish florins would yet be required; and with much zeal the Synod took care to raise a capital, from the interest of which these expenses might be defrayed.

§ 23. Now if (as may very properly be done) we assume the number of German Lutherans to be twice as large, we may easily understand that twice as many preachers also and schoolmasters, and consequently also twice as much would be required for their support, if all the congregations are to be sufficiently provided for. But as we in our church in Germany have no such society or assembly of theologians who could care for such an exigency, with the emphasis as did the Synod in Holland, so without extraordinary help from God himself, we can indeed hardly ever promise ourselves that the condition of our German fellow-believers in all Pennsylvania will be brought into perfect order and proper adjustment. Meanwhile, it is nevertheless earnestly to be desired, that at least the work begun in the congregations already standing under the supervision of the preachers sent from Halle to Pennsylvania, might be perfected and preserved in good order and in faith, we justly confide in the faithful providence of God, that he will thereto further grant his blessing. Only remarking yet, that this which was hitherto cited, was by no means noticed to burden any one who is not himself awakened of God to a liberal contribution, as this would be wholly against the intention of the said servants of God. We have only desired hereby to remove the prejudices out of the way, which are found in many.

§ 24. But on this occasion also, a reminder is to be added for the sake of many members of our congregations. It was mentioned before, that Mr. Schlatter thought it necessary that sufficient aid be extended to those preachers, besides that which the congregations collect for their support, but which is insufficient, so that they may have a moderate honest subsistence. It would also not at all have been unreasonable, and where necessary, it would likewise not have been contrary to the design of the benefactors, if this could have been done from the liberal favors received, at least in the case of several Lutheran preachers. For this reason also, many of the members of the congregation may think that their preachers have hitherto enjoyed the like contributions, as they did not see that they demanded even that which was promised to them with any strictness, but rather were content with that which each one presented them, from his own impulse and free will. But this, until date, has still been wholly impossible, inasmuch as the generous benefactions received were scarcely sufficient to defray the required traveling expenses of the preachers who were sent, and to make a small beginning toward the payment of the church debt. Each year, the preachers also transmitted to the court-preacher Ziegenhagen and to Doctor Francke, a full account of the remittances received by them. In the present year they also transmitted a repetition of this account from the beginning until this time, from which may be seen that all that they received of the moneys collected was faithfully applied to the wants of the churches.

§ 25. The Lord be humbly praised, that he has begun graciously to care for the widely-dispersed and perishing sheep by his Word and by his servants. May he henceforth not cease to send them faithful shepherds, and by these to feed and to save them, and therein do much more than we can ask and understand, for the sake of his grace and compassion. Amen!

CHAPTER III.

SIXTH CONTINUATION OF THE REPORT OF SEVERAL EVANGELICAL LUTHERAN CONGREGATIONS IN AMERICA, ESPECIALLY IN PENNSYLVANIA.

THIS present sixth continuation of the report concerning the Pennsylvania congregations, which is herewith presented to the kind reader, contains the personal reports of the oldest three preachers of both the years 1749 and 1750. What pastor Mühlenberg wrote in said years of his official transactions is the most detailed, although not near so circumstantial as the reports of the two preceding years, communicated in the previous continuation. The reason of this is easily found in his journey to Albany, and in his subsequent journeys to New York, where he remained for several months, as well in the year 1751 as in 1752. For as he is accustomed to make an extract from that which he is wont to write of his official transactions for his own information, and to relate somewhat more amply the most important circumstances, especially of the noticed workings of the grace of God in the soul, it is easily conceived that these journeys and the long absence from his regular congregations, as well as the accumulated work in these afterwards, did not permit him to bestow as much time on writing this report as he could spare thereto from his labor in the preceding years. Notwithstanding this, the kind reader will still find much therein which is acceptable, and which may awaken him to the praise of God for the blessing which the Lord has bestowed upon his work.

Pastors Brunnholtz and Handschuch had indeed also undertaken to arrange the report of their official transactions in like manner. But as these (in the constant contact and commingling of official transactions in their town congregations), had hitherto not so much time left as was required thereto, they excused themselves that they were not as yet able to put their purpose into practice. Of the former, therefore, there are only a few letters subjoined, or rather an extract from them of the things which are most worthy of note, from which, however, his honest intention, together with his zeal for the glory of God, and the salvation of the souls entrusted to him, may be seen, as well as the condition not only of his own, but also of the rest of the united congregations. Now especially, as this faithful servant of God was at that time frequently very infirm, he is so much the more excusable for not having sent such a detailed account of his official transactions as we could indeed have wished for, as it cannot be doubted that it would have been very acceptable and edifying to read. He could not determine in mind to send the diary, which he kept for his own information, without enlarging it, although he even mentions that it would have been sufficiently ample.

As on the contrary, the latter, pastor Handschuch, sent a copy of his diary, just as he had briefly written in it the daily occurrences, so we have communicated an extract from it, in the third article, although he did not send it with this intent, but only for the information of Doctor Francke. If this extract could have been perfected by himself, it would doubtless have become much more circumstantial and acceptable. In many places in his diary he only noted in a few words that he had observed the workings of grace in one and in another during a visit in sickness, or on other occasions, when in an extract made by himself he would doubtlessly have added other circumstances which he remembered, of the good perceived in these souls. But we did not think it best to burden the reader with such naked generalities, but omitted them in the printed extract, together with most of the narrations of his ordinary official transactions. So much generally was otherwise to be seen from it, that he manifested great earnestness in his office. If any fault could be found therewith, it is that he labored almost beyond his ability and strength for the salvation of souls; inasmuch as he, not only for the most part on Sundays, besides the two public services, but also frequently on other days, especially at the time when those announced themselves who intended coming to the Holy Supper, passed the time from early in the morning until the coming night, in attending to the numerous calls, visiting the sick and the well, and in other official transactions. It is also well perceived that he had a favorable reception with the most of them, although it was afterwards not so acknowledged by all, as it justly should have been. As for the rest, this extract is connected with the printed extract in the third continuation of his diary, kept on the voyage, and in the beginning of his residence in Pennsylvania, and therefore begins in September, 1748, but extends only to May, 1750, because the report following that was lost at sea.

In relation to the most recent events reported in the last letters received from Pennsylvania, the following changes only are to be noted for the present: 1. Mr. Heintzelmann was accepted as their second regular preacher, by the congregation in Philadelphia. 2. As pastor Mühlenberg could not leave his congretions in Providence and New Hanover, the congregation in New York called Mr. Weygand as their preacher; to whose place, 3, in the congregation at Raritan, Mr. Schrenck was assigned, who is mentioned several times in these reports, and who in the following years always conducted himself well, and also increased in theological knowledge and in experience from day to day. As for the rest, all the preachers were well, and had recovered considerably from the infirmity previously experienced. But of all this, and whatever else further transpired, will appear in the extended reports in the following continuations, whereof the next will, with the divine aid, be published at the future fair, and will contain much that is edifying and acceptable of the years 1751 and 1752.

But the greatest concern of the preachers consists herein, that for the instruction of the numerous youth so few adequate institutions are at hand, when nevertheless in a country where such a multiplicity of sects and opinions prevail, the highest necessity demands that the young be established and fortified in time in the knowledge of God and divine truth, by sufficient instruction, so that they may not in future permit themselves to be driven about by every wind of doctrine. The preachers have hitherto used all possible diligence and care, but still the means which were required are wanting to lay the foundation in several places of school buildings which are still wanting, and to appoint enough and capable schoolmasters, and also to provide them with the necessary support. In Philadelphia especially, as the chief city of the country, and where the harbor is into which more than a thousand, yea, perhaps several thousands of Germans from Europe, annually are accustomed to come, it is most highly necessary to build a roomy school-house, and the great number of youth require that at least from two to three school colleagues should be appointed to labor in the school; but the school money received is insufficient to maintain even one, and has hitherto only served to pay for the remaining necessaries of Mr. Heintzelmann, except the table, with which pastor Brunnholtz supplied him. The congregation is unable to raise that which is necessary for a school building, as they are yet involved in much debt from building the church. In the meanwhile, the preachers have the hope that the Lord will further have pity upon the necessities of the congregations, and especially bestow the means for a school institute in Philadelphia, when afterwards better arrangements can also be thought of in the remaining congregations.

Now, that it pleases the Lord to continue his gracious providence for these poor congregations, he has manifested by a very clear proof in this, that besides other generous gifts which arrived, a certain patron and kind benefactor out in Germany was awakened to appropriate a respectable capital for these congregations, and actually paid it over, of which he retained the interest for himself until his death; but directed that after his decease it be applied for the benefit of these congregations as necessity requires, especially also among other things for the establishment of good school institutions, and that the entire disposition and administration of it be entrusted to the existing directors of the orphan-house at Halle, according to their best knowledge. The name of the Lord be heartily praised, who has made this dear patron willing to concern himself for the advancement of the work of God among these congregations, by such a generous and considerable charitable foundation. May he reward him for his great benefaction with a superabundant blessing for time and eternity, and grant his rich blessing to the future application of the interest of this capital, which, according to the will of the most worthy benefactor, is to be used as a permanent fund for the Pennsylvania congregations. As this benefaction, acknowledged indeed with all due thankfulness to God and the dear benefactor, is nevertheless quite insufficient to meet the wants, the congregations also only have the benefit thereof after the decease of the kind founder, we also trust his kind paternal providence, that the Lord will further, from time to time, graciously bestow as much as is necessary to carry forward these institutions. Meanwhile, by this liberal foundation, these are established as a permanent work, and the servants of God, who have hitherto cared for these, are thereby very powerfully strengthened in their trust in his providence, and encouraged anew not to let their hands sink, but according to the grace which the Lord will bestow, to advance and support these to the utmost. But they look into the hands of the Lord, and trust alone to his gracious aid and blessing, which he may further bestow on all efforts in behalf of these congregations. May he also remember his messengers, whom he has sent to these congregations, and care for them in their manifold cares, wants, and sufferings, strengthen them amid all labor, and accompany them with his blessing, that his name may be praised therefor, and yet many souls be saved eternally, for the sake of his compassion. Amen!

Continued report of Pastor Mühlenberg's official transactions in the years 1749 and 1750.

In the beginning of the winter of the past year, a change occurred with the schools in our congregations. For, when pastor Handschuch and his congregation in Lancaster were much concerned because they were without a capable schoolmaster in the town for their numerous youth, and I once intimated that our schoolmaster and catechist in New Hanover might perhaps suit that place, the wardens of the Lancaster congregation took the word, and ceased not until he accepted of the service. Now the school at New Hanover was not alone deprived of a teacher, but the congregations of Upper Milford and Saccum were also forsaken, and became dissatisfied that their instructor of the youth was removed.

As to the school in New Hanover, I supplied his place with another young man, who had kept school in the neighborhood for a few years. He had come into this country when young, and was sold to a distinguished Quaker for many years. The little which he collected in his mind of the Evangelical religion in Germany had prevented him from entangling himself with the Quakers, although he served many years among them, went along with them into their meetings, and had many temptations to go over to them, especially as he had no opportunity to attend Evangelical divine service. When he had served out his years, and consequently was free, he applied himself to keeping school; but had in the previous years grown up in darkness and in ignorance, except that he had learned to read and to write English, and had led a free life. He came once and again into our meeting in New Hanover, was convinced by the Word of God, fell into a godly sorrow for his sins, and now in this light, to his salvation, he begins to know the one true God, and him whom he has sent, Jesus Christ. He now attends to the school before-mentioned in New

Hanover, and also gives good hope that he will ever better establish himself in true repentance, faith and godliness.

As respects the congregations in Upper Milford and Saccum, I cannot myself well visit them in the rough winter months, because time and strength will not admit, nor yet allow them to be visited by the present schoolmaster, as by the former. Meanwhile I must hear to my sorrow, that in Saccum a so-called parson again crept in, who, on account of his exceptionally vexatious life, had been removed before, and that already one or several brothers of the Zinzendorfer crept into the houses here and there, and also baptized several children. As soon as we have planted only the least plant, and turn our back, the parasites fasten on it, and devour everything.

In Providence, the neighbors around the church also accepted of a schoolmaster who had come from Germany. He has between thirty and forty children to instruct, whereto, however, the school-house is too small, as it has only one room, and the schoolmaster has a family. We will therefore be obliged to erect another building by the side of it.

Pastor Brunnholtz has taken our old friend Mr. Vigera into his house, and lets him keep school in Philadelphia. Our schools should, notwithstanding, succeed better than they do. The old trees die, and if we plant no young ones, we cannot expect fruit.

January the 1st, 1749. In the beginning of this year, I had a funeral in New Hanover. We interred the corpse this New Year's day. A little girl of five years, who had pious parents, died in the Lord. The child was a joy to her parents and to me, because the Holy Spirit had his temple and habitation in her. She could repeat various edifying passages and hymns, and stammer very sweetly and pleasantly of her Saviour, so that we could not listen to her without emotion. The most of her conversation (proportional to her age and comprehension), was of the Lord Jesus, the holy angels, and a speedy dissolution to be with the Lord Jesus, amid which conversation and prayer the child expired.

In the very same month, the father of the before-mentioned child died also, aged thirty-six years. From a desire to become rich, the man had overdone himself in his younger years by hard labor. But for several years, the gracious God drew him to himself by severe illness, and taught him to give heed to the word. No less also was his pious wife, with her quiet life and edifying speech, at the proper time a promoter of his repentance. She once heard him pray with tears: Alas! blessed God, I have had so much love and inclination to earthly possessions. Root this love and propensity out of my heart, and give unto me a hunger and a thirst for my Lord Jesus, and for his righteousness, etc., etc. At another time, he was in his field, engaged in the work of his calling. When his wife came to him, he let the plough stand, and said: My dear wife, I never could believe that I was a sinner before God, because I led an honest life, and was conscious of no gross vice. But now the world is too narrow for me, and I feel as if I should sink, because the Word of God testifies against me in my conscience, and heaven and earth from without testify against me, and say, that among all men on earth, I am the greatest sinner. Alas! where shall I find counsel and help for the hurt of my soul? The woman answered: Now is the proper time for us to bend our knees, and come to the Lord Jesus, weary and heavy laden. With various passages and verses out of the penitential hymns, she sought to convince him that he was welcome to the Lord Jesus if he approached him with a truly penitential heart, with a longing hunger and thirst for his grace, and with an earnest purpose to amend his life, through his strength. With such like encouragements, she also sought to awaken him, according to the measure of her own knowledge and experience, and remained his domestic preacher until death. When I buried the husband, and observed how the widow conducted herself at the funeral, I found her sorrowful indeed, but nevertheless not like the heathen. She comforted herself with the Word of God, and was very silent. Several of the foolish people who were present at the burial construed her calmness into a want of love to her late husband, in which they however erred, and gave me the opportunity to show the difference between converted and unconverted widows, and to explain it to them in a manner which they could comprehend.

On the 15th of January, I traveled with my

father-in-law, Mr. Weiser, to Philadelphia. Now, as about this time four years ago, pastor Brunnholtz, together with Messrs. Kurtz and Schaum, arrived safely, we called to mind the gracious guidance of God, and encouraged ourselves to praise God for it, and to pray for our highly venerable fathers, patrons, and benefactors in Europe, and for our congregations here, and thereby to be mindful of the whole church militant.

On the 22d of January, I baptized a grown child of an English neighbor in Providence, for whom I had already baptized three adult children. The woman is Low Dutch, comes diligently to our meeting, and also permits her children to go to our school. May God give his increase, that they as branches may abide in the vine, be purified daily, and bear good fruit.

In the month of February, a man of the Providence congregation died. He had been troubled for many years with asthma and a cough, and was miserable in body. When I inquired after his soul's condition, I received for answer, that he was a poor nothing, and yet a sinful worm before God, worthy of condemnation, and comforting himself with his Lord Jesus Christ. He gladly went to church when his sickly condition would permit; he also read diligently in Arndt's True Christianity. During his illness, he said to one of our wardens, that he could not sufficiently thank God that he had awakened our highly venerable fathers to send teachers who cared for the poor scattered souls. Shortly before his death he had me called once more, confessed and received the Holy Supper, and requested me also, in taking leave, that I should bury him, but not to remember his person, as he had nothing at all in himself but corruption and misery. But besides this, it is not our custom to preach concerning the dead. We are wont to tell the attendants briefly, that if they had seen anything good in the deceased, they should esteem it as a gracious gift from God, and let it serve as an example in the order of repentance and of faith. But where they saw anything wicked, they should take it as an example of their own corrupt hearts, and let this serve them for a warning and for improvement. He was buried in the Mennonite churchyard, as he had lived near there. And as there was a large attendance of various opinions and sects present, I preached to them repentance towards God, whereto they were very attentive. After the sermon, one of the Mennonite preachers repeated to me, with a deep sigh, the verse, Deut. v. 29: *O that there were such a heart in them, that they would fear me, and keep all my Commandments always.* This gave me opportunity to have an edifying conversation with him. At the funeral we had a deep snow under foot, and a drizzle over head, and I had to walk several miles to the place, whereby I got into a profuse perspiration, and caught cold by reason of the wet. This made me sick and bed-ridden for four weeks. Nevertheless, I had thereby to perform my ordinary official duties, and twice fainted on the pulpit. I bled myself, but, as there is little communication with the city in winter, because of the bad weather, I had otherwise no medicine wherewith to help nature, except domestic and Indian remedies, which the Lord at length blessed to my recovery.

In the month of March, one of the elders in New Hanover died, whom I had found as an elder, and for good reasons retained. He was brought up in the evangelical religion, and diligently kept himself to the church, both in Germany and in this country, but with all this, did not lead the best life, etc. Yet the gracious and long-suffering God loved his poor soul, and would willingly save him from destruction. Accordingly, he permitted him to fall into a sickness seven years since, which may indeed have been a natural consequence of his sinful life, but was still accompanied with chastening grace unto his salvation. He could take nothing more of strong drink, without recalling the most tormenting incidents. Now he had seven years time to consider his former manner of life, to understand it, and to repent of it, and to employ the present season of grace for salvation. But before he perceived the true cause of his malady, and would come to the right physician, he employed all remedies for the body which he met with. However, nothing would take effect. At length he became silent, came to himself like the prodigal, and testified several times that he regarded his sickness as a special favor from God, as he was thereby drawn away by force from his sinful life, and by the saving grace of God gradually rescued as a brand from the fire. In his last will, he bequeathed three pounds to our church in New Hanover.

In the same month, a man came to me from the same congregation, and desired to speak with me concerning the state of his heart. He had already passed several years in a legal work of repentance, desired to deliver himself from his sins without Christ, and then always fell deeper into them. I spoke with him several times, and directed him to the destroyer of sin, Jesus Christ, which, however, was at no time quite successful. He said that as often as he was in the church and heard the Word of God, his heart and conscience became tranquil and joyful, but when he reached home the anxiety and fear again began. It was almost with him as with the aged Myconius, in the time of the Reformation, who in the agony of his conscience had a sweet dream of justification, and yet continued in the same anguish when he awoke from the dream, until he truly experienced the process of justification, by reflecting upon John the Evangelist, and the epistle to the Romans. When the before-mentioned man spoke with me on this occasion, he assured me that for the sake of Christ, the Heavenly Father had forgiven him all his sins, as one who was weary and heavy laden, and had imputed to him the sufficient righteousness of Christ; and now when he was intent on leading a new life in faith, he had already on various occasions to suffer nicknames and mockery, which however occasioned him more joy than sorrow. He testified that he was encouraged anew by the funeral sermon of the before-described elder, and driven to Jesus with his wounded heart, when he ceased not to ask, to seek, and to knock, until the paternal heart was opened unto him in Christ, and he obtained thence righteousness, peace, and free access to ineffable grace. We prayed with each other in secret, which made him still more joyful and confident. In taking leave, he said that I would see that the Lord would shortly take him out of this wicked world, although he had only lived to see between thirty and forty years, and must leave back a delicate wife and uneducated children. In ten days afterwards, he died with pleurisy, and requested me, by his neighbor, that I should preach his funeral sermon on the text Isa. xxxviii. 17, which he had experienced in life and in death: *Behold, for peace I had great bitterness; but thou hast in love to my soul delivered it from the pit of corruption, for thou hast cast all my sins behind thy back.*

Soon afterwards another man died in New Hanover, who, in the first years of my presence here had been my bitter enemy, and who permitted himself to be instigated against me by associates. He led a profligate life, and pretended withal to be a Lutheran. Now, because I reprimanded him by the Word of God, he conceived a furious hatred against me, and also suggested to his brother's daughter that she should make oath before the authorities that I had desired wicked things of her, and yet to my knowledge I had never seen the woman. But before she could commit the crime it was discovered, and the man appeared publicly before the congregation, and acknowledged his wickedness, said also that he was sorry for it, and he gave it to me in writing before witnesses that he had done this from wilful spite. Afterwards he placed himself at a distance, and again was present at divine service, and also several times declared to me that he would heartily turn to God, whereto he was diligently admonished, and also received from me spiritual and temporal favors in his poverty, so that he might not think that I entertained the least appearance of revenge against his person and his family. He at length still drew nearer, and heard the Word of God with great attention. We also observed a change in his conduct outwardly, but whether a true repentance was effected in his soul I cannot say with certainty. Thus much a man of his relationship, who is somewhat enlightened, testified, that in his last illness he wrestled and contended very much, and also said to his children and to those present, O children, help me pray, for I have mountains of sins resting upon me! I must otherwise sink if prayer does not prevail! The before-mentioned friend said he had assisted with prayer, according to his feeble ability, and thought that the patient had attained grace before his departure. I was far away, and was not sent for, otherwise I would gladly have been at his death. He let them wish me good night, and say that I should bury him with the funeral text, Song of Solomon ii. 16: *My beloved is mine, etc.* I did this, explained the passage, and also the 21st, 22d and 23d verses of the 18th chapter of Ezekiel.

In the month of April, a young married woman of the New Hanover congregation fell asleep. She was enlightened by the Word of God, and was able to give a reason of the faith and of the love to our Lord Jesus, for she had accepted of him in faith, and he had given her power to be called a child of God. In intercourse, I was several times edified by her pious conversation, because she knew by experience how a weary and heavy laden sinner, who has come to Christ and is pardoned, is disposed, and also endeavors in his following to learn meekness and heartfelt humility. Immediately in the beginning of her illness, she thought it probable that she would attain to the rest which is yet remaining, and therefore prepared herself properly for her departure. I was invited to go up from Providence and administer the Holy Supper to her, but on account of other necessary official labor, I could only go to her on the next day. When I came to her, I saw that already some signs of approaching death were present. She said: I heartily desired to be once more strengthened and refreshed in this mortal state with the body and blood of my Lord Jesus before I die, otherwise I might indeed already have departed this life. When I asked her whether she was prepared for a happy departure, she answered: " I have a desire to depart and be with Christ! Lord, now let thy handmaiden depart in peace, for the eyes of my faith have seen thy salvation, etc. But that which makes my departure hard are my minor children, whom I must leave uneducated in this wild and seductive land. Still, I have commended them in prayer to my heavenly Father, and hope that he will lead them in an even path to heaven, and let none of them perish." She confessed and prayed fervently with me, and with hunger and thirst partook of the Holy Supper, and fell asleep in the Lord five hours afterwards, to the sorrow of all acquainted with her. Her funeral text was taken from John i. 47, *Behold an Israelite indeed, in whom is no guile.*

In the same month, I buried a man who maintained his connection with the congregation in Providence, although he lived somewhat remote. He was a diligent hearer of the Word of God, and a benefactor to his pastor, for which he had often to hear mockery and backbitings from the sects among whom he dwelt. At first he held to the body of people with whom parson Andrea stands, but afterwards came to us, and said that he wished membership where he found the most edification for his soul.

In the same month, a warden in the congregation in New Hanover died. He had been an officer in the military service of Saxony for many years, led an honorable and peaceful life, but may indeed have experienced very little of a true change of heart, as in most of his conversation he had the former war history for a hobby, and manifested thereby that of which his heart was full. He suffered for several years from a dry cough, but in the last year especially he lay in the furnace of affliction. I visited him several times, and said that he should turn to God with his whole heart, and pray diligently with David, that the Lord might not remember the sins of his whole past life. He said, weeping:

I never thought that the last days could be so bitter, when sickness and afflictions come, and in addition, conscience awakes. I asked whether one passage and another of the sermons which he had heard in so many years did not occur to him. He answered yes, and acknowledged that God, by his Word and Spirit, worked in his soul, and called him to repentance, etc. He was admonished that he, according to the fifty-first Psalm, should go back with the holy David to the source of his corruption, and to consider well both original and actual sins from his birth to the present time, according to the law of God, and earnestly reflect upon the guilt and punishment of sin, that he might be moved to a godly sorrow, repentance and regret, and thereby be driven to the Redeemer, who is our righteousness, etc. He had time enough thereto, and as I hope, the gracious God on his part tried all possible means for his salvation.

In this oft-mentioned April, the wife of a church elder in New Hanover fell asleep. She had been well instructed in her youth. She could read, write and repeat beautiful choice passages from the Word of God. By very diligent hearing of the Word of God in the church, and studious searching at home, she was gradually enlightened and drawn to Christ. She had a consciousness and feeling of her sinful condition, hungered and thirsted after righteousness, and was also filled with the rich blessings of grace in Christ. According to her confession, the penitential hymn, From my transgression I will, etc., may have been among others, a means to her more immediate awakening and conversion. Now, after she was refreshed in the Lord, she found rich nourishment in the promises of God in the Old and New Testaments, and among others also, made good use of the beautiful hymns; as e. g., Alas all, which encompasses heaven and earth, etc.; O Jesus, my bridegroom, how happy am I, etc.; Wherefore then should I myself grieve, etc.; O thou Triune God, etc. She had to suffer much in her last illness, still she besought her Saviour that he would grant her patience and faithfulness until her end, but melt everything away which had yet been hidden of dross and impurities. When other foolish people regarded the preachers as a burden, and their doctrines as yoke-cords, she on the contrary thanked the Lord with tears of joy, that he awakened our highly venerable fathers, patrons and benefactors in Europe to come to our help. Her own brother, together with his wife, with goods and chattels, had permitted himself to be misled to Bethlehem to the Zinzendorfer, which she heartily deplored, and made many representations to him, in letters and orally, but without the desired result. He thought to bring her, and she thought to lead him, to the right way. In her last illness, she admonished me that I should remain faithful in my office and in the Word of God, and not become weary, that she might see me again with joy before the throne of God. She had selected for her funeral text, Psalm xciv. 19. *In the multitude of my thoughts within me, thy comforts delight my soul!*

In the same month, a young married woman in New Hanover died in child-bed. She was of Reformed parentage, and had several years before, together with her husband, been confirmed by me, and prepared for the Holy Supper. In her speedy departure I could not be present, but still I heard that she calmly submitted herself to the Lord, and I had also before observed something of the living seed of regeneration in her. Her funeral sermon was preached on 1 Samuel iv. 20.

On the 19th of April, a person of about thirty-six years, the daughter of an English widow, was united in marriage to her bridegroom, in my house, by pastor Brunnholtz. The mother was a Quakeress, and had also dedicated this daughter to this sect, and consequently also left her unbaptized. But when, in the year 1740, a certain English preacher filled Pennsylvania with the sound of the gospel, this person was awakened by the Word of God, and led to repentance and faith. Afterwards, she was variously and unceasingly called, especially by the Zinzendorfer, to forsake the right way. But she diligently gave heed to the Bible and to Arndt's True Christianity, was wise as a serpent, but harmless as a dove, and permitted herself to be seduced upon no by-paths. Now, as she stood alone and became acquainted with me, she came diligently to our church, studied the German language, showed a growth in grace, and at length permitted herself to be examined in the congregation in her own language, and to be baptized in the name of the Lord. She had to suffer much on that account from both parties, and the Quakers had already before sent her a written ban or dismission, because she, according to their manner of speaking, had associated herself with the world. My colleague, Brunnholtz, afterwards confirmed her, and admitted her to the Holy Supper. She walked worthily of her calling, and proved herself a Phœbe. Her mother was burdened with a severe illness for eight or nine years, so that she was most of the time in bed, and required attention day and night. This daughter served her mother faithfully, and for that reason refused various seemingly advantageous opportunities for marriage, as she was unwilling to leave her sick mother; and may therefore serve as a pattern to all children, especially how they should show their obligations to poor and sick parents, according to the Fourth Commandment, and comfort themselves thereby with the gracious promises of God concerning his providence. The faithful God grant that these two persons in this newly-begun conjugal life may lose nothing, but daily grow in grace, and attain the end of faith, the salvation of the soul.

Just at this time, a student of philosophy and law moved into my house, who in the month of March had arrived in Philadelphia in a ship from London. His name is Ludolph Henry Schrenck, born in Luneburg. He had heard the rudiments of the new philosophy and some legal lectures in the university at Erlangen. But after he had been at the university several years, his means failed, so that he could not subsist much longer. Now, when he saw a report from Georgia, which was translated from the English into German, and printed at Göttingen, he was induced thereby to go to America, and especially to Georgia. For this purpose he went to London, and tried whether, with the assistance of the trustees, he could get to Georgia, and establish himself there in conformity with his purpose. But he received no attention, and in a few weeks there consumed his remaining money to such an extent, that he could scarcely get on a Pennsylvania merchant vessel, pay for his passage, and land at Philadelphia. When he disembarked, he was an utter stranger, and knew not what to do or where to go, until he was directed to pastor Brunnholtz, to whom he complained of his present condition with tears, asked for good advice, and exhibited the printed report from Georgia, according to which he had hitherto regulated himself. According to universal love, pastor Brunnholtz could not do otherwise than to care for him, according to his feeble ability. But according to the circumstances of this country, it is uncommonly difficult to assist a German lawyer to the extent that he may obtain a sufficiency of bread. An advocate or notary he could not be, because these must be thoroughly acquainted with the English language and laws. Besides, there are Englishmen enough here who learn the art from the lawyers, like the tradesmen in Germany. My father-in-law thought of taking him to the Surveyor-General, but he had only heard in part the theory of surveying, and was without the English language, which, besides, a German does not so easily learn. An Englishman promised to help him to his bread if he understood the English language perfectly; but who would give him bread during the protracted time of learning it? Of book-keepers, there is a superabundance of the English nation. Merchant or shop-keeper he could not be, as there was no capital. For handicraft and coarse farm work the educated are unfitted, and military service there is none at all in Pennsylvania. Tutors and preceptors educated Germans cannot become, as a sufficient number come in from Scotland and Ireland, who are employed for these purposes. The German schools are so constructed that a man can scarcely live thereby, if besides he does not follow a trade or the work of a day-laborer. Thus poor Mr. Schrenck was in a bad predicament, in order to get into a position to serve God and his neighbor, and to support himself honestly. He could neither get backwards nor forwards. Pastor Brunnholtz shared with him according to his ability whatever the utmost necessity required, diligently admonished him to repentance and faith, and so arranged matters that he should have his food and maintenance for a time in my house. Accordingly, he moved to me on the 19th of April, and applied himself to the Studium Biblico-Catecheticum, wherein he improved considerably in a short time, and also gave me to understand several times that it had an influence on his heart.

Now, as above-mentioned, the congregations in Upper Milford and Saccum were wholly forsaken, and were enticed by rude, vicious, uncalled preachers, as well as the Zinzendorfer; so we concluded to place Mr. Schrenck there as catechist, on trial, after previous instruction, and permitted him occasionally to prepare a catechetical discourse, and after we had revised it, preach it in the congregation. We told the wardens candidly, how and in what manner we received the man, and what our object was thereby. The wardens had on each occasion to send a sealed written testimonial of his discourse and of his conduct. They seemed delighted with his discourse and behavior. In the meantime, two very small congregations petitioned to be received into our care, both of which are fifteen miles from Saccum. When, therefore, Mr. Schrenck had in about every three weeks prepared a proposition or discourse, and had the same revised by us, he visited the four congregations successively, and edified them with the one discourse, and again returned. The congregations are poor, live far away in the rocky hills, cannot conveniently maintain a regular preacher, but still they would hear the Word of God, and not become the servants of the Zinzendorfer, tolerably near to whom they live; hence we are forced to do something tending to their welfare.

In the months of April and May, I instructed fourteen young persons in the congregation in Providence, confirmed them, and admitted them to the Holy Supper. Among them was a person of eighteen years, whose parents in the beginning separated themselves from the congregation in Providence, because the man was proud, rude and foolish, and desired to rule everything according to his own notions. The circumstances were these: a small chest of Bibles and hymn-books, etc. was sent after me from London for the three congregations, which were divided into three parts, and one part given to each congregation. The wardens of Providence said that their portion of the books should be sold in the congregations, and the money used for church-building purposes, thus it would be for the benefit of the whole congregation, as there were not books enough that each family, yea, not one in ten, could get one, and consequently nine would grumble wherever the tenth had the preference, etc. This man, however, insisted on it, that we should make a present of the books in the congregation, and when this was not done, he separated himself, proclaimed the church a Babel, and held to those who (like him) were opposed to us. Notwithstanding this, his poor children held on to the congregation, and wept over their father's obduracy, and were often reviled and rebuked by their father on account of their church-going. This person was very attentive to the Word of God during instruction, and experienced salutary emotions by the Spirit of God through the Word. Another person of eighteen years also had indeed been neglected in earlier years, because her parents lived remote from churches and schools, viz: in Oley. She was, however, very tractable and desirous to learn, wherefore I also permitted her to live with me for a time, that she might lay so much the better foundation, which she also did to my joy. Still another, an orphan, who served with scoffers, and was much neglected, but was set free from these people by her guardian, and brought to instruction, so that she might yet perhaps attain to better thoughts, and be saved. The master had put so many lies and calumnies into the head of the poor maid-servant concerning me, and among other things made her believe that the parson would flay her and strew salt into the raw flesh, that her guardian had to bring her into my house almost by force. I kept her in my house for about five months, let her go to school, gave her to eat and drink in the dear time, when I had to pay even seven shillings and sixpence for a measure of wheat, and advanced her so far, that she could make her confession of faith tolerably well, and be confirmed with the rest. She attained a fine knowledge of salvation, showed herself pliant and affected, and afterwards moved to her guardian. The rest manifested themselves as usual, and were young plants of the congregation, etc.

Towards the close of the month of May, I visited the congregations in Upper Milford and Saccum, exhorted them to unity, and made known to them what we intended with Mr. Schrenck, in their behalf. They were much pleased with the proposal, and said, if we did not set some one on the watch, the congregations would gradually be scattered by vagrants.

The congregation of York in Pennsylvania, where Mr. Schaum has hitherto been stationed, earnestly petitioned us that we should ordain their teacher. Now, as we had already previously had permission from our highly venerable fathers, we appointed the 4th of June for the ordination, and the 5th for the conference of the congregations, in the town of Lancaster.

In the month of May, I was obliged to revisit the Swedish-English congregations, impossible as it seemed for us. The Quakers and other sects around there had already published various calumnies, and said the preacher had not received money enough the year before, and therefore he remains away. The English members, however, blamed the Swedes, and these blamed the English, that I did not come to them again, etc. Now, when I preached there again for the first time, I removed these prejudices, and showed them wherefore I had to hold back somewhat, and that my purpose with God is one more summer to take the burden upon myself, and to care for the salvation of their souls. They were very glad on this account, heard the first sermon with tears, and entreated that I should not forsake them. Thus are we entangled beyond our ability. If I had an assistant to aid me in my regular congregations, I could take care of the poor forsaken little side-masses along with the rest; but so it is impossible.

On the 29th of May, pastor Brunnholtz came to us in Providence from Philadelphia. On the 30th and 31st, he, together with Mr. Schrenck and myself, rode fifty miles further to Tulpehocken.

On the 1st of June, we remained in the house of Mr. Weiser, edified ourselves with the Word of God, and sought to rest ourselves.

On the 2d of June, we traveled, in company with Messrs. Weiser and Kurtz, thirty miles further to Lancaster, and presented ourselves to our brother, pastor Handschuch.

On the 3d of June, we examined Mr. Schaum, finished the Vocationis Instrumenta, and had them signed by the wardens and elders present from York.

On the 4th of June, the second Sabbath after Trinity, all the preachers and deputies of the united congregations assembled at the residence of pastor Handschuch, and amid the ringing of the bells, went to church in procession, in the following order: 1. Pastor Handschuch and his church council; 2. Pastor Brunnholtz, Mr. Weiser, and the delegates from Philadelphia and Germantown; 3. Myself and the delegates from New Hanover and Providence; 4. Deacon Kurtz and the deputies from Tulpehocken and Northkill; 5. Mr. Schaum and his church board of York. My colleague urged me to preach on the gospel of the Great Supper. After the sermon, all present formed a semi-circle around the altar, and were our witnesses, and prayed with us when we ordained Mr. Schaum. Afterwards we preachers, together with some members of the congregation, partook of the Holy Supper, and closed therewith the forenoon service. In the afternoon service, Mr. Kurtz preached. In the evening at 6 o'clock, I had to preach a sermon in our church for the English, as they had no preacher, and earnestly desired this.

On the 5th of June, all the preachers and delegates went to church once more Mr. Schaum preached, and afterwards we held a conference for the improvement of our Evangelical congregations. The congregations at Raritan, Upper Milford and Saccum, had sent no delegates, because they are so distant; but they sent letters instead, which were read before the conference.

On the 6th of June, pastor Brunnholtz, Mr. Schrenck, and the deputies from New Hanover and Providence, rode home with me, and had a fatiguing day, on account of the penetrating heat of the sun. We had also to ride through the broad stream of the Schuylkill by night; but notwithstanding this, by the help of God we arrived in Providence at 12 o'clock, after we had traveled nearly fifty miles.

In this month of June, parson Klug visited us, who already stood in office for several years in a German Evangelical congregation in the province of Virginia. From this country, Virginia, which otherwise is also called Spotsylvania, several Germans (among whom was one especially, called Stœver), went collecting some years ago in all Germany, and gathered a sum of nearly three thousand pounds. They received the one-third part for their traveling expenses and trouble, and for the rest they built a wooden church, and bought a tract of land and a number of black slaves, from which land and slaves the parson receives his salary liberally, and is not the least burdensome to the congregation on account of his support. He complained that he stood so entirely alone in that large and extensive country, as most of the inhabitants are English, and was without the opportunity of being cheered and edified by his German colleagues in office. He also said, that one and another of the Zinzendorfer passed through his congregation, but had obtained no firm footing. They also could not easily get into that country, as the laws of the land are very severe against such rovers, who are unable to show a lawful calling and satisfactory testimonials. He promised to visit us again, if his life was spared, as he felt encouraged therefrom, although he lived perhaps three hundred miles away from us.

In the month of July, I was called two different times to an English married woman, eighteen miles distant from my residence. The woman was an assiduous hearer when I preached in the Swedish-English church. The woman lay very sick with violent epileptic paroxysms. Both times I was unable to speak with her, as she lay senseless in the paroxysm for several hours. When I came to her the third time, she remained sensible for half an hour, wrung her hands, accused herself before God in prayer as a poor sinner, and asked the Lord Jesus that he might have compassion on her, pardon her sins for the sake of his blood and death, and set her free; and desired that I should continue the prayer, as she was too weak, which I willingly did. Weeping, she yet prayed perhaps for a half-quarter of an hour with me, and fell into the paroxysm again, and soon after died. The husband desired that I should preach a funeral sermon for her, which I did, on the text 1 Kings xix. 4: *It is enough*, etc., in a large assembly of various nations and sects.

In the same month, I was invited to visit the small congregations in Upper Milford,

Saccum, and Perkasie. I found in all the three congregations one soul and another concerned for their salvation, and eager for the Word of God, which gave me joy, and moved me still to send Mr. Schrenck to that place. It is to be noticed that I had always to make these trips on week-days, and on Sundays hold divine service in my own congregations.

In the month of August, I administered the Holy Supper in the said congregations at Upper Milford and Saccum. I also visited the two small newly-received congregations at the great river Delaware and in Perkasie. In Upper Milford I examined and confirmed seven persons, for the most part adults, of whom we have good hope, and admitted them to the Holy Supper with the rest. In Saccum, I confirmed two English married women, after they had, during the examination, made their confession of faith before the congregation, and promised to live conformably to it. One of these had been baptized the year before. The merciful God did not permit himself to be unattested in those souls, who gave room to his gracious workings. I had fatigued myself much in one day, but towards evening I had to travel on, and as yet ride upwards of fourteen miles, as I had to be in the third congregation on the day following. They gave me two men along as companions, as I did not know the road in the pathless forest. Now, when night overtook us, we lost our way, and came to a long mountain, into dense thickets and bushes, had to lead the horses, and with much trouble creep around miserably for several hours. I lacerated my face and tore my clothes in the bushes, and once also hung fast between wild grape vines until my companions again cut me loose. As for the rest, God preserved us from serpents and other vermin, and at length let us find a house where we could stop. Several had told me in confidence that one of my companions, who was unknown to me, was wont to speak edifyingly, but did not always conduct himself conformably to his words. On the way, I also noticed in conversation that he had read edifying books, which delighted me. But when we got into thickets, and knew not what to do, and also in creeping through were torn by the bushes, he became impatient and cursed himself and his horse, for which I reproved him in love and earnestness, and said a good tree yielded good fruit, and a bad tree bad fruit; a fountain doth not send forth at once sweet water and bitter. The blessed God enabled me to accomplish this journey without perceptible injury to my health.

In the same month of August, I had once more to enter upon the difficult journey to Raritan, in Jersey, because it was promised and was necessary. I there found Mr. Weygand still active and well, and had a meeting of the twelve church elders, and inquired: 1. How Mr. Weygand had conducted himself in the past year in doctrine and in life? They all answered, that he had taught sound doctrine, assiduously cared for the young, and also visited the old, according to his time and ability, and had conducted himself without offence. 2. Whether they intended to accept of and to retain Mr. Weygand as their regular teacher? Answer: Yes; they desired for themselves no other and no better, if he remained thus. 3. Whether they would release us, and permit Mr. Weygand to be ordained by the New York preachers, because my colleagues in office are infirm in body, and I am too feeble to make such a long journey alone? Answer:

No; they would have nothing to do with the New York preachers, but they entreated that we, in their name, should most humbly request our highly venerable fathers in Europe to consent to his ordination, and to retain Mr. Weygand under our supervision. 4. Whether they intended to give Mr. Weygand a regular call, in order that I could send out a copy of it? Answer: They were afraid, as they had already been unfortunate with Mag. Wolf, and apprehended it might also fail with this one, because he was not regularly called by us, and also not sent thus. Nevertheless, I should find a middle way and preserve them from misfortune. I accordingly wrote a call in the English language, wherein he was called according to the pure doctrine of the apostles and prophets, with this condition, to be their preacher as long as he teaches and lives according to it. But in case the contrary should appear, he shall be obliged to submit himself to the examination and judgment of our highly venerable fathers. But as the ordination had not as yet taken place, and we had still further to test Mr. Weygand, so this call, which was signed by most of the members of the congregation, was to be preserved by the elders of the church in the church-chest, and only a copy of it be given to him, so that he could not at any time misuse the original before the authorities for a sword, as did Mr. Wolf. This was acknowledged as proper by Mr. Weygand, and by the congregation. On the day following, preparatory service and confession was held with the congregation, and the young people, in part married and in part single, about thirty in number, were examined by me on the Order of Salvation. I found that Mr. Weygand had shown considerable diligence and faithfulness to those young people in their instruction, and I also observed that they were much affected. In a word, the renewal of the baptismal covenant and confirmation took place amid many tears of the old and the young, and of the preachers. After divine service, Mr. Weygand conferred with me particularly, and I delivered to him the testimonial which we had drawn up to the Governor of Jersey at his desire and the desire of the congregation, concerning a collection for their church. He then conversed with me concerning a Dutch married woman who was already engaged in a difficult work of repentance for about three months, and was as yet without peace, but against her will was harassed with dreadfully wicked thoughts. I had an opportunity to speak to the woman herself, and found that some bodily infirmity contributed much to her anxiety, whereby the Spirit of God, by means of the Word, did not leave himself unwitnessed, only nature and grace, according to their operations, are difficult to distinguish in such persons.

On Sunday, Mr. Weygand preached before a numerous assembly, who sat so crowded in an old wooden church building, that many could scarcely guard themselves against fainting in the exceptionally hot weather. After the sermon, I made an address, and briefly presented the following: 1. I showed under what circumstances we became acquainted with them, and were invited to care for the congregation, besides our own. 2. How we have hitherto been concerned for their souls' best welfare. 3. In what manner Mr. Weygand came to us. 4. That he was tried according to his doctrine and life, first for a quarter of a year by us in Pennsylvania, and now three-quarters of a year by them. 5. That accordingly, on the day previous, the elders of the church and the members of the congregation present prepared a regular call, with the desire to obtain from our highly venerable fathers in Europe a confirmation of the same, and permission for his ordination. 6. According to our infirmity, we had now done our part, given heed to the footsteps of God, and heard what God spake with us by the circumstances. 7. They might indeed think with others—with the multitude abusing their liberty—that there was no ordination necessary, as the cause itself prospered so far. But if they desired to be and to remain a part of our Evangelical church in Pennsylvania, and we altogether a part of the Evangelical mother church in Europe, it was proper for us to observe all good order. I have no doubt but that the highly venerable fathers, after understanding the matter in connection, would kindly give their consent, so that the ordination could take place at the next conference. I would not promise to come again, and I also had no certain order from my brethren in office to make such a promise. Thereupon, I directed myself (8) to Mr. Weygand especially, testified briefly what care and anxiety we have had in our other official burdens for these wild and forsaken congregations, and how readily young persons sometimes at first take upon themselves a call, and the burden of office, when they do not sufficiently understand and consider their own weakness, the importance of the difficult office, and the heavy responsibility, etc. I asked him whether he trusted himself, by the grace and aid of God, to propagate the pure doctrine according to the foundation of the apostles and prophets, and our Symbolical books, and to adorn it with a godly walk, as an example to the flock? Weeping, he answered yes; and thereupon gave me his hand, and I said, if he by false doctrine, and a disorderly life, should injure anything by neglect, the Lord would demand that blood at his hands; but if he was faithful, exercised his office in divine power, and with all his heart, then also would grace, mercy and peace from God through Jesus Christ be multiplied over and in him, etc.

After this, I delivered a brief exhortation to the congregation, and especially to the communicants, and administered the Holy Supper. After the close of the divine service, I again collected myself a little, and then preached to the dispersed English church people, and to the Hollanders, in the English language, on Luke xv., of the son who was lost and found again. Although I was indeed very faint, yet as it seemed, the Holy Spirit accompanied the word to the hearts of the hearers. May God permit it to result in fruit and blessing to the glory of his name! The people of Raritan have already built their church until it is under roof, and it is a handsome massive brickwork. They desired that I should once more visit the fourth congregation in the hills, and see whether they would not come hither again, and unite with the new church. I did this, but could accomplish nothing. They said that they had in part from twelve to fourteen miles to the new church, and could not take their old people and their young children so far without injury to their health, etc., and desired that Mr. Weygand should preach for them every third Sunday. The three united congregations said that they had for this reason built the new church as nearly as possible in the middle of the four congregations, and had themselves also in part to travel from ten to twelve miles; that they could not let them have their preacher on the third Sunday, as this would curtail and scatter the three congregations, and then the new church would again stand there, empty and useless. They said, that if they regularly held to the new church, then Mr. Weygand might occasionally, during the week, preach and hold instruction for the young with those living in the hills. But they did not want this, and desired that I should direct them to a preacher of their own, etc. I took leave, and on the following day traveled towards home. Late in the evening of the next day, we reached the great river Delaware, which divides Jersey and Pennsylvania, and rode past a tavern where there was a tumult and a clamor, as in Sodom and Gomorrah. We had, therefore, to apply for quarters for the night to a Hollandish widow near there.

In the month of September, I was taken to an English Quaker, five miles from New Hanover. The man is of tolerably rich parentage, and had also married a woman, perhaps for the sake of riches, who was born of English church people, baptized and raised by them. Some years ago, the woman came to New Hanover to church on several occasions, when I preached English. But she was ridiculed on this account by the friends of her husband. Now, as she led a quiet, honorable life, and still occasionally manifested a desire to hear the Word of God in our church, the friends employed flattering words, and said she had no need of going to church, as she was surely a pattern of virtue without this, and therefore would be eternally happy. She at length permitted herself to be lulled asleep, until she came upon her dying-bed, when she said that she must once more necessarily speak with her preacher. The friends desired to bring a Quaker preacher, wherewith, however, she was not satisfied, but insisted that I should come to her. Now, although they indeed regarded it as almost disgraceful, still they dared not refuse her dying request. When I entered the room, I found a considerable number of the Quaker relationship assembled, in part also women preachers. The woman herself indeed was still in the full possession of her reason, but nevertheless, we noticed some signs already of approaching death. I inquired: What is your foundation, on which you would live and die ? Answer: The church. Question: The word church has many different significations ; do you perhaps mean the means of grace which God has entrusted to his church, viz., the Word of God, *i. e.*, the law and the gospel and the holy sacraments, or do you mean the head of the church, which is Christ Jesus, the Saviour of the world? Answer: I found my salvation upon Jesus Christ. Question: Have you also experienced repentance toward God and faith in the Lord Jesus? Answer: I am no gross sinner. Question: Have you not sinned against the holy Ten Commandments of God? Answer: No; I have committed no gross sins against the Ten Commandments. Question: Have you not sinned against the commands of God in thoughts, desires, and inclinations ? Answer: O, I have been very quiet and gentle from my youth up. Those present corroborated this, and said that she had been a singularly good person ; if only all mankind were such as she, then they could not fail of eternal salvation. I answered: You are very near unto death, and therewith your soul is in a dangerous condition, and if you have no other and better righteousness than the Pharisees, you will not enter into the kingdom of heaven. The Pharisees trusted to their outward honesty and piety, and yet, according to their inward corruption, they were an abomination before God, so that the Saviour of the world, who tries the hearts and the reins, uttered an eight-times-repeated woe against them in the twenty-third chapter of Matthew! Your own righteousness, which you would present before God, is only a filthy garment. It may be that you have been preserved from the grossest crimes against the Ten Commandments, but where has there been a true, living fear of God, a perfectly pure love, and a filial confidence in God? How feeble, slothful, and indolent have you not indeed been to acknowledge the most holy name of God, to honor, to praise, and to glorify him. How little respect have you manifested towards the sermon, the Word of God, and the Holy Sacraments. And so examine yourself further, according to all the Commandments, which are spiritual, and of right require of us that which was entrusted by God unto our first parents. We are carnal, and how shall we stand before the most holy God with our tattered morality and honesty? When you have considered this, think further wherefore the most holy Son of God, as Saviour of the world, suffered so much, as you may have read in the gospels. He was surely most innocent. Now there must certainly be reasons wherefore he suffered so much and died. He himself says: Thou hast made me to serve with thy sins, thou hast wearied me *with thine iniquities. I, even I, am he that blotteth out thy transgressions, for mine own sake*, etc. She at length admitted that she had omitted much good, and committed much evil in thoughts and desires, wept and said: Did I then think the Lord Jesus would reject and condemn her? I replied: That he would certainly not accept of her for the sake of her own righteousness, and he also would not reject her on account of her sins, if she acknowledged herself as a sinner worthy of condemnation, and manifested repentance and sorrow therefor, and took her refuge in the perfect righteousness of Jesus Christ. For as Moses lifted up the serpent in the wilderness, so also was the Son of Man lifted up on the cross so that all *who believe in him should not perish*, etc. *For God so loved the world*, etc. If she would have part in it, she should indeed instantly reckon her own righteousness and unbelief to the most grievous sins, and with the poor sinful woman, Luke vii., call to the Redeemer, who is near to her heart, and with the Publican, Luke xviii., smite upon her breast, and pray for grace and reconciliation. In this order, the Lord Jesus would not cast her out, but graciously receive her, forgive her her sins, clothe her with the garments of salvation and with the cloak of righteousness, and conduct her as a bride to the Heavenly Father. She began to pray penitently, that the Lord Jesus might indeed not reject her on account of her sins, but let grace and mercy prevail. She also said, that if she should yet live somewhat longer, that she would regulate her life somewhat differently, and through his grace walk more seriously before him. Afterwards, I bowed my knee, and prayed a penitential prayer with her. Those present remained standing, as they are not accustomed to kneel, neither think favorably of loud prayer. After prayer, I inquired how it was with her? Answer: She only desired the one favor, that the Lord Jesus may not reject her! I took leave, and admonished those present that they should spare her with their encomiums, and read something for her out of the Bible of repentance and faith. In going away, the man offered me a piece of money, but I did not take it, and left him with a word of exhortation. The next night she died. She intimated that she wished to be buried in our churchyard. A person connected with the government of the relationship, who loves the right, earnestly advised that they should bury her, and let her repose with those of her faith. But it was not done. The Quakers had to make a show therewith, and bury her in their place of interment, as she was such a pattern of morality. To me it was a matter of indifference as respects the body, if only the poor soul found its right home.

In the months of September and October, besides my regular labor, I had to instruct a small number of young persons in New Hanover for the Holy Supper.

As one member and another of the Indianfield congregation, which parson Andrea had served hitherto, held to us in Providence, and desired much that I should occasionally visit them in their place, and edify them with a sermon and catechisation, I was compelled to concede to their request. But I feared a disturbance by Andrea's party, who had possession of the church, and threatened very much, and I therefore several times had a meeting with a small number in a private house. But when this became too small, the Reformed opened their church for us, where before winter we met several times during week-days. I once made an appointment to preach there on a Sunday afternoon, when so many people assembled that the Reformed church also was much too small, and I had to preach under the open heaven.

In the month of November, I confirmed the young persons whom I had instructed in New Hanover, and admitted them to the Holy Supper. They were twenty-six in number, for the most part adults, among whom was one married man. They had memorized the Order of Salvation pretty well, and were also diligently led to the sense and understanding of it, and unceasingly admonished to bring all into their prayers and into practice, and therefore they can have no excuse before God, that they had not been sufficiently moved, and pathetically affected. Most of them also assured me in special conversation, that they had often at home on their knees prayed in secret, and had experienced the effective power of the Spirit of God in their souls by means of the Word. At their confirmation, kneeling, they renewed their baptismal covenant before God and the congregation with many tears. We can only plant and water; God is willing and ready to give the increase, if only men themselves do not forfeit his grace, and cast it to the winds.

On the 18th of November, I traveled sixteen miles from my house to the Swedish-English congregation, held divine service there, and again returned ten miles to New Hanover, and preached the following day as usual.

On the 20th of November, Mr. Schrenck came from my house to New Hanover, and was ready to go further with me. The extreme necessity of helping the mountain congregations, the good hope of Mr. Schrenck's growth in grace, the consent of my brethren in office, and the suppliant entreaty of the congregations, induced me to introduce him there as catechist on trial for one year. Accordingly, we traveled on said 20th of November, fifteen miles further to Upper Milford, where I administered the Holy Supper to the congregation after previous confession and preparation. A couple of newly-arrived Würtembergers, who had given offence to the congregation, by sporting and dancing, were refused, and exhorted to repentance, and another was again received, who had been before excluded.

After the affairs of this congregation were brought into the order possible, we traveled four miles further to Saccum, where, on the 22d of November, I had confession and the Lord's Supper with delight, because the communicants showed themselves orderly, tractable and hungering after grace, and the members of the congregation stood in pleasant harmony. His new lodgings were pointed out to Mr. Schrenck, who was much afraid, as he was not accustomed to such poor circumstances. As it seems, there is still the largest number of pliant souls and souls hungering after grace in this congregation, although obstinate ones also are not wanting.

On the 23d of November, we set out early, and rode sixteen miles, in terribly cold weather, to the recently-accepted congregation at the river Delaware, at the Fork, as it was called. I there held confession and the Holy Supper with the members of the congregation, who had been examined and recorded several weeks before by Mr. Schrenck. I set things in order in the congregation, and in the evening rode through the river, for the purpose of visiting a good friend in Jersey, and to pass the night there.

On the 24th of November, we traveled twenty-two miles back to the fourth congregation in Perkasie, as it is called. In this congregation we became acquainted with one and another well-meaning soul; but as for the rest, they seem to be a rude, wild multitude, who had been much corrupted and hardened in wickedness by the vagrant preachers.

On the 25th of November, I held divine service in Perkasie, and endeavored to bring the multitude somewhat into order.

Now, as I had to hold divine service in Providence on the 26th of November, and had as yet to ride twenty miles to my residence, I was obliged to set out from Perkasie on the 25th of November, in the afternoon at 3 o'clock. They gave me a guide. Night soon overtook us, and therefore we could not ride rapidly, and only came to the Perkiomen creek at 11 o'clock at night, which is still two miles away from my house. To our great surprise, we perceived that the stream since my departure was frozen over hard, and covered with ice, by reason of the cold weather. My companion only had a small horse, which in addition was unshod, consequently I had to go before and break the ice. I did this at the peril of my life, and remained in the saddle, notwithstanding the leaping and rearing of my horse, and let my companion follow in the footsteps and holes which my horse had broken. In breaking the ice, my horse had always to raise himself up in front, and at the same time break a hole with the fore-feet, and keep the piece of ice on the bottom until he leaped after with the hind feet, and then went still further forward. I got over safely, but on account of the dark night, I missed the outlet on the other side, and came with my companion to a bank, which was high and almost perpendicular. Back I would not again venture, for the broken holes were not easily found again in the darkness. We took off the saddles, and by the aid of some bushes clambered up on land, and resolved to make an attempt with our horses also. We tied the girths to the bridle of the small horse, and compelled him to stand on his hind feet, so that he could reach on the bank with his forefeet. We pulled, and the horse helped himself bravely onward with the hind feet, and safely reached the shore, as he was young and nimble. But when we would do the same with my horse, that was old and stiff, the bridle broke, and the poor beast fell backward with all his weight into the ice, so that he lay on the ground on his back in the water, with his legs up, and locked in by the ice, and must thus have been drowned. I gave up the poor beast, because I saw no possibility to help. My companion, however, would not rest, but in great anxiety he cut a leaver with a small knife, sprang down with it, and made a great opening in the ice, helped the horse, that he laid on one side, and at length worked himself on his feet again. Thereupon the horse anew broke through again, and would go back on the other side, but on account of weakness stuck fast in the middle of the stream in the ice, so that we could help no more in any manner. We laid our saddles and baggage upon the one horse, and wished to go the rest of the way home on foot, lost ourselves in the dark thickets, and walked around for about half an hour in a circle, until the stars once appeared in the heavens, and showed us the country where we were, when we then got home about 3 o'clock. Early in the morning I sent several neighbors to the stream, who met the horse as yet in the middle of the stream in the ice. They released him with trouble, and brought him home half dead. I was active, so that on that day I was able to perform divine service, but had to endure a sickness afterwards, from which the gracious God also permitted me to recover. I have cited this so circumstantially, not to abuse therewith the patience of my highly venerable fathers and patrons, but only to show how we sometimes get into difficulty and danger, but are also mercifully protected, if we remain in our path of duty.

In the month of December, a young woman of eighteen years fell asleep, whom I had baptized and confirmed a few years before. Now, as she had a father who ignorantly slandered the holy Sacraments, I retained her in my house with me for some time, and indeed noticed in her a feeble life in the faith of the Son of God, but could perceive no special growth until she came to a sick bed with her parents. As soon as the sickness began, she entreated her mother that she should kneel with her, and help her to wrestle and contend. The mother did this, and was surprised at the penitential prayer of the child. She accused herself before God as the greatest sinner, lamented her slothfulness and unfaithfulness towards the many calls of grace, and would not relinquish her Lord Jesus, except he bless her with a sufficient righteousness in his blood, and an ever-enduring peace. The remaining days she constantly occupied herself with the hymn which I gave her, when she visited me the last time, viz: *Wrestle thou aright when*

God's grace now doth thee draw, etc. In her remembrance of her past sins and errors, she confessed to her mother, that in my family she unawares melted a hole in a pewter plate, and kept it secret; that her mother should make an apology for it in her name, and make compensation. She was uncommonly melted during her illness, and persevered in the faith. Before she died, she desired to speak with me once more. But I was sick myself and feeble; still, after much solicitation, I had to enter on the journey, as the mother sent me word that she had already wrestled with death for two days, and could not die. When I arrived, her sight was seriously enfeebled, her hearing had nearly passed away, and her speech was impaired. Her mother called to her that I was present. She raised herself up, fell upon my neck, and wept bitterly, wished to say much with her stammering tongue, but I could understand nothing of it, and therefore exhorted all present to pray with me. I commended this poor sheep into the arms of the Lord Jesus, and to the perfect enjoyment of his purchased possessions. As her mother told me, she had been much grieved by her foolish father, with these and such like blasphemies: What good does your Baptism and Holy Supper do you now? you must indeed suffer more than others, who are not baptized, etc. After I had commended her to the Lord in prayer, I took leave, and heard afterwards that on the following day she delivered up her spirit into the faithful hands of her Redeemer, and had found her Bridegroom, as a favored and wise virgin. The poor child had many trials. On the one hand they would gladly have drawn her into the net of the Zinzendorfer, on the other to the rude world, and from her own father she had more offense than edification. The faithful God delivered her out of all, and hastened with her into a place of safety. I also was not a little edified by the mother's Christian frame of mind and assured heart. When I asked the mother whether she would still gladly retain her daughter, as I wished to adapt my prayer accordingly, she answered: no, as she has almost entirely overcome, I would rather if the Lord would take her home, still I will prescribe nothing, but say: *Thy will is best.*

In the same month, the father of a family of

the congregation in New Hanover died. In his youth he had been tolerably well instructed in the fundamentals of the evangelical religion, and had also filled the office of church warden in Germany for several years, and also held no less strongly and firmly to the confession of the doctrine in Pennsylvania. He neglected no opportunity where he could hear the Word of God in his church, testified several times that he could not sufficiently thank God, who inclined and moved our highly venerable fathers and so many patrons to care for the poor scattered and despised Lutherans in Pennsylvania, and to send shepherds, etc. In the first years, he came to me wholly perplexed, and said he had heard from several as though I also would at last let myself be misled, and be made a Zinzendorfer. If I did this, he would move where no human being should see him again, and in all his life he would neither believe nor trust any clergyman again. I replied, that he should only be assured and faithful, and pray the blessed God that he should make his heart as evangelical in a living faith as is his confession, that he may not only have the language of Luther, but his faith also, and the fruits of it, so that he may be saved. As respects myself, he should not regard the verdict of men, pray for me, and believe in love that the blessed God would not permit me to fall so far, but preserve me faithful unto death, etc. He returned home again comforted and joyful. When other sects provoked him to disputation, and attacked his religion, he was almost too passionate; still it was serviceable hereto, that they afterwards left him untouched. Persons who think nothing of the evangelical religion and denomination, are frequently unwearied in disputation, and when they perceive that one is not grounded in the doctrine, they cease not until they have entangled him and led him away from the church. On another occasion, I asked him whether the Word of God, which he heard so diligently, also produced repentance and a living faith in his soul. He replied, that that which he heard on Sundays in the sermon, he could not again tell immediately after the sermon, but during the week in his calling, on the field, or wherever he worked, there everything occurred to him again, one part after the other, in such reality as if he had heard it again. In the great heat of summer, he had injured himself by a drink of cold water, and was still more injured in health by violent medicines, and thence he was gradually enfeebled and became ripe for death. I visited him several times, and observed that the faithful physician of souls, Jesus Christ, operated in his soul by his Word. He was afraid of death, because he yet had small uneducated children and a weakly consort. When I came to him the last time, and inquired somewhat strictly concerning his inward condition, he said, weeping, that various sins which he had committed in his youth occurred to him, and which he otherwise had long since forgotten. He had wished to banish such thoughts from his mind, but could not rid himself of them. I asked him if a woman came to the time of birth, and felt the labor-pains, would it be advisable and proper if she suppressed them or ceased thinking of them? He answered: No. I therefore continued: Now he should thus allow himself to be directed and advised. He had heard much good in his lifetime, and observed the operations of the Spirit, all which happened that there might be awakened and wrought in his heart repentance and sorrow for all his sinful misery, a hunger and thirst for the sufficient righteousness of Jesus Christ, pardon of sin, and peace with God, and a new life, etc. He should bow his knees in secret, and with the prodigal penitently ask for grace and forgiveness; smite upon his breast with the Publican, and flee to the bleeding wounds of Jesus; so would he find rest for his poor soul, and die with an assured mind. We prayed with each other, and after prayer I inquired of him how he felt. He assured me that he already perceived some relief, and promised still to persevere, which he also did, and a few days afterwards fell asleep with a joyful and confident heart, as those informed me who were present at his death.

During the past year, I publicly administered the Holy Supper twice in all my congregations, and in each separately, and so far as it was possible for me in my infirmity, I spoke with each one specially, and exhorted them to repentance and faith, as their condition required. Moreover, I baptized more than one hundred children, buried fifteen persons, and married twenty-three couples. In catechisation, I went through the five principal articles of the catechism of Luther, and therewith concluded.

May the Lord not enter into judgment with me on account of my innumerable sins of office and station, but let grace be substituted for justice, and mercy for judgment, for the sake of his blood and his death!

If I have done aught amiss, from my heart do I grieve;
As antidote, the blood and pains of Christ I receive.
For this, this is the ransom for all my transgression:
If I bring this 'fore God's throne, I'm crown'd with salvation!

In the month of January, 1750, after instruction, I granted holy baptism to an English woman of twenty-one years. Her father was called a member of the English church, but was very seldom present at divine service; yea, did not even do so much as to bring forward his children to holy baptism, and at length was also miserably drowned when attempting to ride through a much-swollen stream. His daughter, as a poor orphan, had to serve among other people, and abode with English Quakers, who despise baptism. But as this person could read, and held to the church, she obtained a desire for it. She learned the chief articles of the small catechism, and desired the sooner the better to execute the covenant of a good conscience with the Bridegroom of souls. I therefore held a meeting in her father's house, where Quakers and various sects were present. I preached in English of the necessity and use of holy baptism, asked her concerning the principal articles of faith, let her make her confession, prayed with her, and to her consolation and joy in the Lord, I baptized her, enjoined upon her her duties once more, and closed with an English hymn.

In the same month, I was taken fourteen miles, in the night, to an old man who had for many years past adhered to the congregation in New Hanover, and who was now dangerously ill. He desired the Holy Supper, which I could not refuse him, as he had led a quiet life, and in his sickness had learned to give heed to the Word, and testified with tears that he was a great sinner, and also knew of no other comfort and counsel than in the sufficient righteousness which Jesus Christ had purchased. Among other things, he lamented that he went to church and to the Holy Supper for so many years in Germany, but thereby walked in blindness, and did not rightly know his Saviour, etc. He showed himself penitent, and partook of the Holy Supper, as it seemed, with proper hunger and thirst, asked his Saviour to shorten his sufferings and soon set him free, take him home out of the wicked world, and set him in a place of safety. This also came to pass, as on the second day after he commended his wearied spirit into the faithful hands of Jesus, and attained the end of faith. At my leave-taking, he wept, and complained that I so seldom visited him, and thought that perhaps I had an aversion to his poor sick person and circumstances. But I represented to him how fortunate the most of the preachers in Germany were, who had the sheep entrusted to them living together in towns or villages, whom, without exception, they could successively visit once or several times each year. But as he knew, I had my hearers scattered over a district thirty miles in length and about twenty miles in breadth, dwelling in the valleys and on the mountains, was but seldom at home, and could scarcely perform the most necessary official duties even if I employed many a night to help me, etc. He agreed with me, and said, that under the circumstances I had indeed neglected nothing in his case. As for the rest, he wished me to say good-night to our beloved fathers and benefactors, and to give them thanks for their unmerited love and assistance, with this addition, that he hoped to see them all face to face before the throne of the Lamb.

In the month of February, I prepared a fine young man of twenty-two years for holy baptism, who was born in this country of Dutch parents, who had him taught to read and write English. I asked the father why he did not have his son baptized in his infancy. He replied: Because there were so many sects in this country, he did not know which was the right one and the best; for if he asked the teachers of all the sects one after the other, each would say, Here is Christ, There he is! Each one professes to have the best medicine for the soul, and the nearest road to heaven, etc. He himself had been baptized in his infancy by the Reformed, but was not instructed afterwards, consequently he did not know of what advantage baptism was to him, etc. For this reason also he waited until his son attained his understanding, so that he afterwards might himself choose, and select the best religion for himself. Now, as I knew that the father inquired more diligently after the value of money than after the nearest way to heaven, so I sought to convince him according to his comprehension, and asked him: Do you know gold well? Answer: Yes. Question: What color is gold? Answer: It is yellow. Question: Is gold all equally good and of the same value? Answer: No. Question: How and whereby can we certainly know what is real or spurious; what is good, better, or the best? Answer: Whoever understands the art, can tell it by the touch-stone and in the chapel. I made the application of it to himself, and said: You have an impressed desire to be happy and at rest, but you do not find this in yourself, much less in the perishable things of this world, but rather disquietude, accusing and excusing thoughts, and a fear of death, etc. Experience sufficiently teaches you and all mankind that we are creatures wholly dependent on the Supreme Being. I hereupon more extensively showed him that the general revelation of God, in reason and in the works of creation, was not sufficient to teach the way to salvation, but that a nearer revelation thereto was necessary, which, however, is to be found nowhere else than in the Holy Scriptures, and directed him to his duty often, and diligently to read this most venerable and most holy book with seriousness and eagerness, and in calling upon God, and to try his state and condition by this touch-stone, by which course he would soon discover which is the true religion. Thereupon I briefly presented to him from the Holy Scriptures the principal truths which belong to the order of salvation, and added, that he must not just read and consider all this superficially, or be satisfied with merely knowing, but through the revealed word, and the Spirit of God connected therewith, to let his whole heart be thoroughly changed, and prepared and cultivated unto a living faith in the blood-surety and Redeemer, Jesus Christ. For without faith it is impossible to please God, Heb. xi. 6, and without holiness we cannot see him, Heb.

xii. 14. Now, if he had experienced such practical truths in his soul, then he has an infallible touch-stone in the Word of God, by which he can try all sects and their composition. Now, whatever accords with the Word of God is genuine gold. On the contrary, not everything is gold which appears yellow or red. He was affected thereby, and promised to give the matter further consideration. The young man was well read in the New Testament, and increased in knowledge. He manifested repentance and sorrow for his past walk in ignorance, and a desire to be united to the Saviour of the world, through faith and holy baptism, and to be a living branch in the vine, Jesus Christ. I therefore examined him on the most necessary parts of the Order of Salvation, allowed him to make his confession of faith, prayed with him, and imparted holy baptism unto him. He received this amid many tears, and promised, by the aid of the Holy Spirit, to walk conformably to his calling. May the Lord powerfully assist him, that he may not fall by the cunning of Satan and so many temptations, but that he be preserved.

In the months of March and April, I had

forty-two young persons in instruction in New Hanover, that they might be confirmed, and admitted to the Holy Supper. Among these were two married men, who in their earliest youth had been neglected. One of these was weak, both in comprehending and in retaining anything, but still was desirous of obtaining a new heart. I taught him in a simple manner how he must conduct himself with God in prayer, and what he must ask of him. When I once asked him whether he followed my advice, he related to me how and what he had prayed to the reconciled Father in Christ, at home in secret, and out in the field, in the work of his calling, and what thereby was the disposition of his mind. It was very delightful to hear, and gave evidence of a simplicity of heart. Generally, I have frequently admonished all and each young person during instruction, that they should make each day's lesson the subject of prayer at home, and apply it to themselves, and when I thereupon inquired of each one privately, whether they had followed my counsel, they for the most part confessed in simplicity of heart, that they bowed their knees, and in secret asked of God a new heart, the one in the barn, the other in the field, the third in the stable, etc., wherever he could find a chamber and remain undisturbed. Although I see innumerable hindrances and temptations, which waylay the poor youths, and which I cannot remove, but only fear and deplore, still it cheers me, when young persons in their instruction and confirmation receive a living impression of the Order of Salvation, and I commit it to the heavenly Father, and to the faithful chief Shepherd, who will try everything possible to save whatever will yet permit itself to be saved. About seventeen of this number have come here from distant places, and the rest are out of the congregation.

Towards the close of April, I made a journey to Lancaster, and as I had to baptize a child on the way on my return, on the 2d of May, an English Justice of the Peace, who was present at the baptism, said that there were many serving men and women of the German nation, with the English, in that region, who desired that I should come and preach, as the poor people did not understand the English, and for a long time had no divine service in their mother tongue. The Justice said that he and his English neighbors would open the church to me for the Germans on this condition, that I also preached an English sermon for them. Now, as they had a regular preacher in the church, I answered, that I would not make use of the church for the Germans until they had asked the teacher himself, and obtained his consent thereto, so that no dispute may arise between the preacher and his congregation, especially as I had hitherto lived in concord with the preacher. The Justice said that they had already asked him before, and obtained his full consent thereto, consequently I promised to come there in several week.

In the month of May, I visited the four small congregations in which Mr. Schrenck has hitherto stood as substitute. I had to administer the Holy Supper to them and also confirm young people, whom Mr. Schrenck had instructed with considerable diligence and faithfulness. In the congregation at the Delaware, I confirmed a woman after an examination in the English language, who was of Reformed parentage, and married to a warden of the congregation, and attained to an excellent knowledge and to faith in the Lord Jesus. As for the rest, I was delighted with the diligence and faithfulness which Mr. Schrenck had hitherto showed to the congregations. May the faithful chief Shepherd make him continually more able and apt for the office, and ever grant him more blessings! By riding in the great heat in the previous journey to Lancaster, and also in this, I was so affected by the circumstances that I felt great pain, and was nearly laid up before I had finished the work in the congregations. I knew not what to do, and entreated the heavenly Father that he should remove the plague until I could reach home again, and in grace chastise me there as much as he found necessary for the good of my soul, according to his paternal faithfulness and wisdom. The Lord heard my sighing in my distress, and took it away from me in the same hour, so that I was enabled to finish the work vigorously, and get home well. The providence of the Lord extends to little things, and he hears the prayer of the miserable. This I have experienced.

In the same month of May, an aged member of the New Hanover congregation died. The man had a considerable knowledge of the Order of Salvation, and was concerned also to experience repentance and a living faith in his soul. But he was naturally very passionate, and when he had formed a good resolution and made a beginning in repentance, he was at times overtaken by his passion, and everything overthrown, which afterwards caused him great distress and anguish, that he had again to begin anew. In charity, I hope that the Lord Jesus, who was so often portrayed before his eyes, may still as yet have taken form in him. For he entreated God to break asunder the power of his sinful nature, and set him fully free in his Son. He was also much purified by a long and severe illness, as he suffered much annoyance from a cough and asthma. The more his body wasted, the more room there was in the soul for the Spirit of God, by means of the word, to work repentance and faith in him, and lead him to righteousness and peace through Jesus Christ. At the time when the Zinzendorfer were at their highest renown, and were most flourishing, they had drawn him along with them up to Bethlehem, and showed him their glory, and promised to point out a nearer way to heaven. But after he had seen one institution and another, and continued several examinations, he inquired whether they had something more and better than that which was in the New Testament, and which was proposed for salvation and life? One, however, was so honest and said: No! Thereupon he answered, thus, it is not necessary for me to seek my salvation with you and in Bethlehem, but only need to follow the Saviour who has said: *Search the Scriptures*, etc. *Him that cometh to me I will in no wise cast out*, etc. Afterwards they let him go away from them, nor further looked after him. As long as I have been here in office, he was diligently present to hear the Word of God, and also partook of the Holy Supper with devotion; and except being overtaken by his passion, he manifested himself as a Christian in his walk, and also assiduously kept his family thereto. He was one of those who rejoice in the Evangelical divine service, and who acknowledge before God the hearty endeavors of our highly venerable fathers and benefactors in behalf of the forsaken, and who observe the time of visitation.

In the month of June, preparation was made for the annual meeting. Providence was appointed as the place of meeting, and the 17th and 18th of June as the time.

On the 11th of June, pastor Brunnholtz arrived in Providence to consult with me about necessary matters, and to refresh himself by the country air.

On the 15th of June, Mr. Weygand came with three elders from Raritan, as also pastor Handschuch from Lancaster; but his congregation sent no delegates, although requested to do so. Moreover, the adjunct, Mr. Schaum, came with two delegates from his congregation. At length came also the adjunct, Mr. Kurtz, with three delegates from Tulpehocken; the substitute, Mr. Schrenck, with four men from his congregations; and in the evening three more elders appeared from Raritan.

On the 17th of June, being the first Sunday after Trinity, there assembled in and before my house Messrs. Brunnholtz, Handschuch, Kurtz, Schaum, Weygand, Schrenck, Rauss, as also the delegates, viz.: from Philadelphia, eight; from Germantown, six; from Providence, twelve; from New Hanover, six; from the Swedish-English congregation, one; from Tulpehocken and Heidelberg, Mr. Weiser and four others; from York, on the other side of the Susquehanna, two; from Lancaster, one, who, however, came of his own accord, and was not sent by the congregation; from Upper Milford, Saccum, Fork, and Sacony, four; from Indianfield, two; from Goschenoppen, two; from Tohickon, two; from Macungie, two; from Raritan, six; from Cohansey, two. All these went in procession from my house into the church, and had divine service in quietness and devotion before God. We had taken out the windows, and made a shelter with green bushes around the church, as the church would not hold the multitude of people. Pastor Handschuch preached the principal sermon. After the sermon, I delivered a short address to the people concerning the footsteps of God, how these now in the eighth year drop fatness among our dispersed Lutherans. Afterwards, I as yet delivered a brief Latin discourse to my colleagues in office. After divine service, the members of the congregation of Providence, who lived nearest, took their strange brethren along with them home, and for their refreshment shared with them, from love, whatever the Lord had given; and I entertained the preachers and other good friends, as many as the house could hold.

On the 18th of June, we together went into the church again. Mr. Weygand preached, and afterwards we held a long conference concerning the external regulation and improvement of the congregrations. Of the necessity, purpose, and use of such an annual meeting and conference of the preachers and deputed elders of the congregations, much might be written, if it were not apparent to every one how and wherefore this is necessary. After the conference, about eighty persons were entertained at the table according to their need, and the preachers were divided among them, who during the meal sought to edify the deputies and other members of the congregations with good conversation. After the repast was over, the conclusion of the conference was prepared in writing for each congregation, and given along, and the delegates set out on their journey home. In this meeting and conference everything proceeded in a very orderly and Christian manner.

Afterwards, I made a trip of seventeen miles into the region where many of our German domestics are at service with English people. The English church was opened to me, where, according to promise, I first preached an English sermon, and afterwards a German. The English hearers were very attentive and affected, and desired that I should frequently come. The wife of a warden desired to speak with me alone, and confessed that she had been awakened before, but again fell asleep. Now she would begin anew to seek the Lord, who from infinite love and compassion purchased her with his blood, etc. She requested me to visit her, but the way is too far and the time too short. The Germans also wept among each other, as it is wont to be on such occasions, when they for a long time have heard nothing from the Word of God. The English were astonished at our singing, and almost enraptured, as some people had fine musical voices, and sang harmoniously.

Since the past spring, I had to visit the English and Swedish congregations on Sunday afternoon from New Hanover. But I feel that it is injurious to my health.

In the month of July, I examined and baptized an English married man in the Swedish-English church. The man had an excellent understanding, and could publicly give a reason of the hope that was in him; leads an edifying life, as those testify who live near him and have intercourse with him. May the Lord preserve this engrafted branch and purify it daily, that it may bear fruit and abide in the vine! John xv.

My father-in-law, Mr. Conrad Weiser, was ordered by the royal government of Virginia to undertake an embassy to the savage nations dwelling upon the borders of Canada. He had to travel upwards of three hundred miles to that place, through the provinces of Jersey and New York, and he offered to take one of us along, free of expense, to the place where pastor Hartwick lives, as he had to pass near by him. Now pastor Hartwick had maintained pleasant relations with us, and several times visited us at his own expense, and on that account suffered diverse calumnies from evil-minded persons and enemies. He had always encouraged his congregation that one of us would pay a visit in return. Now, as this had not as yet taken place, some also made insinuations to the well-disposed as though perhaps he did not visit us, but the Zinzendorfer, in Pennsylvania, etc. It was therefore almost necessary that one of us should go to that place. For this reason I conferred with my colleagues in office, and would gladly have seen one of them undertake the journey, but as it would not suit either of them, it fell to me. I had to ride about two hundred and ten English miles to pastor Hartwick's, and I still had my old stiff horse, which had stuck fast in the ice the preceding year. On the 16th of August, I entered upon the journey in the name of God, and rode thirty miles to Mr. Schrenck in Saccum, whom I met well and active at his post. On the 17th of August, I traveled six miles further with Mr. Schrenck, to Bethlehem, where Mr. Weiser also arrived with his companions, and was invited to coffee by the Zinzendorfer bishop Kammerhof. We were courteously treated by him, and entertained with a political discourse, as the time was too short to dispute about the plans. They have erected several large, massive buildings as churches and common halls, and have a considerable number of grown people, and especially of children, at that place; and the country is pleasant to the eye, as a broad water flows on the one side, called the Lehigh, and on the other side lies a land which rises gradually until it becomes high mountains. In the afternoon, Mr. Schrenck again returned home, and we continued our journey, and passed over a beautiful level road ten miles further to Nazareth, the other celebrated place of residence of the Herrnhuter, but which in comparison with Bethlehem has the appearance of a farm only, and is inhabited by agriculturists. Mr. Kammerhof related to Mr. Weiser that he had been among the savage nations a few weeks before, where he was going, which seemed doubtful to him. In the evening, we traveled still five miles further, to an inn, where we lodged for the night.

Early on the morning of the 18th of August, we continued our journey, ascended the first chain of the Blue Mountains, and had to lead our horses for several miles between rocks and stones. We traveled about thirty-six miles, and in the evening stopped with a Dutchman of distinction who knew Mr. Weiser, and invited him together with his company to remain with him. The man lives on the borders of Pennsylvania, and had been a Justice of the peace for several years, but had retired and was already very old. I could not speak with him, on account of a heavy cold on my breast, and great hoarseness. My father-in-law however entered into an edifying conversation with him. He spoke in a very Christian and edifying manner, prayed before and after meals, and also on retiring, so devoutly and impressively that it cheered and heartily delighted us.

On the 19th of August, we left Pennsylvania, passed over the great river Delaware, and came into the province of New Jersey, and traveled about thirty-two miles on that day. In the evening we visited a Reformed Dutch preacher, and spoke of various edifying matters, as far as there was opportunity. However, my hoarseness still increased.

On the 20th of August, we proceeded about forty miles, and came out of the province of New Jersey into that of New York, through wild and untrodden forests. We dined with a distinguished Dutch Justice of the peace, and

Major of the militia of the province. He was an old acquaintance of Mr. Weiser, and knew much to speak of. In the evening we were still in the forest and saw a bear, which took flight before us, and also met a number of savages, with whom Mr. Weiser spoke. We thereupon rode yet somewhat further, and had to pass the night with a man whom they call the Spaniard, because his father had come into this country as a captured Spaniard; but his mother had been a Dutch woman. We received no supper, and had straw only to lie on.

On the 21st of August we set out on our journey early, and rode the whole day in hot weather, and were fed at an inn with raccoons, or American badgers, and pumpkins, and after riding forty-one miles we came to the town of Kingston at the Hudson in the evening. We had now passed over two hundred English miles from our home in five days, and were indeed tired of our journey, but praised God, who graciously preserved us by his aid from all harm.

On the 22d of August we lay still, because of violent rain. Mr. Weiser could have proceeded further on in his journey on this side of the Hudson river. But he also much wished to visit pastor Hartwick, and once more to see good friends and his former place of residence, where he first lived with his parents on their arrival in this country.

On the 23d of August we rode a few miles from the town of Kingston to the Hudson river, and had ourselves together with our horses conveyed over in a boat, and rode from there to Rhinebeck, where Mr. Hartwick lives.

Our arrival awakened joy in all those who still knew Mr. Weiser, and who entertained a good opinion of the Pennsylvania preachers. Many now came together in the dwelling of pastor Hartwick, who desired to see the so-long-expected Pennsylvania preacher, and had much to say to him; but speech was very difficult for me, on account of my continued cold on my breast, which was a great plague for me, as the people ceased not, but for all that much desired to have discourse and answer from me. I found pastor Hartwick indeed sound and well bodily, but the affairs of the congregation were in considerable confusion. For pastor Hartwick, partly by his friendship maintained with us, and partly by the earnestness manifested in his office, from a good intention, had drawn upon himself the envy and opposition of several neighboring preachers, who accused him of being a secret adherent of the Herrnhuter, merely for this reason, because he sought and maintained an acquaintance with us. Such accusations were made known in publicly printed letters, whereby many of his congregation were prejudiced against him, and were ever more provoked against him, by evil-minded persons. It was easy for the opponents to raise all manner of complaints, which consisted in part of narrations of unreliable people, collected together in part, of acts wrongly construed and perverted, and also in part of errors of infirmity magnified, which, however, relate only to subordinate things, and not to main points. These complaints were sent by a certain preacher to Doctor Kreuter, preacher of a German congregation in London, through whose mediation pastor Hartwick was at first called and sent, but who was too discreet to pass judgment on such ex parte complaints, and sent these which had arrived against him to pastor Hartwick for his reply. But with this the former was not satisfied, but continued to publish his revilings in print, and proceeded so far that he, with several other preachers whom he had drawn to his side, came into pastor Hartwick's congregation, and assembled all the opposing members of the congregation, and assumed to remove parson Hartwick by a diffusively written declaration. The cause of his removal was the Crypto-Herrnhuthianismus, or the secret cherishing of Herrnhuter errors. But as it was impossible for them to prove such charges, and as Mr. Hartwick also as yet had some members on his side, who through his office, by the blessing of God, were brought so far that they loved the truth in Christ, they could not attain their object, nor wholly dispossess him of his congregations. Shortly before my arrival, the notorious imposter, Carl Rudolph, who calls himself the prince of Würtemberg, and who already endeavored to create disturbance everywhere else, also came into Mr. Hartwick's congregations, and increased the confusion. In one of his congregations called Camp, where Mr. Hartwick has the most opponents, they let him preach in the church, on which account Mr. Hartwick recalled his office in that church, and would have nothing more to do with them. This in brief was the condition of affairs, as they were on my arrival in Rhinebeck.

On the 24th of August, Mr. Weiser left Rhinebeck, and we two preachers accompanied him twenty miles, until beyond the Camp, to a distinguished English gentleman, to whom the land in part properly belongs on which the Germans live. We were well received, and were informed by him that the French of Canada had brought over on their side most of the savage nations to whom Mr. Weiser was going, and who otherwise stood in alliance with England. This intelligence occasioned anxiety to Mr. Weiser. In the evening we took leave of Mr. Weiser, left him with the English gentleman, and rode back five miles to the Camp.

On the 25th of August, several men of the congregation came to us, and desired me to preach in Camp on the following day, it being the eleventh Sunday after Trinity. Mr. Hartwick thought that I should not refuse, although he had given up the congregation on account of their irregularity. I had therefore to accede to this demand for preaching, in the hope that a new union might be formed.

On the 26th of August, we went into the church. I well saw that there were two parties; the one came into the church, and the other remained outside, and harkened at a distance. My voice was still somewhat hoarse, therefore I had to exert myself to the utmost to be only somewhat intelligible. Now, as Carl Rudolph had last preached in this church, I first of all entreated the blessed God that he should again cleanse this house, gather the poor scattered sheep, and forgive those who introduced such a stain as the imposter Carl Rudolph is, and let him preach therein. I also told the people what kind of a man he is, and afterwards I preached as well as I could. After the sermon, one and another old warden came and promised that they would again begin anew to help care for the continuation of the divine service, although there were so many opponents in the congregation, who let themselves be incited by other preachers, and by the printed slanderous letters. Hereupon, we in the same week visited yet another out-parish, in Tarbush, so-called, about six or seven miles from Camp. This region is called Tarbush because the Germans whom Queen Ann sent into New York in the years 1709 and 1710 had to burn tar or pitch for a time. Camp is the tract of land along the Hudson where these same Germans first established their encampment, and called it camp, or encampment. In Tarbush only a few came together to my preaching, because nearly the most of them hold to the opponents, and the whole number also were not a little dispersed by Carl Rudolph. After we had again returned to Camp, I made use of some medicine, which had a good effect in a few days, so that my voice was again restored. During the last days of the week, we traveled back again fifteen miles to Rhinebeck, where we were diligently visited by the well-minded members of the congregation, and we ourselves also visited several.

On the 2d of September, I preached before a large congregation in Rhinebeck. There were several Dutch in the meeting, who assured me that they satisfactorily understood everything. As far as I could perceive, a general joy and encouragement arose among the people on that day, and it seemed as if all might be harmonized again. In the afternoon Mr. Hartwick delivered a beautiful catechetical sermon, and afterwards instructed the numerous youth.

On the 3d of September, a general conference was held at Rhinebeck, to which Mr. Hartwick invited the elders and wardens of all the four congregations, as also all the members of the congregations who were willing to appear, and requested me to be present. In this conference, two points, among others, were specially treated of. First, pastor Hartwick took up the complaints which were made in writing to Doctor Kreuter in London, but again returned by him to Mr. Hartwick for his reply. We asked the friends and the enemies present concerning the points of the complaint, and presented one after the other for their answer; when, to speak impartially of the matter, according to my weak insight, I could not understand it otherwise than that pastor Hartwick indeed, in several unimportant matters, with good intention, was somewhat hasty in the *modo procedendi*, or in the mode and manner—that he may not have acted with sufficient circumspection; but that with this exception the complaints are false, and perverted by manifest enmity, unjust and brought in and magnified, contrary to the truth; as any impartial lover of the truth can easily see, that if there had been no enemies and instigators there, that which gave occasion to the complaints either would not have been seen or noticed at all, or rather would have been reckoned to the proper zeal of a pastor. The second point was whether they thought it best that Mr. Hartwick should resign his call, and go with us to Pennsylvania, or whether he should go there for six months? To the former many well-meaning people would not consent, but to the latter all present assented, with this condition; that we of Pennsylvania would send some one in his place, who in the meanwhile would administer his office. Thus matters remained. The most important matters discussed in this conference were written and subscribed to by all the elders present.

The remaining days of the week I employed in visiting some dissatisfied members, and tried whether they might not be mollified. But the opposition to pastor Hartwick seemed to be already too deeply rooted, and to be maintained by the appearance of those who were opposed to him, as also by many passions of private conceits. It is very sad when such contentions and disturbances arise in congregations. For the members of the congregations are almost universally allied with each other by marriage, relationships, and the like, but the dissatisfied cease not until they obtain an ever-increasing faction, and attain their object, and the preachers have no refuge anywhere, nor help nor aid.

On the 9th of September, I preached in another out-parish called Ancram, which lies in the mountains, about eighteen miles from Rhinebeck. The divine service was held in a large barn: German in the forenoon, and in the afternoon English. I found several souls in this small congregation who testified that they had been awakened by the sermons of pastor Hartwick, and gave him a good testimonial.

On the 10th of September, I traveled fifteen miles with a guide, and again came into Camp, visited several discontented members, and preached there once more, after much solicitation, on the 12th of September, where both parties, as also the English proprietor, were present, and showed themselves much pleased.

On the 13th of September, I took leave in Camp, and again traveled to Rhinebeck.

On the 16th of September, I preached in Rhinebeck in the forenoon, and Mr. Hartwick in the afternoon, and also took leave there. Generally, the souls seemed much delighted by my visit, and to be encouraged thereby, and also desired to get into closer friendship and communion with our Ministerium of Pennsylvania.

On the 17th, we visited the fourth small congregation in Staatsburg, so called, held divine service there, and I took leave of all who were there assembled yet once more in crowds, from the other congregations.

On the 18th of September, we had our things taken to the Hudson river, into the house of a member of the congregation living not far from it, for the purpose of waiting there for a vessel to take us to New York. The whole time which I spent in pastor Hartwick's congregation, as much as possible according to my weakness and the grace of God, I sought to contribute my part towards the general pacification and edification, and otherwise did not concern myself about the personal circumstances of the quarrel, or enter into their investigation.

My old horse, which has now carried me hitherto until into the seventh year, through mountain and valley, through thorns and bushes, I could not take along again by water, consequently, I was obliged to sell saddle and bridle for the payment of traveling expenses, and to make a present of the horse to a poor man.

From the 18th to the 22d of September we had to tarry at the river, as we had come somewhat too late, and the vessels from Albany were already past. During this time we had many visits, by both old and young people of the Rhinebeck congregation, and we also visited the consort of a certain gentleman, who refreshed us on her estate with edifying conversation.

On the 22d of September we left the place where we had been staying, in a small boat, and came again to Kingston. We there visited the Dutch Reformed preacher, who received us in a very friendly manner. He complained that he also, several times, had strife in his congregation, and there were still some dissatisfied persons in it. In the evening about 8 o'clock, we sailed further in a small ship, and thanked God that he granted us an honorable ship's company, such as we very seldom meet with.

On Sunday the 23d of September, we sung an English Psalm, and Mr. Hartwick delivered an English discourse, as the most of our ship's company were Hollanders, who also understood English, whilst we were not sufficiently master of the Dutch. In the afternoon at 4 o'clock we were already beneath the fortress of the old renowned city, which was formerly called New Amsterdam, but is now called New York. Within twenty hours we had made about ninety miles. The Lord be praised for this also.

I would gladly have passed by the town, as I was well aware that old and new vexatious disputes prevailed among the few Lutherans there; but I had nevertheless to stop, and wait another opportunity for our further journey. Whilst we had to lay by, I endeavored to obtain a proper knowledge of the circumstances of the Lutheran congregation, of which we present the following in connection: The small Evangelical Lutheran congregation in this city of New York had almost taken its origin at the same time with the first peopling of this country. When the country as yet belonged to the States of Holland, the few Dutch Lutherans had to hold their divine service secretly. But after the city and country came under the sceptre of Great Britain, they obtained liberty from all the successive governors to hold public divine service, without hinderance. As may be seen from a certain protocol, there were in the more recent times, from 1703 until this present year, three preachers in this congregation, viz.: Messrs. Justus Falckner, Christoph William Berkenmeyer, and Christian Knoll. In the times of pastor Berkenmeyer the old wooden church was removed, and a new massive stone church erected in its place. But the members of the congregation of that time, among whom our esteemed friend Mr. Schleydorn had also been, found themselves unable to build the church by their means alone; but through the intercession of pastor

Berkenmeyer, they received kind donations from other denominations of New York, and from our fellow believers in Europe, especially from London, Amsterdam, Hamburg, Denmark, and other places. In the times of Messrs. Falckner and Berkenmeyer, the congregation was as yet pretty numerous, but in later times it gradually declined. The old Dutch separated themselves in part from the church, and the young persons were also for the most part scattered and joined other denominations. As respects the external order, usages and ceremonies in divine service, the before-mentioned preachers introduced a church service, which they prepared according to the pattern of the church service in the Evangelical Lutheran Church in Amsterdam, and which all the elders and deacons subscribed to, and hitherto they used the Liturgy of Amsterdam, which was very conveniently and edifyingly arranged according to American circumstances. Now, as in later years a considerable number of Germans settled in and around New York, who indeed in part were studious of the Dutch language, but in part continually complained that they could neither learn nor understand Dutch, and thus much dispute arose whether pastor Knoll should not occasionally hold divine service in German for the latter. The elders and wardens frequently consulted about the matter, and also formerly obtained an opinion from our Pennsylvania Ministerium, and consented to a forenoon or afternoon sermon, or a sermon between times, in the German language, sometimes on the third, and occasionally on every other Sunday. One part of the Germans were satisfied with this, and have remained in the church until this day, with the congregation and their arrangement. But the other part of the Germans, which consists of people who are led by several quarrelsome heads, have never been at rest or satisfied, held to the church at one time and at another time separated themselves from it without just cause, as the church register shows. A few years ago this disorderly multitude attached themselves to a vagabond, who here called himself Hofgut, but who under his proper name was degraded from office in Würtemberg, on account of a gross violation of the sixth commandment, and had come to America with a young woman. They held divine service with him, for a time, in a private dwelling, until the kingdom divided and the preacher went from thence further into the country, to those who are like him, after the government had interdicted his preaching until he produced proof of his ordination. Thereupon they again began to treat with pastor Knoll and his Dutch and German congregation, about German divine service. According to the register, their desire was acceded to once and again; but it was without permanence, for as soon as they heard that a young preacher, by the name of John Frederick Riess, had arrived in Pennsylvania, they called for him and accepted him as their preacher, and at length bought a building set apart for a brewery in a distant part of the city, and obligated themselves to pay £250 for it in time. Afterwards they borrowed £50 more, to arrange the house somewhat more conveniently for divine service, and also obtained permission from the Governor to collect alms in New York, under the pretext that they did not understand the Dutch in the old church, and that the Dutch would not allow any divine service in German, etc. Now the division among the Lutherans was completed. That part of the Germans which went over to Mr. Riess, sought to acquire the one-half right in the old Lutheran church, so that they might prescribe laws, and set up every vagrant as preacher, and use one-half of the alms and church property, according to their own will and pleasure. But the church council replied to them, that they dared to alienate neither the half nor a part of the church and its property in this manner, but that the church was built and dedicated by their mite and the liberal contribution from Europe, for an Evangelical Lutheran church, according to the unaltered Augsburg Confession, and had its established order and liturgy, and according to these was at the service of all fellow-believers, from whatsoever nation they may be, etc. But the leaders of the opposing party were not satisfied therewith, but when they could not attain that object, they desired to have a church of their own, and expected to take up many collections for that purpose, both here and in Europe, under various good pretenses. To this end, an emigrant, lately arrived, as he told me himself, had already represented to a teacher of consequence in Germany, as impressively as it was possible for him, the imaginary wants of the Germans. It is sad that in this country some of our German nation are so readily found, who according to their life and conduct are not even worthy to be called Lutherans, but yet put themselves forward, separate themselves from churches which are built and well regulated, and from good order, and desire to build their own churches, not indeed at their own expense, but in the hope of receiving aid from Europe. By such disorderly heads, and by the uncalled preachers, our Evangelical denomination suffers the greatest injury. The Lutheran Church in New York is at present still large enough for both parties, and there is opportunity enough for both Dutch and German divine service, if the people had in view only the general good of our religion, and not their own hatred, pride and selfwill, and interest! But now, the disorderly party has, without necessity, involved itself in debt, and must also support its self-chosen preacher.

As respects the small number of the Dutch

and German nation who still hold to the church, they have already lived in a misunderstanding with pastor Knoll for several years past. Shortly before my arrival in New York, he settled with the church council, laid down his office for a certain sum of money, and gave up in writing all demand on the church and congregation, whereupon the money conceded to him was paid out of the church treasury. I found an advertisement in the English newspaper, which he had inserted himself, and therein announced that he had resigned his office, and had resolved to keep school. From which, then, it was clearly manifest, that the Lutheran church and congregation were at the present time without a preacher.

On the 24th of September, Mr. Hartwick and I went out and visited Mr. Riess, the preacher of the party which had separated. He was very glad to see us, and called several of his wardens, hoping that I would stand by their party, and that I would preach for them on the next Sunday, in what had been a brewery. I however refused, and put him in mind that I advised him in Philadelphia that he should have nothing to do with the disaffected in New York, as pastor Knoll was still the lawful preacher there, so that he might not give occasion to the separation, as it is now manifest. Mr. Riess acknowledged to me that two heads only of his party managed the whole affair; that the men set themselves up as chiefs, and that otherwise they had a very bad name in the city, on account of their gross sinful lives. Nothing the less, they were all in good spirits, that their German church would shortly get the upper hand, as the Governor had granted them liberty to take up collections in New York, that the men had already gone out for this purpose, and already obtained something from those who did not know their circumstances. Others, however, refused the collectors, with the answer that there was a Lutheran church there already, and that it was unnecessary to build another. It is said that shortly one or several men are also to go to Germany to make collections there.

On the 25th of September, we visited several elders of the church and congregation, whom we knew by name, because they several times sought an opinion from us in reference to their matters in dispute. They desired that I should preach in their church on the next Sunday, as they were without a preacher at the present time, as Mr. Knoll had resigned his office. Now, as I had seen from the above-mentioned advertisement that it was so, I could not well refuse them.

On the 26th of September, we took a trip to a place called Flushing, to visit an acquaintance there, a gentleman of our religion, viz., Mr. Melchior Joachim Magens. His father had been Danish preacher in St. Thomas, and had left many possessions to his son, who had studied law. Now, as he thought the climate of New York, and other circumstances, more suitable to his health and that of his family, he purchased a landed estate for himself in said place. He understands Latin, Greek, and also many European languages, and is especially well versed in theology, and holds firmly to the Evangelical Lutheran doctrine and denomination, and is also anxious to raise his children well. He had heard that pastor Hartwick had been persecuted on account of his zeal for the power of godliness, and was therefore induced to write to him twice, and to call him for his domestic preacher, which pastor Hartwick however was unwilling to accept, and to leave his congregation without urgent necessity. He received us in a very friendly manner, edified himself with us in conversation, and on several evenings allowed Mr. Hartwick to hold a meeting for edification in the English language.

On the 29th of September, we again returned to New York. Towards evening, we understood that pastor Berckenmeyer had arrived in New York. The elders and wardens had written to him a few weeks before, and requested him to come and give advice how the ruined congregation could be best aided. For this reason, I wished again to decline the sermon with which I was commissioned, so as not to forestall him. But as the wardens again requested me in this behalf, I went to him in the evening, related the circumstances to him, and inquired whether I could preach with his permission, otherwise it would not be proper. He received me courteously, and gave his consent in the presence of two witnesses; stipulated, however, that for certain reasons he could not be present at the service.

On the 30th of September, I preached in the church, German in the forenoon, and in the afternoon in English, as I was not sufficiently master of the Dutch. In the afternoon, there were three awakened Englishmen of the Presbyterian congregation present in the church. One of these, who was a merchant, invited us to his residence, and together with the rest carried on an edifying conversation, and in the evening took us along into their church, in which the celebrated Mr. Pemberton is teacher. But a new preacher preached on this occasion, whom the congregation had recently accepted as an assistant or deacon.

On the 1st of October, we took leave in New York. We went by water, and arrived in Brunswick towards evening of October the 2d. We could there find no room and night's lodging in the inn, because just then a meeting of Freemasons was held there. On that account we turned in with an English Presbyterian preacher, Mr. Arthur, who received us in a very friendly manner, and kindly lodged us. He entertained us with edifying conversations concerning the kingdom of God, gathered his household, and offered an excellent spiritual and instructive prayer for every condition throughout Christendom. This good man soon after died, in his best years, to the great regret of his congregation, and of all others who are concerned for the hurt of Joseph.

On the 3d of October, Mr. Hartwick continued his journey to Philadelphia, but I went aside by way of Raritan to visit Mr. Weygand, whom I met in ill health on the 4th of October, and tarried with him over night. We encouraged ourselves with necessary conversation and with prayer.

On the following day, I continued my journey, and lodged with an awakened widow from Holland, and at length came home safely on the 6th of October. Our first business after having finished our journey, was to prepare the young candidate, Mr. Rauss, with instructions, and send him to Rhinebeck and Camp for six months on trial as a catechist. Now, as Mr. Rauss was to do the work in Mr. Hartwick's congregations, so on the contrary Mr. Hartwick promised to take his place with us, sometimes to relieve pastor Brunnholtz of some of his labor, and at the same time attend to the country congregations in Old Goschenhoppen and Indianfield, which had dismissed parson Andrea, because he had successively given two living husbands to one woman, on which account he fell into the hands of the authorities, and was imprisoned twice. Now, Andrea is still in the congregation in New Goschenhoppen, and a few congregations attached, and also as yet continues to slander us bitterly.

In the remaining part of October and in November, I cultivated my regular congregations, administered the Holy Supper, and in the special examination of the communicants, I found to my consolation some traces of the power of godliness. I also once more visited the Swedish-English congregation, my relations, and the adjunctus Mr. Kurtz in Tulpehocken, and came home again in good condition.

Towards the close of November, the colleagues in office, Messrs. Brunnholtz, Hartwick, Handschuch, Schaum and Kurtz, all together came to my house, to start from here on the journey to Raritan in Jersey, and at the desire of the congregation to consecrate the new church, and to ordain Mr. Weygand.

My dear colleagues in office wished to spare me this time, as I was still fatigued with the former journey, and I was not willing to leave my congregations so soon again. So far as I have heard, the transactions at Raritan were satisfactorily accomplished before a very great multitude of people, in a very orderly and edifying manner, and so as to be happily remembered by the numerous youth who had never witnessed such a thing before. May God's great and holy name be hallowed also here in the wilds of America—praised and glorified now, henceforth and forever. Amen!

Many vessels with Germans arrived during the past autumn, who were distributed and scattered in the country in crowds.

In the month of December, I unexpectedly received a letter in the Dutch language from the elders of the congregation in New York, dated in November, in which they gave me a call to become their preacher, and in which they set forth at length that they are in danger that their congregation (as it is already divided and distracted) be wholly ruined, and many souls not only for themselves, but with their children also, be estranged from the pure doctrine of the gospel, if they do not soon receive an honest man, yea, rather a father, for their teacher; who, as they express themselves, might again gather the scattered souls under the shelter of the pure doctrine of our gospel. They therefore entreated me most earnestly that I should care for them in this trouble, and not refuse this call. But if I should not be able or willing to accept of it permanently, they requested that I should at least accept the office of teacher with them for one, two or three years, or as long as I should think it best, so that in this time, if possible, the separated members might be brought in again, and they afterwards obtain another honest and zealous man for their teacher, through my interposition, who would set me at liberty again. That I should hereupon declare myself as soon as possible, and then seek to come to them—the sooner the better.

I understood at the same time, from various special letters which I received on this account, that after my departure, the elders and wardens (pastor Berckenmeyer also being present), had a long conference and consultation, how the fallen church affairs of that place might be helped up again. Now although, among other things, the advice was given them, that they should again call a preacher from Germany, still the most of them, and the most judicious of the church-board, objected to this, that as their congregation was at present in such doubtful circumstances, it was quite too critical a matter to await an unknown teacher from Europe, of whom they could not know how he would turn out. For if they should not succeed well with him again, entire destruction and ruin would be inevitable. Now, when the elders and wardens afterwards had much consultation among themselves, although warned against the Pennsylvania preachers as dangerous people, they nevertheless came to the conclusion to try whether they could get Mühlenberg for their preacher. But first of all they had found it necessary to invite Mr. Riess and his party, which had separated from the congregation, to a conference, and make the proposal whether they would again unite with them, and in common with them call Mühlenberg. But they would consent to no union, unless Mr. Riess would be accepted as preacher by both parties; but to this it was objected, that on the one hand he was incapable, on account of the English and Dutch language, and on the other, that he had also given an offence hereby, inasmuch as he aided in causing the separation in the congregation, and had hitherto maintained it.

This proposal and call, which reached me contrary to anything I could have conjectured, placed me in not a little embarrassment, inasmuch as I did not at all wish to be precipitate on the one hand, but on the other, I could not regard such a call as wholly accidental, which came to me without my seeking, and I did not know whether God had not his wise designs thereby, which I would not willingly hinder. I especially lamented the ruin and distraction of this congregation, and as the orderly part of it must so much the more have had a good design by this call to me, as from prejudice and affection they were warned against me by those who were in repute with them, so I held myself bound in conscience to care for them as much as possible. I directed my answer accordingly, and testified that I esteemed myself wholly and entirely unworthy, and also that I did not possess the necessary facility in the Dutch language, nevertheless I rejoiced that the Lord had still preserved some zeal in their hearts to be concerned (at this time, when faith, love and hope have almost vanished) for their own and for the salvation of the souls of their descendants, and for the maintenance of the pure doctrine of the prophets and apostles. That the circumstances of their congregation and church are mournful enough, and so constituted that it is difficult to improve them, although not wholly impossible through the power of God in faith; but for me it would be very hard to leave the congregations committed to me and my worthy colleagues and brethren in office, as also my relatives. But as it seems that they had foreseen all these difficulties, and therefore only desired that I should make the experiment for one, two or three years, my answer to this proposal is the following: 1. I know that the congregation needs speedy help. 2. I am prepared to renounce all ease for the sake of the things of God. 3, I depend alone on the grace and aid of the Lord, who alone can fit me for the holy office. 4. I must care that my congregations in the meantime are provided with a faithful teacher and laborer, so that I do not close a hole on the one side of the sheepfold, and on the other let the door stand open for the wolves. 5. I am under the supervision of Doctor Francke and the court preacher Zeigenhagen, to whom I must give notice thereof. 6. I must have liberty to be present with our united Ministerium in Pennsylvania at the annual meetings, and on other occasions, and to visit here and there a forsaken congregation, where, by my feeble interposition, some improvement could be made. 7. I could at first only preach German and English, and would require two or three months to attain to a readiness in the Dutch language. 8. I would first have to set in order my external affairs. Now, as all these circumstances require some time for preparation, and a further investigation of the gracious will of the Lord, I would meanwhile await another answer from them, and leave it to their choice whether they, according to their best and impartial insight, leave me, and look around for a better man, or send me a regular call for a trial for two years. In the latter case, I would inquire into the will and pleasure of God, and amidst heartfelt prayer seek to become sure of it by observing the circumstances, and if I should be assured of it, come over as soon as it is possible, according to the will of God and surrounding circumstances.

Alas! how afraid I often become when I think of the heavy responsibility of the preacher's office, and my great unfitness for it. Alas! only be not thou terrible to me, but gracious and merciful, and for the sake of Jesus Christ and his merits, cast my sins of office and station behind thee, O Lord! and let grace be instead of righteousness, and mercy instead of judgment. Amen! Kyrie eleison!

The following is an appendix to the report of pastor Mühlenberg's official transactions, consisting of an extract from a letter of the same to the court preacher Ziegenhagen, at London, and to Doctor Francke, at Halle, of December the 29th, 1749.

The mercy of God in Christ permits me to hope that my humble letter shall find our venerable fathers still alive, in good spirits, and confident at their important posts in the church militant and in the kingdom of the cross of Jesus Christ. Whoever sees with enlightened eyes, and can judge impartially in what condition the evangelical church at present floats upon the boisterous ocean, and considers how few sit at the helm who have sufficient experience, ability, and will to steer between the waves and the rocks, will heartily call upon the Lord with us, for your further preservation. Now, as earnestly as we desire and pray that the highly venerable fathers may be commanded by Jehovah, our gracious Father in Christ, to tarry yet many years in the church militant, to labor for the whole; so eager you may also be to hear from our small and unimportant part, whether here and there a stone has been found among the rubbish prepared and fitted to fill up a gap in the completed building of the kingdom of Jesus Christ. You highly venerable fathers have a right to this, as well as all other estimable patrons and benefactors, because your great efforts and gifts of love had this for their object, that forsaken and scattered souls be sought, and be turned from darkness to light, and from the power of Satan to God.

But here I must immediately make complaint by way of anticipation, and acknowledge a truth which daily experience in my office furnishes me with, viz.: *with true repentance and conversion according to the Word of God, the progress is difficult and peculiar.* I can by no means ascribe the fault to the most holy God, and to his powerful Word, and to the Holy Sacraments, much less to the ceaseless intercession of our Lord Jesus Christ and his dear children; but I indisputably find it in the wicked heart of man, which in truth, according to its innate corruption, loves darkness more than the light and the truth, as also in the thousand-fold obstacles which Satan and the world cast in the way, and not less also in my inexperience in my important office. But experience also teaches me this fact, that it is easier to convert men to a sect or denomination wherein certain limits are fixed to which the natural temperaments may attain by their own powers, find sustenance and a false rest, and avoid the ways which are unpleasant to the flesh, viz.: of repentance and faith, together with godliness, which the rule of the Divine Word requires. How easy it is to convert unconverted people to Quakerism! for here in this country so many respectable persons of the magistracy, who govern the country, who possess honor, respectability, power, and riches, profess to belong to it. In this denomination, the people need not trouble themselves with the written Word of God and with the Sacraments. They need give salary to no preacher. They wear the very plainest dress, and all can teach and prophesy when they have good ideas. They love each other, if they are loved in turn. They help the poor of their denomination, and a naturally honest life they fix as the basis of eternal happiness; and they remain good converted members, if they only appear twice a year in the great meeting. Is such a repentance still too cumbersome for the flesh?—then an easier way is found. For we have many here who separate themselves from all things visible, and pretend to worship God in Spirit and in truth, and call themselves *the silent in the land*. These belong to no denomination at all, permit themselves to be reprimanded by no one, have no compassion or feeling for other members, as they are separated, explain the

Bible according to their pleasure, darken the very plainest truths with their strange speech, and find therein great mysteries which the ordinary man indeed must leave unsolved. They write books and lament and deplore it, that all mankind do not find the light and the Saviour in themselves. As silent however as they and theirs are, when they are to care for the common and special want and poverty, they are still found loud, active, and efficient enough at the markets where there is trafficking. If there are melancholy natures, who would gladly be wholly out of the world, there is a convenient denomination provided by various crafty men, which is called the denomination of the Seventh Day Baptists. There is a beautiful and rich tract of land purchased, large common halls for single men and women, and the like; also brew and bake-houses are built by the sweat and blood of the self-denying members. O what wonderful institutions and converts are these! According to their pretension, we dare look upon Christ no further than as an example, but only give heed to the men who have become like to Christ in holiness, and thereby obtained the power of regenerating, so as to be able to beget spiritual children. We have nothing there of a righteousness apprehended by faith. If they only affect a righteousness of life by fasting, mortification, hard work, and a ridiculous manner of dress, give their goods and chattels into the common treasury, let themselves be dipped in their community, and ruled for life, body and soul, by the chief taskmaster, then they are such a convert, and pity all others who do not also wish so to enjoy life. But this denomination is still much too circumscribed, and adapted only to one or two kinds of temperaments; and for this reason Count Zinzendorf has contrived a still more convenient denomination, wherein all sorts of temperaments find sustenance. Here in this country many a wanton fornicator and adulterer has given his house and farm in order to be absolved by such new teachers from his gross vices, without repentance and faith, and to be assured that his natural disposition is well adapted to the remaining cross-bills and beasts, if he brings goods and chattels, and makes himself friends with the unrighteous mammon. The last conversion would be still far more universal if it did not act so hard on property, and left more food for the natural disposition. If one would rather himself control his goods and chattels, and still become something extraordinary, that has more show than the common church life, he can be converted to the denomination of the so-called Dippers. With himself he has soon finished, if he can only repeat a few passages of the Revelation by John, concerning Babylon and the beast and the whore, makes an outward figure therewith, and allows himself to be publicly immersed by them. Their lessons are easy to nature, and convenient to learn. They have only to scoff at infant baptism, and to judge all others who do not hold with them, especially the parsons and the church people, and among other things believe that the devil and the damned shall again be released from hell. Conversion to the Mennonite denomination is also very easy, convenient, and advantageous, and well-nigh one of the most tranquil.

But I must also lament over those of our own religion, and confess that the greater part entertain the erroneous opinion that they are already converted when they have performed the *opus operatum*, external worship of God, and have sung: Now praise God it is finished; although on other occasions, under cover of human weakness, they curse that heaven might shudder at it, get drunk, and follow other worldly vanities. These poor people are strengthened in their misconception by nine or ten so-called Lutheran preachers, who have here in part set themselves up to teach, and in part were degraded from office in Germany on account of gross vices, and came here to this country—they are falsely assured by these of the certainty of their salvation, for the sake of a handful of barley, and lulled to sleep; yea, indeed, very diligently persuaded that other preachers, who so earnestly insist on repentance, have deviated from the Lutheran doctrine. We dare not think that the people first fell into this error here in this country, but they brought it with them from various places in Germany. In a word, in this country, Satan, who deceives the whole world, has his complete fair, and almost all possible kinds of sectarian forms; still they all agree herein, that they have the semblance of godliness, but deny its just power. So far, the unbridled so-called liberty of conscience, may serve this mortal and sinful generation.

And now, highly venerable fathers, you, and other worthy patrons and benefactors might justly ask, what have we hitherto built up? To building belongs as well the removal of obstacles, the preparation of materials, the digging of the ground, and the raising of the scaffolding, as the actual symmetrical placing together of the parts. How many hindrances does not Satan occasion us, and also the rude and subtle world, the unbridled liberty, and especially the condition of all human hearts which have lost the original image of God, and become instead as an involved and tangled mass of weaver's yarn. We had to spend several years before they even let us pass for honest people, because the preacher's office has been far too much prostituted, and rendered suspected in this country by those so-called clergymen, who lead a vexatious life, and under the black coat perpetrate subtle frauds. How difficult it is to dig a deep and permanent foundation in hearts which our Master compares to the wayside with stony and thorny ground! We bravely dig into them with the holy law of God, and animadvert upon all possible kinds of sin, but there is very much resistance. External preparation, *i. e.*, the building of churches and school-houses, wasted much time for us. Our dear colleagues in office in Europe have a great advantage over us, because the outward scaffolding already stands. They receive their necessary support without care. They have an external hedge around their congregations, and are protected by Christian governments, though at one place more or less than at another, so that they may dig on with confidence and unhindered with the law in the hearts of those entrusted to them, and build up with the gospel as a power unto salvation! In many Protestant places it would be just as difficult as it is with us, if they had at present first to build their churches and school-houses, without any certain charitable foundation from voluntary contributions. For the rich have nothing left for churches and schools, for the maintenance of preachers and school teachers, but many indeed rather wish that such were banished from the country. The poor would sometimes willingly give, but are unable. Now, although we know the difference between particular churches, those which have the outward equipment and those which have it not, those which have a hedge and those which have none, those which have governments as nursing mothers and those which have none, yet it is exceeding well with us beneath the shadow and protection of the Most High, and we have hedge and wall enough, if we believe the promise of our Master: *Lo, I am with you alway*, etc. We also will not murmur that we are without aid from Bracihio seculari, the secular arm, but most humbly thank our Jehovah, that he is the help of our countenance and our God! We do not wish to be understood as though we thought that we alone have made and still make the outward preparation here; but it remains an everlasting memorial, that in this century, the essentially good God awakened many honest souls in the Protestant church of various stations, dignities and honor, and endowed them with distinguished faith, and who quickly strove to be active through love, and especially had, and still have for their object, the spreading abroad of the kingdom of Jesus Christ among the heathen, the Jews, and even in lukewarm Christendom. This most gracious God, and his dear children in Europe, the dispersed, erring and forsaken Lutherans in Philadelphia, Germantown, Providence, New Hanover, Upper Milford, Saccum, New York, Perkasie, Tulpehocken, Heidelberg, Lancaster and York, have most humbly to thank, that in the midst of the most dangerous time of war, they with much trouble and heavy expense, sent them five preachers free, and when the mites contributed by the first united congregations did not suffice by far to provide the most necessary buildings for divine service and for schools, the highly venerable fathers, benefactors and patrons gradually sent over so much, that, by the donations in connection with the mites of this place, a church was repaired in New Hanover, and a new school house built, and several acres of land purchased, and in Providence a substantial stone church and school house were finished from the foundation. In Germantown the second half of a church was erected, and in Philadelphia a piece of land was bought, and a church built on it, which last, however, alone is yet involved in the most debts, as building in the city is exceedingly expensive. The members of the congregation are for the most part poor, and as yet young beginners. The house had to be built the largest, and according to a close comparison, a pound in building reaches no further in the city than one dollar in Germany. As many groschen as are given to a laboring man a day in Germany, so many shillings must be given here to English tradesmen. The accounts and receipts which pastor Brunnholtz has already sent, and will still send to the highly venerable fathers, will certify all the before-mentioned. Now, whether some souls are won and saved by the many efforts, gifts of love and institutions, or that we, since God is with us, waste our strength among them, only as a witness, still, according to the infallible promises of God, the great endeavors and gifts of love, yea, the least drink of cold water of our highly venerable fathers, and of all worthy benefactors, will not remain unrecompensed and unrequited. All our endeavor and care, although in great weakness, accordingly tend to this, that we (conformably to the blessed design of our highly venerable fathers, patrons and benefactors, and of our office), so believe, teach, live, pray, wrestle and fight, that our congregations entrusted to us, and each member of them particularly, be won and saved if possible, by our service.

In this order, our dear colleague in office, pastor Brunnholtz, labors, now in the fifth year, with all faithfulness and patience in the congregations in Philadelphia and Germantown. He preaches publicly, not with the words of human wisdom, but in demonstration of the Spirit and of power. He holds special prayer-meetings in his house. He is edifying in intercourse with his own people and all kinds of sects, and concentrates all his discourse to the improvement of the understanding and the will. He visits the sick by day and by night, if necessary, often also when he himself is weak and faint. He meditates, prays, contends and wrestles in his chamber for all congregations, and for those entrusted to him especially, for the fathers, and for all the members of Jesus Christ in Europe. He is very much occupied with the instruction of the young. He is greatly burdened with the correspondence, as all our letters are delivered to him for distribution. He faithfully cares for the external burdens of the church and for the debts, and attends to it, that the interest is collected. He is satisfied with that which the members of his congregation from good will offer him, and spares the poor, duns no one, shifts along from hand to mouth, and if he has anything left, he shares it with the poor. He shows himself in all things a servant of God, and a faithful steward of the mysteries of God. His labor also is not without a blessing. For the preaching of the gospel will be unto some a savor of life unto life. God, however, does not upon the whole make known to him the blessing, in order that he may remain in poverty of spirit and in humility. He has already removed many obstacles out of the way, dug a deep foundation in some, and laid the foundation by the grace of God. The fire of tribulation will preserve and reveal it. But now I must announce it with sorrow that he has already nearly consumed himself, whilst he shone as a light to others. For he has been sickly nearly the whole of the past summer, so that I was anxious on his account. I took him with me into the country for a few weeks, whereby he again recovered somewhat. At length, in autumn, he had a very dangerous attack of malaria fever, that twice already we expected his death. He indeed employed English doctors, but next to God the *essentia dulcis* helped him to his feet again after a long and severe illness, by which however he was very much enfeebled. In these circumstances a lessening of labor is indispensably necessary to him. But none of us are able to assist him, for we are scarcely able to help ourselves situated as we are. Pastor Brunnholtz and myself have in our calls the first united congregations. He and I are both scarcely as yet strong enough for one man, therefore we both need an adjunct. Now, highly venerable fathers, if according to your paternal love to us, and to our poor congregations, you could select a suitable person and send him in, pastor Brunnholtz could at least for a time stay with me in the country until he recovered, and labor as much as his strength permitted, and thus I and all the four congregations would be all the better aided. He might also for exercise now and then visit the other colleagues in office, and give them advice and comfort. Although my income is pretty small, yet God will not forsake nor neglect us. For we have a rich Father over all. I know that he will be satisfied as God directs. He shall have as much privilege in my house and surroundings as I have myself. In relation to the expenses of the voyage, the Heavenly Father will also provide in time.

As fearful as pastor Handschuch was at first to go to Lancaster, he still finds a good entrance, and already labors with a blessing. He suffered a severe sickness in the latter part of this summer, so that we almost feared his death. But God graciously averted it, and bestowed him unto us again. Mr. Schaum, who was ordained this year for the congregation in York, also had a severe fever, and otherwise one trial and another; still, as yet no temptation but human has perplexed us, but God is faithful, etc. Mr. Kurtz I suppose has reported his circumstances himself. He has hitherto faithfully performed his office, and enjoyed reasonably good health.

In the past summer, I had to travel to

Raritan once more. Mr. Weygand finds a good entrance there, and has hitherto as yet conducted himself well. The three congregations there gave him a formal call in my presence, and ask our highly venerable fathers through me, whether they would let this rest, and grant full power to us to ordain the said Mr. Weygand at our next synod. We have lifted the Darmstadt collection, and decreed the one-half to Providence and the other to Philadelphia.

As for the rest, I commend my family, especially my dear colleagues in office, congregations, and all other concerns, to the further love and favor, and chiefly to the earnest intercession of our highly venerable fathers, patrons, and all acquaintances in the Lord.

HENRY MELCHIOR MÜHLENBERG.

CHAPTER IV.

SEVERAL LETTERS FROM PASTOR BRUNNHOLTZ, IN PHILADELPHIA, DURING THE YEARS 1749 AND 1750.

I. Extract of a letter to the court preacher, Mr. Ziegenhagen, in London, and Doctor Francke, in Halle, of the 11th of April, 1749.

My last letter to the same address was dated in November of last year, wherein there were several supplements. I hope all may have arrived safely, although I have no intelligence as yet of the ship wherewith it was sent. As the Delaware was frozen over for a long time, no opportunity occurred from here from that time until now, when a ship again leaves.

Now, as we all hope and wish that our fathers and other patrons and friends in Europe may still be alive and in tolerable health, so we may announce that it has pleased the good God to preserve us all in life and unity together.

Our dear brother Handschuch has now labored for nearly a year in the vineyard in Lancaster, with all faithfulness, but also under diverse circumstances, which generally are not wanting in the kingdom of the cross of the Lord Jesus Christ, and especially also not in this country and among these people. We write to each other on every post-day, and comfort and encourage each other as God gives us ability. We have not many servants and children of God here, at least not near together, with and among whom we might have pleasant intercourse and constant encouragement. Still the hand of the Lord is not too short, and his Spirit is not far from us, and is able to compensate for the want of all this the more abundantly and purely. As we have ever to learn as long as we live, so we have fine opportunities here to learn that which we indeed as yet never knew, and also perhaps had never learned in the old country. And although obstacles are met with here which are not there, so also there are advantages here which are wished for there but are not obtained. Christ, the head of the Church, faith and trust in and to him will so support us, that in the end his wisdom and goodness will be extolled. May he give unto us the spirit of love, of power, and of discretion, and make us wise, courageous, and patient, triumphantly to finish the fight and the race set before us.

The said brother Handschuch has obtained pastor Mühlenberg's schoolmaster from Hanover, Jacob Löser for Lancaster. He had indeed been deathly sick recently, but God has helped him up again. He is a fine man, conducts the school in that place, and is at the same time chanter and sacristan in the congregation.

Mr. Schaum is still in York, and as Mr. Handschuch has written, it seems that the congregation there, intend to call him as their regular preacher and to have him ordained. In these days pastor Handschuch goes over there to administer the Lord's Supper, and to see how matters stand. Mr. Kurtz, as far as I know, is still well, keeps school in his house during winter, and as is known, regularly officiates in Tulpehocken.

The young candidate, Weygand, of whom we made mention in our last, is stationed at Raritan, and on his account we made inquiry of your highly venerableness, and still await the answer. He writes occasionally. During the past week he and an elder from that place were with me over night, and reported the condition of things there. He seems to be honest. But he must pass through many trials yet, so that the true character in him, may be so much the more established. The congregation is well satisfied with him. There is a gentle spirit in his delivery, and this winter he diligently instructed the children on week days. This spring the congregation there purpose building a stone church in common for all, and pastor Mühlenberg will doubtless have to go over this summer to visit the congregation.

Pastor Mühlenberg and his wife were with me on the 15th of January of this year, just when I entered upon my fifth year in this country. They were with me for several days when we animated and cheered ourselves with prayer and supplication to God. He is indisposed now and then, and had also been sick this winter. He cannot endure the labor any more as he did formerly, inasmuch as his constitution becomes weaker. As we cannot often meet, we make amends for the want by letters, and confer about that which is most needful.

Since my last, God be praised, I had no need to miss a sermon on account of infirmity, except on New Year's day, when I, in riding out to Germantown, was so frozen through by the furious cold, that I could only preach for fifteen minutes. God in great mercy so strengthened me in my weakness, that in my sermons I could feel the aid of the Holy Ghost. And when I obtained a little more rest, as the most disquietude of the external church building is past, I am enabled to labor more for the internal. When I examine myself before the Lord, I must confess to the praise alone of unmerited grace, that in so far as I know myself, I am solely concerned for the eternal salvation of my own soul and that of others, and therefore I hope that the blessing can fail as little as the holy cross and the assaults of the arch enemy. I am according to my feelings the weakest and the most miserable without and within, and to know this is also grace. Still this will not hinder the work of God, for I place my trust not in myself, nor upon any other thing in the world, but upon him who is all in all, worketh all in all, and will eternally be all in all. On account of my infirmity I cannot indeed do as much in external matters as I willingly would, and if I could, I indeed might accomplish more good. In case of necessity, I still ride around to visit the members. Still I hope that the Lord himself will compensate for this deficiency, by either, giving me more strength, so that that which is not done now, may be accomplished in future, or that he himself, by the gracious influence of his Spirit (who at all events must do all) will succor the souls. In my public preaching, one of the principal points I urge, is to direct the hearers to the Bible, to search in it diligently at home, to read in it, and with prayer to bring that which they read into their lives. I also observe some profit in many, and especially in young families. The hinderances to true repentance and to the progress of the work of the Lord in the soul I point out to them according to ability, and show them how we may overcome them. Those who are moved and affected, I publicly request to come to me for more particular instruction. Some also actually come.

At the afternoon service in Philadelphia, which is every two weeks, I endeavor to direct the children and the poor servants (*i. e.*, those men and maid servants, who are sold for several years on account of their passage, who come diligently and of whom there is a large number in the city) to Christ and to true piety. I represent to them the great danger in which they especially stand, on account of their youth and the circumstances of the country, etc. On Easter, as is done in Halle, I had passages printed and distributed among the smaller children for their encouragement. In the evening prayer meetings, which I hold on Wednesdays in the schoolroom in my house, I repeat in a regular manner the sermon which I preached the Sunday previous. In the summer I may do it in church, as there is not room enough in the house. Various English people have indeed desired me to preach English, and inquired when it could be done. It seems to me, however, that it is not as yet the time, in case I were able. My office is principally with the Germans, among whom I have more to do than I am able to accomplish.

Now, as there is a regular printing office in

the city, which the English printer and postmaster, Mr. Franklin, has purchased, and appointed a German printer over it, we have opportunity, when useful and necessary, to have anything printed. And as the printer, who is of the Lutheran religion, desired to print for sale the small catechism of Luther for children, and had requested me to arrange it, I did so, and am now enabled to make use of it in the instruction of the youth. The first edition is for the most part sold. Perhaps we may shortly have a new appendix printed to the Marpurg hymn-book, as many spiritual hymns are wanting, and we cannot readily introduce another entire book. The printer also intends to print John Arndt's True Christianity, if he can get subscribers enough. I very often publicly recommended it, and in this and that matter, direct them to it. As the grace of God worketh unto true repentance in several in my congregations, so this also particularly is taking place in Mr. N., in whom I now observe a very marked change within a year, and I hope for permanency. His eyes are opened more continually, and he is very eager for instruction, and has also already enjoyed some true grace, and now also labors with all earnestness in his family. He weeps over the deception in which he lived until old age, and yet esteemed himself an earnest and a true Lutheran. God help him through, together with others. His example has a good influence upon others. Another Mr. N., who is our friend, and who has much love for us, is, and often indeed becomes uneasy; he also neglects no sermon, but his reason is too exalted. Men would rather dispute about matters of controversy, and decide these, than attack the heretic within us. It is easier for many to praise a sermon, or to criticise it, whether it was regularly arranged, than to examine his heart by it. It is a difficult thing to give up the old Adam unto death, to deny the worldly spirit, and regard all our own prudence and fancied wisdom as foolishness and ignorance. Still God is able to humble us when his time comes. More particulars of this and of that one I cannot at this time give, for many reasons. My highly venerable fathers know already from longer experience how it is in the congregations of to-day, when we must often be satisfied with the gleanings, and generally watch and wait for the divine workings, where, when, and in whom, and whether the Spirit would give an abundant harvest.

Mr. Vigera has had a fine school this winter, and so instructed the children, that it was a pleasure to the parents. God has at length so ordered it, that he can now remain here, and continue the school in the city.

I have inclosed an extract from the Philadelphia church accounts, etc., so that my fathers may also see from it that which is the most necessary. As the concourse of hearers multiplies, especially since many Reformed go to our church (as on the Sunday when I am in Philadelphia, they have no sermon in the forenoon), and as our own congregation increases, necessity requires it that the elders of the church build a massive gallery this summer, when it is to be hoped that we shall be fully done with the building. If we should further receive any collection, we would need it most in this place. I am but little burdensome to the congregation, as I desire nothing from any one except that which anyone gives me from his own free will, as moved by his own conscience. I am only glad when the revenues of the church do not suffer. When the church is once out of debt, he who comes after me may indeed have it better. May God only rule according to his pleasure.

PETER BRUNNHOLTZ.

II. Extract from a second letter of the same, of the 3d of July, 1749.

After I had finished with the catechumens, and Whitsuntide was past, I went to Cohansey, thirty-six miles from here, in Jersey, beyond the Delaware river, to put things somewhat in order there, and also promised to visit them twice a year.

Immediately thereupon we held our annual synod, or general church meeting, of all the united preachers and wardens of the united congregations, in Lancaster. On application of the congregation in York, at the Codorus, where Mr. Schaum has hitherto been stationed, and after finding it necessary, we, after examination, ordained the said Schaum, Dom. II. after Trinity, publicly and in presence of the delegated elders of the united congregations, and called and installed him there as our colleague. The synod was held the Monday following, and everything, thank God! passed off to the delight of us all. I only mention this preliminarily.

It continually becomes more manifest to us, that God in his supreme wisdom and omniscience destined the dear brother Handschuch for the service of the congregation in Lancaster before we could think of it. Still his infirmity affects him much. When we had returned from Lancaster, we had a visit from pastor Kluge, from Virginia, three hundred and thirty miles from here, who went there ten years ago. He desired to see our arrangements, and to become acquainted with us. We received him kindly. He left rather quietly and pleased. God grant that the journey may be a blessing to him.

The heat is extraordinary at this time, and I cannot easily express how difficult it is for me to preach on Sundays to a large assembly. Yet God still gives support so that I am enabled in some measure to penetrate the consciences of many. I have, God be praised, no distant journeys to make until autumn. But pastor Mühlenberg will perhaps have to go to Raritan in August. Thus much I have been enabled to announce for this time dutifully, in weakness and in haste, as the ship will leave this afternoon.

PETER BRUNNHOLTZ.

III. Extract of another letter from the same, of the 21st of May, 1750.

It is of the goodness of the Lord that we are not utterly consumed, and his mercy is still without end, for it is not only new every morning, but everlasting. Hallelujah!

What relates especially to my own circumstances here as well as to those of my brethren and colleagues, I mention in passing, that we three preachers and two assistants, Messrs. Kurtz and Schaum, flow together in paternal love, and that envy, suspicion, mistrust, and the like are far from us which occasions us great encouragement in our occasional and annual meetings. This is a rare and great grace. In relation then

1. To my own circumstances, and indeed (*a*) to my person, I have been very infirm since July, 1749, until the present time. Besides the sickly turns which I have had from my youth up, the changeable climate here and the

confused circumstances of the country, and of the office here, contribute much to the impairing of my bodily constitution. Besides the yearly illness which I have had, I have often been confined to bed for several days, whereby I lost about five Sundays this year, in which I could not preach, which occasioned some grumbling with people, who know not what it is to be sickly. In this time also the general correspondence with Europe, Georgia and in the country here was considerably interrupted, because under such circumstances we are fitted for, and delight in nothing. (*b*) My congregations considered according to outward condition, it may be observed that the congregation in Philadelphia has had a regular school hitherto in my house, of which Mr. Vigera has the oversight, and whom I also employ in case of necessity, to read a sermon before public congregation, here and in Germantown, where there is a school likewise, but there are more difficulties connected therewith, because the people are so much scattered, and the smaller number of the congregation live in Germantown. The young student Rauss, mentioned in my last, is with me. After I had kept him in my house for a long time gratuitously, and he had nothing to do but to study for himself, and the congregations signified a desire to have divine service every Sunday, and wished that I should accept of an assistant; so brother Mühlenberg and I together, took this young man for a year and a half, in which time he is to assist me in preaching, and in other similar occupations, for which I am obligated to pay his passage of about £16, provide him with decent clothes, food, drink, and everything. Now when he was accepted, the wardens indeed desired to have church every Sunday; but to make me any contribution, for the payment of his passage and other expenses, they were neither able nor willing, whereas food and raiment cost much in the city, especially as Mr. Rauss was badly provided with clothes. The Philadelphians say they have enough with one preacher, they wish to have him alone, that the Germantown congregation was attached to them to their damage, etc., on which account they also presented a petition to the Synod, etc. I now help myself through with Mr. Rauss as well as I am able, although it is burdensome to me, in respect to diverse things. He has a good gift in preaching, whereto he has sufficient help in my library, as he is not as yet sufficiently versed in theology, although he is well skilled in the humanities, philosophy, and the like. He preaches in my congregations every Sunday, and now and then I send him to pastor Mühlenberg to assist him.

If Germantown were out of debt, and able to keep another preacher, I would immediately, with the consent of my fathers, resign the place to another, and remain in Philadelphia alone; but it is as yet too soon. In both congregations there is still considerable tranquility and unity. They come to church diligently. The church reckoning of the year 1749, is herewith presented. They have now at length resolved to build the gallery, for which they have already purchased the materials. In Germantown they have stipulated for the making of the pews for £56 of Pennsylvania currency, and have built a small sacristy for me at the side. But to obtain the money I had to spend about eight days indeed, riding around among the members of the congregation, to make them willing thereto. This congregation has occasioned me more trouble in relation to the building, than the congregation in Philadelphia, on account of the disagreement of the members of the Church council. The Darmstadt collection, which amounted to £107 of our money, was divided on the 14th of November, a. p., at a meeting of several elders from Philadelphia and Providence. In relation to the internal state of my congregations, it is so, that it might indeed be better. Generally, it seems the present time in Pennsylvania is a time of lethargy, shamelessness and security among all sects. Avarice, drinking and all kinds of vice prevail. The judgments of God may not be far off, from which we have hitherto been spared in this province. That which is good in some in the congregations, is in danger of being choked. This humbles one much, when we think of it, and look upon our own weakness, and the great power of the devil. Still, I hope as yet upon the Lord, whose right hand can change all. At Easter and Whitsuntide, I, this year, instructed and confirmed a considerable number of young people of from twelve to fifteen years, in both congregations. We must sometimes receive them when young, and in hope that they may not afterwards, if we permit them to get too old before they are confirmed, grow entirely wild amidst the Pennsylvanian masses. Every Sunday afternoon I publicly instruct the young in Germantown as well as in Philadelphia. With the smaller children, I use Luther's small catechism; but with the larger, I review the order of salvation, and lead them into the Bible. In Philadelphia there are a great many servants, *i. e.*, sold domestics, and I also hope for some benefit to these by the instruction. If only all of them had small Bibles! When I am well, I would gladly instruct the youth twice during the week, but the children over ten years, must work; therefore, we cannot get them together during the week, and much less the servants. The prayer-meeting is continued every Wednesday evening, when I am well. O Lord, Lord! forsake us not for thy great name's sake. Break the wrath of Satan and his great power, and preserve thy kingdom from him. When all seemed to dissolve, I was still conscious of thy aid.

2. In relation to pastor Mühlenberg, who has at the present time gone on a journey, with his father-in-law, Mr. Conrad Weiser, to Albany, in New York, where Mr. Hartwick is stationed, I observe that he is tolerably well; still he has various sickly turns now and then. Matters stand moderately well in his congregations. He has besides several out-parishes, and an extensive circuit. In Saccum, Upper Milford, etc., where he formerly preached on week days, he has a catechist, viz: Ludolph Schrenck. He came into this country in February, 1749, is a Luneburger, and had studied law at Erlangen. He wished to go to Georgia, but came from London to Philadélphia, and addressed himself to me. At first I did not accept of him, but when he staid in Philadelphia about ten weeks, conducted himself quietly, and had nothing more to live on, Mr. Mühlenberg took him on my recommendation, and that of Mr. Vigera. He was with him for half a year, and diligently read the Bible and theological books, until he, under the direction of Mr. Mühlenberg, became catechist in the above-mentioned congregation, where he has now been stationed for

almost a year. We are well satisfied with him. I provided him with the necessary books.

3. Our dear pastor Handschuch, whose diary herewith also follows, is weakly, but labors faithfully and patiently among the wild people in Lancaster. Our dearest fathers will see more from his journal.

4. Mr. Kurtz is well. He succeeds well in Tulpehocken, is earnest, zealous and obedient. I hope, as he is of sound constitution, and continually grows more in experience, that he may continue the work begun after our decease.

5. Mr. Schaum is also still well. His congregation declare their satisfaction with him. He grows in knowledge and experience. The town of York, which has now obtained a county, or the name of a Shire, increases. Many people from here move over there. In Conewago, twenty miles from there, he is now also to preach every four weeks. Thus he has to labor enough.

6. Mr. Weygand is also still in good health. Everything was arranged for his ordination on the day previous to the Synod. But for good

reasons it was deferred until the dedication of their church. Otherwise, the building of their church progresses finely. They have also purchased a plantation near the church for £120, where Mr. Weygand may live, but whereby they involved themselves in debt very much. How it may be in the future, time must tell.

7. The Archbishop has recently sent over three preachers, of whom the one is provost. All three seem to be honest men, and show love towards us. They are willing to hold friendship and communion with us, because he, as the new Provost told me, had orders to this effect in his instructions. The just-mentioned Provost, Acrelius, is in Mr. Trauberg's place in Wilmington. The second, Mr. Unander, is where the late Provost Sandin was stationed, and the third, Mr. Perlin, came here into the city in the place of Mr. Nässmann. From the Swedish tracts against the Herrnhuter, brought along with them, of which they presented several to me, as I understand the Swedish language, I see that the letter of Mr. Weiser to me has been translated into the Swedish language and printed. The former

parson of Lancaster, Mr. Nyberg, goes to Europe, likely to Count Zinzendorf.

8. Last autumn about twenty-five ships arrived here with Germans. The number of those who arrived alive was 1049, among whom there were also about twelve who were in part regular schoolmasters in the old country, but on account of small pay, and in the hope of improvement, moved into this, and in part they had been engaged in other pursuits. They would have better remained where they were. Some come who in part have public certificates, and in part letters to me from their parsons. I, however, can help them but little. In this month, ships again frequently arrive with Germans, so that about ten have already come. The province is crowded full of people, and living becomes continually more expensive. Those who come in free—who had something in the old country, but consumed that which they had, on an expensive voyage—and see that it is otherwise than was represented to them, whine and cry. Woe on the emigrants, who induced them to this! One of these in Germantown had wished to shoot himself recently from des-

peration. The Newlanders, as they are here called, are such as do not work, and still wish to become rich speedily, and for this reason they go out into Würtemberg and vicinity, and persuade the people to come into this country, alleging, that everything was here that they could wish for, that such a country like this there was none in the world, and that every one could become as rich as a nobleman, etc. These deceivers have this profit in it, that they with their merchandise are brought in free, and in addition, for every head they bring to Amsterdam or to Rotterdam, they receive a certain sum from the merchants. The owners of these vessels derive much money herefrom in freightage. They pack them into the ships as if they were herring, and when they arrive, there are so many sick and dying among them that it is pitiful to behold them. Those, however, who have nothing, and are in debt also for their passage, are taken into small huts, where they lie upon straw, and are corrupted like cattle, and in part half deprived of their reason, so that they can scarcely perceive anything of the parsons consolations. The government and assembly have meanwhile made some ordinances and institutions, but whether the difficulty will be remedied thereby time will show. It would be just and right if a regular report of such things were put into the German newspapers here and there in Europe. Still what good would it do? The farmers don't get to read the papers, and many indeed would not believe it, as they moreover have a mind to come.

PETER BRUNNHOLTZ.

CHAPTER V.

EXTRACT FROM PASTOR HANDSCHUCH'S DIARY FROM THE 7TH OF SEPTEMBER, 1748, TO THE 16TH OF MAY 1750.

On the 7th of September, 1748, I went with two wardens and a mother to the plantation of a Mennonite, to speak with him concerning his servant, the son of this mother, whether he would not permit him to come twice a week, from one to four o'clock, to a preparation for the Holy Supper, to which he was quite willing, on certain conditions.

On the 14th of September, I rode to Earltown, preached there, and held instruction for the youth. After divine service, a so-called new-born woman addressed me, whose three adult children I found extremely ignorant in the instruction given to the youth. She apologized for the children, and complained that they were not even baptized, nor their father, but that she had a great desire to have them instructed and baptized, and that her husband would have nothing against it. Her husband, who heard all at a distance, came up to us, and I represented to him his great indifference for his own and for the souls of his family. He excused himself herewith, that his father also held him to nothing, and permitted him to grow up thus, but that he now understood indeed how injurious it was, and that he should do much better by holding to the church. There was no good done at home surely; and in future he would at all times send his children to church.

On the 23d of September I was not at all well. Still I had to preach a funeral sermon. In visiting her diligently, the deceased woman had given me some hope of a true repentance, and of a simple longing after grace.

On the 7th of October, the usual meeting of the elders and wardens, or as it is here called, the church council, was held, which was continued from two o'clock until late in the evening, inasmuch as a matter in dispute between a father and his sons was amicably settled. Much was also spoken concerning a school-house, which was to be rented of a schoolmaster, who was to be accepted, and of his business and pay; and finally, the prelection in the church the following Sunday, was entrusted to a warden in my absence and in the absence of the schoolmaster.

Early on the 8th of October, at the most urgent request of Mr. Kurtz, I rode to Tulpehocken. In the evening, at six o'clock, I arrived safely at the house of Mr. Conrad Weiser.

On the 9th of October, the eighteenth Sunday after Trinity, I baptized three children. After the sermon, Mr. Kurtz examined thirty-one young people, who stood the test tolerably well. I still as yet submitted several questions to their consciences, and confirmed them after renewing their baptismal covenant upon their knees, in the name of the Triune God. Thereupon we administered the Holy Supper to one hundred and thirty communicants. The many persons present, both young and old, seemed to be considerably affected by these holy acts. It was four o'clock before we had finished with all. The day following, I again returned.

On the 22d of October, I, in company with several wardens and members of the church council, inspected our church, the sills of which had wholly rotted away. We also examined several houses which were proposed for a school house. Soon thereafter, Jacob Löser came, who had been school master hitherto in New Hanover, and who had been proposed as school masterfor this place. He brought letters along with him from pastor Mühlenberg, He was this day as yet presented to the church council, which met with me, and a conference was held with him in his presence, and finally it was resolved to let him give a proof publicly on the morrow.

On the twentieth Sunday after Trinity, I rode to Earltown early, baptized a child, preached, had a rehearsal and instruction for the young, and easily perceived in both young and old that my labor hitherto had not been wholly without blessing.

On the 25th of October, I preached in Lancaster, and presented to the people that which was most needful in reference to the education of the youth, and the necessity of a good schoolmaster. After the close of the divine service, the congregation tarried, and I spoke with them (1) concerning the choice of a new schoolmaster, (2) concerning the renting of a convenient school house, and (3) of the speedy repairing of the church, which begins to sink quite rapidly. But nothing could be determined, as many of the members of the congregation and the principal persons of the church council were absent. Still, some of those present, at my request, promised to contribute something certain thereto.

On the twenty-first Sunday after Trinity, after divine service, we spoke again with the regular members of the congregation, concerning a new schoolmaster of his yearly salary and of his dwelling, and at length we arrived at a settled conclusion in everything. In the afternoon, there was a meeting of the church council again. The call to Jacob Löser to the service of the school in this place was written, and signed by the members of the church council, and by the wardens.

On the afternoon of the 6th of November, I visited a certain Herrnhuter. This man had been one of the greatest enemies of our church in the church quarrel of this place, who would immediately hew into everything with his axe; therefore, also, so many of our people are opposed to him. He now indeed confesses that he was deceived by the Herrnhuter, but still he will not fully side with our church, as he alleges that they are all dead people. At the bottom of his heart, the reason may indeed be self-righteousness. In the meanwhile, he neglects no sermon. In church he looks for a passage in his Bible, and repeats the sermon with his wife and children.

On the 19th of November, I had preparatory service and confession with the people in Earltown, who announced themselves for the Holy Supper.

On the twenty-fourth Sunday after Trinity, confession was as yet held with some before the sermon, and afterwards the Holy Supper was administered to forty-one communicants. I then gave notice to the congregation, that on account of the distance, the violent cold of winter, the deep snow, and the streams to be crossed, and also on account of my infirmity, I was obliged to discontinue during the following three severest winter months. I also appointed a reader, and exhorted the whole congregation to peace and unity.

On the second Sunday of Advent, after the

sermon, I examined and confirmed the youth, thirty-four in number, which lasted until towards 2 o'clock, and as I hope may not have been wholly without blessing. During the remaining time, many living at a distance announced themselves to me for the Holy Supper.

On the 5th of December, the people announced themselves the whole day until evening for the Holy Supper. The same on the 6th of December also, so that not a quarter of an hour remained to take a meal, as I sought to speak with all fully concerning the state of their souls.

On the 7th of December, I summoned two women to my room, to inquire into their stiff-necked rancor of many years standing, and finally to put an end to it. Although these women reproached each other with everything, still they conducted themselves pretty sensibly, and forgave each other, whereat I rejoiced, and praised God in prayer. During the time remaining, people of various sorts as yet announced themselves for the Holy Supper.

On the 8th of December, I had a church council meeting from 2 o'clock, p. m., until evening, in which one of the church council was very much awakened, and with affecting words asked of all present pardon for his offences which he had hitherto given. A recent misunderstanding between a church councilman and a warden was also disposed of, and all was concluded with prayer, and by all with purely good resolutions.

On the 9th of December, many again announced themselves for the Holy Supper.

On the 10th of December, it continued thus until I went to church, at about 1 o'clock, to preach a preparatory sermon and engage in penitential and confessional devotion. Between the sermon and the confession, a young person who was sick of late, was confirmed, and a man publicly spoken with, who was unwilling to appear before the church council. I still had many calls afterwards.

On the third Sunday of Advent, I had many calls before divine service. After the sermon, I administered the Holy Supper to 144 communicants.

On the 28th of December, there was a meeting of the church council, in which the man several times mentioned, who had been a Herrnhuter, and who had shown himself hostile enough to our people in the former church dispute, declared that he, from the present time forward, would conduct himself as an honest brother in the faith, and help to advance the best welfare of the congregation, as much as possible. After adding a hearty admonition he was again regularly received into the congregation.

On the 1st of January, 1749, I baptized three children and preached. In the afternoon I had a repetition and instruction for the youth. The growth of both great and small gives me considerable joy.

On Epiphany, the 6th day of January, I baptized a child, the conduct of whose father had otherwise been very bad towards me, but who now asked pardon, and promised amendment.

On the 7th of January, in the afternoon, our present schoolmaster, Jacob Löser, arrived here safely, together with his family, and brought letters along for me from pastor Mühlenberg. It can scarcely be credited what trouble, difficulty and anxiety, this schoolmaster business occasioned to me and to the beloved Mr. Mühlenberg, before it could be accomplished.

The afternoon of the first Sunday after Epiphany, I spent in visiting the sick. When I returned home again, I met four men who were waiting for me; one of whom was affected by the sermon of to-day, whose wife and two children (one of four and the other of one year) were not as yet baptized, requested me to baptize his children on the next Sunday. This evening was edifying to me and to the others present, for the Lord filled my heart with comfort, and my lips overflowed abundantly in consolation and prayer.

On the 11th of January, I was visited by the above-mentioned man, who had been much affected, who with his wife, an English Baptist, and their children desired to go over to our church.

On the second Sunday after Epiphany, during divine service, I baptized three children, of whom two belonged to the man mentioned on the first Sunday after Epiphany and the 11th of January, one of which was over four years, but the other one year old. I was unable to perform this baptismal act without emotion, because the mother, an English Baptist, brought the one child in her arms, and was very attentively present in the whole transaction before the baptismal font, although she understood little or nothing of the German. Thereupon I preached to a large congregation of people of various sorts and sects.

In the days from the 17th to the 21st of January, I had sundry experiences of the power of the Word hitherto preached, whereat I rejoiced. On the contrary, I have had many a grievance from some people.

In the forenoon of the 28th of January, I was quite unexpectedly visited by Mr. Spangenberg, who calls himself Baron of Watteville, otherwise denominated Langgut, and by another Hernnhuter named Schnell. After they had introduced themselves, they declared to have had a desire to know me. Spangenberg was very hard on the Constitution of the Lutheran Church, and thought that no honest servant of Jesus Christ could teach it untrammeled, nor remain in it with a good conscience. He especially reviled our Universities very much, which he called *scholas diaboli*, schools of the devil; the methods of the theologians, which he called weapons of the devil against the Saviour; the consistories and their unconverted members, and the preachers in Berlin, etc. I contradicted him briefly, but according to my best knowledge, with sound arguments, wherein Watteville himself gave assent to me, and he said nothing more. I afterwards asked him upon his conscience, whether he could go and move along in this, his chosen way, with true conviction and joyfulness of heart. To this he was silent for a time; but he at length assumed the joyfulness in words and gestures, with which he assured me he could not do otherwise. Watteville boasted much of the heathen congregations planted in America and in St. Thomas. He could represent everything right lovingly and charmingly, so that if I had not known this sort of people and their repentance, I would have believed many things. Schnell was altogether quiet. In taking leave, I entreated them, for the sake of God, not to be so frivolous in the conversion of the people, to urge the true divine order of salvation better and more earnestly, and to propound the doctrine of the Triune God and his works and benefactions more clearly and scripturally. To do this, they promised with their lips.

On the 30th of January, the people began to announce their children to me to be prepared for the Holy Supper.

On Sunday, Estomihi, two Englishmen came to me in the afternoon, with the request that I should baptize the debilitated child of an English widow. I went there without delay to do this. Soon after my return home, two of the members of the congregation came to tell me of the hard trials of the wife of one of them. They entreated me much to visit her on the morrow as soon as possible.

On the 6th of February, as soon as I had spoken that which was most necessary with several who had come with me, I went out to the tempted woman, mentioned yesterday, with whom I had a very edifying and pleasant conversation. She seemed to me to be a miserable person taken in the true sense. Although she cannot read, she knows how to speak very properly of spiritual things, from her own experience.

On the 14th of February, after I had various visits nearly the whole of the forenoon, I held the first meeting for preparation with the youth in the church. After its close, I spoke many edifying things with a member of the congregation, until late in the evening.

On the 16th of February, I also began the meetings for preparations with our youth in my room, whose number this time is only fourteen.

On the 17th of February, I spoke much with several Mennonites who came to me, and who desired to be edified by me, because they were awakened by my preaching, as they said.

On the 28th of February, the father of two of the girls who come was present all the time along with them at the meeting for preparation, and afterwards as yet remained a good while with me, when he related many good things to me of his wife, and assured me that her great earnestness in Christianity was blessed both to him and to his children.

In the afternoon of Sunday, Lätare, I joined in marriage a Mennonite with a Reformed woman, whose associates, by questions, presented me with a fine opportunity to speak to all their hearts. The whole Mennonite company seemed to go away pleased. Thereupon

I had many another call, and very late I was taken to a man, D. K., who was suddenly taken sick, and whom I met in a fine and awakened frame of mind.

On the 7th of March, I was early taken to a plantation above six miles from here, to perform a marriage with a wedding sermon. People from far and near of various sects were present who, during my address showed themselves very polite and attentive, especially several aged respectable Quakers and Mennonites, who, contrary to their custom, so long as I was there, had their hats off, and otherwise, amidst a very large bridal party, a loud word was scarcely heard.

On the 10th of March, I went early with three of our church council to an aged sick woman, whom I had visited yesterday, and to whom I administered the Holy Supper, after a previous admonition to repentance and self-examination. As she gave proof of her hearty contrition, in her great weakness, the entire act was very edifying to me and to the others present.

On the 24th of March, viz., Good Friday, four of the church council came to my room early, and soon after two, who had been Herrnhuter, who, after perceiving their sinning against our church and the holy doctrines of faith, asked pardon for the offences which they had given, and promised with hand and lips to be more faithful fellow-believers in future, together with their families, and to seek the welfare of the church. They were therefore regularly received into the congregation, and permitted to go with us to confession today. After divine service, I had almost constant visits until I went to church again, and preached a preparatory sermon, and held penitential and confessional services with one hundred and eleven who made confession. The whole evening I was overrun by many people, so that my strength was failing me.

On the first day of Easter, I preached to an unusually numerous congregation, and afterwards administered the Holy Supper to the above one hundred and eleven communicants. Afterwards, I had many visits from strangers until I went to church to baptize three children, and to repeat the sermon. In the evening I again had much company.

On the second day of Easter, after divine

service, I went with the schoolmaster to visit the sick D. K., who with time gives still more hope of a change of heart. This great change is already manifest to the eyes of all people; he speaks and conducts himself wholly otherwise than he did even half a year ago.

In the afternoon of the 28th of March, I had a wholly unexpected visit from an aged man, who had been a Seven Day Baptist, but is now a Mennonite, who says he heard me preach several times, and to have had a feeling of the spirit by which I speak to the people; and therefore he could not avoid visiting me once himself. This old man related how, twenty-three years ago, he was powerfully awakened in Switzerland, and thereupon he soon came here into this country, and fell among the Seven Day Baptists, whose whole concern he found much too light and superficial, and therefore left their fraternity and went to the Mennonites, with whom also he did not meet the right thing, but only decay and ruin among them. Still he would as yet remain with them only for the purpose of belonging to some particular denomination—that he esteemed me highly, and admonished his children to come in to my preaching; and that if it were not so very far for him (the old man), he would himself come more frequently.

On the 14th of April, in the forenoon, I had a funeral, and preached a funeral sermon to a numerous assembly. As soon as I had eaten a little, I rode to York, as I promised to have confession there to-morrow, and to celebrate the Holy Supper the day after. Beyond the Susquehanna, I was met by Mr. Schaum and a warden from York. I arrived there safely before night, with my company, although much wearied; and had for several hours the most necessary conversation with the wardens, elders, and schoolmaster.

On the 15th of April, I preached a preparatory sermon, and held penitential and confessional services with more than two hundred people. The whole afternoon, however, I spent with the wardens and elders, to consider the state of the congregation with them.

On Sunday, Jubilate, I still had penitential and confessional services with some twelve persons, who had come from a distance. After the sermon, I administered the Holy Supper to two hundred and six communicants, among whom was a fine Moor, as also one who several years before had gone over to the Mennonites, but before we went to church, declared his regret for it in the presence of the elders and of the wardens; and with the giving of his hand promised, from a true conviction, to hold to our holy doctrines of faith, and thereon to live and die. This then was also publicly presented to the congregation, and they were requested to receive him again in love as a brother in the faith. The rest of the day was spent in consultation, how the best and permanent planting of the church could be promoted. Accordingly, the elders and others, with many arguments, represented to me the necessity for the speedy ordination of Mr. Schaum, and entreated me to urge it in the strongest manner. I had also to write a petition for this purpose, in their name and presence, to our united preachers, to which they all subscribed.

On the 17th of April, I rode away again in company with Mr. Schaum and several others. I had to wait above two hours at the Susquehanna, to which a Catholic father came, in whose company I was conveyed over the two miles wide and very dangerous river. His intercourse was modest and frank. Some miles from the river, several of our church council met me.

On Sunday, Cantate, there was a meeting of the church council after divine service, in which the highly necessary repairing of the church and of the organ, as also the intended election of several new wardens, were considered.

On the 24th of April, the repairing of the church at length began. Oh! how difficult it is to move the people to anything in church affairs.

On the 29th of April a young man was buried. Three months ago he had been at his brother's wedding, at which very scandalous conduct continued for three whole days and nights. The bride died suddenly five miles from here, and was to be buried on the day before I rode to York, whilst another funeral occurred here in town. These two deaths are remarkable to me and to others, because all my entreaty at the time, and admonition in the room, and publicly in the church, were so utterly ineffective that, according to the declaration of the people, a like ungodly wedding there had not been since the existence of Lancaster.

On Sunday, Rogate, in the forenoon sermon, I published the confirmation of the youth on next Sunday; and the Holy Supper on Whit-Sunday, and the election for new wardens on this afternoon. After the review, we proceeded to the latter this afternoon, and, with the congregation, elected two old and two new wardens, which passed off pretty orderly and quietly.

On the 1st of May the people began to announce themselves to me for the Holy Supper. On this afternoon I had the last meeting for preparation with the youth, and not without emotion of heart and abundant tears on their part.

May the 3d. Yesterday and to-day the people were with me announcing themselves, from early until late in the evening, with all of whom I spoke as fully as I could, and also baptized one child in my room, which was brought from a distance.

The festival of the ascension of Christ. This forenoon I preached to a numerous congregation, consisting also of many strangers. The Word preached also manifested its power, as I heard of several, and, among others, of a Mennonite. During the remainder of the day I had many calls from all sorts of people.

Sunday, Exandi. In the forenoon, after the sermon, fourteen young persons were confirmed and consecrated. Between the forenoon and afternoon service, I could scarcely eat on account of the many visits; and in the afternoon the schoolmaster had to attend to the instruction of the youth. After this was over, I married a couple and visited several sick.

On the 8th of May I had a severe attack of spitting of blood, and had to be bled on this account.

In the forenoon of the thirteenth of May, I have had, as in the days hitherto, many visits; and in the afternoon I preached the preparatory sermon, and had besides penitential and confessional services.

Whitsunday. Seven children were baptized before the sermon, of which one was three years old, and after it the Holy Supper was administered to one hundred and seventy-nine. An extraordinary multitude of people of all kinds were in the church and before the doors of it. In the afternoon I preached again to a great number.

On Whitmonday, after the sermon in the forenoon, the two old and the two new wardens were placed before the congregation, their duties presented to them, and their observance promised by them, with hands and lips. On account of my debility, I permitted the schoolmaster to attend to the instruction of the young, and after that I married a couple.

May the 22d. In the afternoon I had a session of the church council, wherein many necessary things were agreed upon, and, among others, many external circumstances relating to the impending church meeting; and afterwards the church account was rendered.

On May the 24th, I was visited by various married persons, who have not as yet been to the Holy Supper, and who announced themselves for instruction and preparation thereunto. In examining their case, I found, especially in the instance of one woman, a fine awakening and conviction.

On the first Sunday after Trinity, D. K.,

who had been sick, was in church again for the first time after his severe illness. I also visited him afterwards. As some time before, so during his sickness, the Lord worked powerfully in his soul; and from his own experience, he begins to speak so properly of spiritual things, that I heartily rejoice, and hope that he, by diligent faithfulness and constancy, may be an instrument of the mercy of God in our congregation.

May the 30th. In the forenoon, I viewed the work in the church, which was enjoined the day previous, where I was informed by several of the church council that a man of the Reformed church had been with them, who entreated them much to say to me that his sick and likewise Reformed wife had a particular desire for a call from me; and that I should come to her without delay. Now, when I had visited our sick warden living nearer, I also went with one of the church council into the house of these Reformed people, where more persons speedily assembled. This sick person could not sufficiently express in words her love towards me, and her strong desire for my visit; and alleged that neither she nor her husband readily neglected any of my sermons, and that she had therefrom obtained a great blessing for her soul, and wished that the Lord would abundantly reward me for all the good which she had from thence felt in her soul. I sought to repress that which was violent in her love and in her expressions, and spoke with her of the true motive of her heart, etc. She complained that her husband and herself had permitted themselves to be taken in by the Herrnhuter, and had been among them for a time in Bethlehem, really persuaded that these persons were a peculiar people of God; but that they had found themselves mistaken. Since I was in Lancaster, they had nothing more to do with them, and could edify themselves sufficiently by the Word of God and by my sermons, whereby she related many things from my sermons of nine or ten months ago, which I myself did not even rightly remember any more. Of her husband, however, she complained, that to her great sorrow, he still went with them, until he began to hear my sermons six months ago, since which time he endeavors to free himself from them; but they let him have no rest at all. The man himself related how they follow him everywhere. I sought as much as possible to ascertain the state of the woman's soul, and found that she had a considerable degree of scriptural and evangelical knowledge.

June the 2d. As the ordination of Mr. Schaum, the preacher in York, was appointed for the next Sunday, and also the general meeting of the synod here in Lancaster on the following Monday, so my beloved colleagues, Messrs. Mühlenberg and Brunnholtz, together with their companion, Mr. Schrenck, a fine candidate of law, arrived this afternoon. Towards evening, Mr. Schaum, from York, also came. As soon as we had outward rest, on account of the people, the whole evening, until late into the night, was passed in necessary conversation.

June the 3d. We went to the preparatory service in the afternoon. Mr. Brunnholtz preached, and I held the penitential and confessional services. Among the twenty who confessed, there was a man, at whose request and in whose name I entreated the congregation to pardon the vexatious life which he had hitherto led. He also was not satisfied that I alone did this, but he did it himself also, in his own words, amidst many tears. Whereupon he was again heartily admonished by me; and he earnestly promised that by the grace of God he would radically amend his life. Towards five o'clock, we preachers took Mr. Schaum, who had hitherto been our assistant, in hand for examination, which was done by us alternately, amidst many profitable recollections. After its close, we let the elders, wardens, and other members of the congregation in York, on the Codorus, who were present, come before us, and spoke with them concerning Mr Schaum's call and ordination. Pastor Mühlenberg, as the senior, chiefly led the conversation. The Yorkers then drew up their call to Mr. Schaum.

On the second Sunday after Trinity, I baptized a child; and Mr. Mühlenberg preached. After the sermon, he also made the address to him who was to be ordained, set before him the duties of his office, etc. Mr. Brunnholtz prayed, and after the prayer we consecrated him by the laying on of hands. During the act of ordination, each and all authorized church counselors and wardens of the congregation united with us, stood around the altar as witnesses. Before divine service in the afternoon, I buried a child of one of the church council of this place. The funeral attendance was extraordinarily large on account of the many strangers. Afterwards Mr. Kurtz preached, methodically and unto edification. About five o'clock in the evening, Mr. Mühlenberg preached for the English in their language.

On the 5th of June, at 8:30 o'clock, all the members of the church councils and the wardens of the united congregations, assembled before our dwelling, with whom we went to church by pairs, each preacher with his own. Mr. Schaum delivered the synodical sermon. After the close of divine service, our ecclesiastical convention was held, God be praised! in good order, love, and unity. About three o'clock, p. m., the present church meeting was concluded, and we went out of the church three and three, each preacher with his own, through a part of the town, into the house of one of the members of our church council, where a meal was prepared, and upwards of sixty people fed. During the repast, they alternately began to sing edifying hymns in each room, and everything terminated in beautiful tranquility, love, and contentment. Mr. Cockson, one of the most distinguished governmental personages in the country, and Mr. Conrad Weiser, during meal-time, passed from one room to another, and showed their satisfaction with the good order.

Very early on the 6th of June, many people came to take leave of my most worthy colleagues. About seven o'clock they again departed, accompanied by strange church councils, and by the church council of this place; and I was grieved that I could not at all properly enjoy them, on account of the many labors, disquiet, and the press of the people. At noon our school children were fed at the same house with that which was left. The schoolmasters and several members of the church council had the superintendence.

On the 9th of June, several members of the church council brought Mr. Samuel Kluge, parson in Virginia, to me, and who, to my gratification, remained a long time with me; and whom I again accompanied down town.

On the third Sunday after Trinity, I baptized a child, preached, and after the sermon, I read the resolutions of our last synod to the congregation, and thereby duly inculcated that which was most necessary. At noon, parson Kluge, who had yesterday been with me nearly the whole day, dined with me again; and I had him to preach for me in the afternoon. On the next day, he took leave of me, and continued his journey to Philadelphia.

From the 13th to the 17th of June I daily visited our sick warden. On his sick bed, for three weeks, his bearing was such that I hope, that the Word of God laid to his heart may not have been in vain. To-day, before nine o'clock, he had me called to him once more. That which was most necessary I yet enjoined upon him, prayed and thanked God for the mercy manifested to him in the last weeks of his life, all of which he gave ear to, in the full exercise of his reason, as in all his illness, and this whilst he wrestled with death, which, however, I could not wait for on account of my other official duties. About twelve o'clock I heard that he gently fell asleep.

June the 23d. Yesterday Parson Kluge came to me again, on his return from Philadelphia, and to-day took leave of me.

On the 7th of July, four men, sent from a small congregation at Beaver Creek, twelve miles from here, visited me to request me to take care for their souls, and to accept of their congregation. After having spoken the most necessary matters with them concerning this thing, I directed them to come to me again at another time for a decision.

On the 19th of July, I rode five miles from here to people, with whom a sick young man is lying, who had wished for me very much. I had scarcely arrived home again, when I heard that a little while before the most respectable head of the Herrnhuter had shot himself.

On the 20th of July, one related to me that he had been at the funeral of the shot Herrnhuter, and heard how his brethren pronounced him blessed, and said the Saviour wished to have it so, they desired to be where he is, etc. I was also assured by others that, a few days before, he requested his Herrnhuter wife that she should let me be called, that he desired to speak with me concerning his soul; but the woman resisted in every mode and manner, and always said: What will the brethren say to it? etc.

On the 26th of July, I was taken to the above-mentioned small congregation at Beaver Creek, twelve miles from here, where, after several inquiries concerning the condition of the congregation, and the manner of life of persons who were to hold children at baptism, I held divine service; and after the sermon I put them in mind more fully of whatever else I thought necessary for the true improvement and Christian regulation of their congregation.

On the 31st of July, I was visited, among others, by a Seven Day Baptist, who is the son of a Lutheran preacher from Cleves, and who associated with the Herrnhuter for seven years. I was likewise visited by a Sunday Baptist. Both pretended to be friendly, but the latter sought to excuse himself with his ignorance, when I reproached him and asked him wherefore he separated from the Lutheran Church. Both entreated me very much soon to visit them and their neighborhood, ten miles from here, because there were many souls in that place who were hungering after grace, who long for me, and by whom I would not be unblessed.

On the twelfth Sunday after Trinity, after

the forenoon sermon, I let all the men and young lads remain who desired to hold faithfully to the church, and proposed to them the following eight points, giving the reasons therefor, which, according to the resolution of the church council, was required from all who desired to be members of the congregation and enjoy the rights of the congregation, viz.: (1) Each one shall have his name publicly recorded by the schoolmaster. (2) The members of the church council and the wardens shall be acknowledged as such in love and obedience by every one. (3) Every one shall firmly and steadily hold to our good and Christian church discipline, so that the one may give heed to the other, and duly notify the pastor of whatever is of importance. (4) The young people of both sexes shall not come to the church in levity, and shall visit the instruction for the youth more diligently. (5) At funerals all drinking to excess shall be prohibited; everything proceed quietly and orderly, and two and two follow the corpse, first the men, and afterwards the women. (6) The church account shall be heard by the congregation every year. (7) The preacher's salary shall be received by a member of the church council appointed thereto. (8) Every one retains his full liberty to unite with the congregation, or to leave it again, only notice must always be given of it to the pastor. Whoever would not consent to these points could not be regarded as a member of the congregation, nor partake with us of the Holy Supper. The recording of names now proceeded quietly and orderly. One who had been a Herrnhuter also publicly united with the congregation, who sought to excuse himself herewith, that he, like many others, was misled through ignorance. Everything was commenced and concluded with prayer.

August the 18th. A woman whom I joined in marriage to an Irishman, and who is of Lutheran parentage, but was neglected by her step-father who is a Dunker, and not kept to the church, entreated me with tears that I should instruct her, and prepare her for the Holy Supper.

On the 14th Sunday after Trinity, I again requested the congregation to remain after divine service. I again set before them the points established two weeks ago, and added thereto the necessary admonition, directed to the improvement of the whole congregation, whereupon the names of the rest of the men and unmarried (male) persons, and then, also, the names of the women, were recorded by the schoolmaster. All this continued until after ten o'clock.

August the 29th. In the afternoon I, in the name of the Lord, began the preparatory meetings with the youth, and with three married women. A certain man, of Separatist origin, who had otherwise been very rude and restless, came and heard a part with considerable attention, also afterwards conducted himself very properly and discreetly towards me, although he had since I am here occasioned me great trouble. This one was still there, when the widow of a man who was buried to-day, and who had only been a wife for two weeks, came with her step-son, who was sold to a Mennonite, and entreated me most earnestly that I should receive her and her poor child.

On the fifteenth Sunday after Trinity, in the evening, towards eight o'clock, when I had scarcely returned home again from visiting the sick, I was taken to a plantation to a poor strange English widow, to baptize her three children who were born to-day, of whom I found the one, and indeed the strongest, already dead; but I administered holy baptism to the other two.

On the sixteenth Sunday after Trinity, I found myself uncommonly weak, as I was for several days already; still, I ventured on the all availing power of God to hold divine service myself in the forenoon. After the public service, I continued to speak to the whole congregation concerning their improvement, and to let the names of those still left to be recorded by the schoolmaster. I also, as yet, inculcated the following admonitions, viz.: (1) By the grace of God they should introduce (and the sooner the better) a cordial, brotherly love among and towards each other, and no longer remain rams, which only push and rub themselves against each other, as they had hitherto done. (2) They should advise and aid each other according to ability and the opportunity which each one may have, in all simplicity and from sincere brotherly charity, and no longer permit themselves to be made ashamed herein by other sects. (3) They should anticipate each other with civility and respect, and lay off all rude behavior. (4) If one has cause to reprimand another, or to make information to the preacher of his conduct, he should first enter into his own heart and sigh to God that he should have compassion on him himself, and at the same time grant him love, wisdom and humility for the necessary correction of his brother. Thus all unbecoming bluster, and all hard and rude words, would be avoided, and, on the contrary, the one would become kind, friendly, gentle and humble towards the other. (5) They should hold together as much as possible, and permit no separation or schism to arise among them. (6) Since we cannot know how long I shall live, as my strength daily diminishes more and more, whereto the grief occasioned to me, by many among them contributed not a little, I would beseech them for the sake of God, and for the sake of the numerous youth, that in case I unexpectedly died, they should with all their ability according to all grace, which the Lord will willingly give to every one, firmly and constantly hold among themselves, to the regulation introduced—love and honor their schoolmaster—be satisfied with the occasional assistance of my beloved colleagues, and fervently call upon God the Lord, that he may lead the hearts of our fathers and superiors, again to call and to send another in my place. I hereupon dismissed the congregation for this time, and promised, if the Lord granted me life and health, I would let them tarry again the next time, and have all their names read off once more, so that the longer we might get the better acquainted with each other, and know who properly belongs to our congregation; and then those yet remaining shall also be received who are content with our order, and are willing to comply with it. Thereupon I prayed, and blessed the congregation. All this was done in the extremest weakness, so that I had to sit before the altar. But the name of the Lord be praised for his help bestowed to me in my infirmity.

On the 20th of September, several members of the church council came and related to me with emotion and joy of heart, how yesterday at the election of the new town magistrates, it was so quiet and orderly as never before since the existence of Lancaster; and one of our church council, D. Adam Simon Kuhn, was elected chief burgess of the town and the whole county or shire; another Lutheran, and member of the congregation, viz.: Jacob Schlauch, was elected second burgess of the town; and yet another member of the congregation high constable; and three of our church council as assessors, together with another member of the congregation. I rejoiced heartily that nearly all of our Lutherans, on my heartfelt entreaty and representation on the past Sunday, avoided all the otherwise usual disorders in this election. Whilst formerly none were more complained of than our Lutherans. From this government we may promise ourselves much good for our town and congregation, if they administer their offices faithfully and honestly.

Early on the 18th of September, the newly-elected chief burgess came to me and took leave, as he, together with the high constable, had to take the oath of allegiance with the Governor in Philadelphia, and he had to be confirmed in his office. I gave him the admonitions most needed. This man has hitherto let grace have room in his heart, so that a noticeable change is observed in him. God grant that he may in future permit himself to be drawn by it through the Word.

On the 5th of October, I baptized the child of an Englishman in his house, in presence of many English and of five Jewesses, who showed themselves very orderly and devout outwardly, so that I would not have thought them Jewesses if I had not been told afterwards. Before and after the baptismal act, I had opportunity to have a long conversation with Mr. Cockson, who is one of the principal persons connected with the government in the country, and is favorable to our church, and also assists our congregation as much as he is able. I thanked him for this, his good inclination manifested hitherto, and requested his further aid, which he promised, and declared himself to me as most friendly towards our church.

On the twentieth Sunday after Trinity, at the close of the sermon, I was taken with a violent pain in my left shoulder, and was seized with a severe chill, so that I had scarcely strength enough to close with prayer and the benediction. In the utmost feebleness, I baptized a child in my room, whose sponsors, on account of a fever which they had, did not trust to go to church.

From the 9th until the 14th of October, on account of extraordinary pains in my limbs and back, I could find no rest neither day nor night for the poor body, nor speak with any one.

On the twenty-first Sunday after Trinity, the schoolmaster had to hold divine service both in the forenoon and afternoon, and publish to the congregation that although I was extremely weak, yet I would venture it, on the repeatedly-experienced special help and strengthening of the Lord my God, and permit those who needed it most to announce themselves to me for the Holy Supper in the first four days of the week, and to speak with each one as infirmity of mind and body permitted; and if it is only in some measure possible, to preach a penitential sermon and hold confessional services on Saturday, and on the Sunday following administer the Holy Supper. From this afternoon until the 21st of October, there were more than one hundred and fifty people with me, among whom perhaps the half had recently arrived, and to speak with all according to necessity, I had to force myself much in the continued pains in my limbs and in my great weakness. But my hope and heartfelt desire were for holy reasons not fulfilled for this time by God the Lord. For on Saturday and Sunday, I was so miserable and sick that I waited for my happy end every hour. I had therefore to let the schoolmaster again hold divine service on the twenty-second Sunday after Trinity, and excuse me to the congregation.

On the twenty-third Sunday after Trinity, the schoolmaster again read in the church, and in the beginning of this week my illness increased not a little.

On the 4th of November Mr. Kurtz came here to take my place in the forenoon and afternoon of the twenty-fourth Sunday after Trinity; and, as I heard from many people, he preached a regular and edifying sermon.

On the twenty-fifth Sunday after Trinity, the schoolmaster again held divine service, as I, like the whole week previous, was extremely feeble. On Monday, however, I was somewhat better. In this, my severe illness, and great weakness of soul and body, I still perceived some special gracious care of God over me, inasmuch as in many cases of necessity I was enabled to regain strength through his strength, and provide for that which was necessary in my office—attend to the repeated visits of the people in relation to their own and the affairs of the congregation. I also baptized nine children, married six couple, made the external arrangements for about twelve funerals, and afterwards let the schoolmaster attend to them. In like manner I wrote various letters to my colleagues, and a letter of congratulation in Latin to our Governor, James Hamilton, who, on the 2d of this month, visited Lancaster for several days as his proper town. God also awakened various persons in the congregation to bring me some refreshment, and among those such of whom I indeed would least have expected it, which, although I often could eat nothing for eight days together, except chicken and plum broth, was still acceptable to me as a token of their love. As for the rest, I must confess, to the praise of the Lord, that during the past nine months, the congregation has improved much, which also is manifest to all the rest of the inhabitants of the town, and to the whole region. In relation to internal Christianity, I have observed various traces of the power of the preached Word in the hearts of my hearers. Now all this the Lord my God hath wrought; but I can ascribe nothing to myself, except official mistakes and infirmities, which may my heavenly Father forgive me, through grace, for the sake of Jesus my Redeemer. Amen!

On the 23d of November I married an English couple who, with their very numerous company, showed themselves very devout. Shortly afterwards, I was entreated, with many tears, to come to a very sick member of the congregation, who has a great longing to see me. I ventured, in the name of God, and went out again for the first time after my severe illness, and found this man very weak, and filled with a desire to see me.

On the twenty-seventh Sunday after Trinity, the schoolmaster had again to hold divine service, as I was much worse during the whole week after my going out the first time.

On the forenoon of the 28th of November I ventured it once more, and went out a little to visit our school and school children.

On the first Sunday of Advent, although I could not sleep much during the past night, still I ventured with the new church year (which may God bless to me and to all my hearers) publicly to begin my office myself again.

On the 9th of December, an old father, with his already grown up son, came here some twenty miles, with the request that I should accept of his son and confirm him to our church, so that he could come to the Holy Supper at the next opportunity. For he was strongly tempted by various sects, and especially by the Zinzendorfer, and enticed over to their party. Now, after I had examined him, and laid that to his conscience which was most necessary, and he also thereupon declared himself very properly, and not without emotion. I promised, when he has exercised himself still more in a literal knowledge, to confirm him on the holy eve of the coming Christmas, between the preparatory sermon and the confessional services, and permit him to come to the Holy Supper on the first holy day afterwards. The aged father desired to have his daughter, twenty-two years old, to be examined along with him and confirmed at the same time, if she got well again; and also that he would himself go with them to the Lord's Supper, as he had not received it in fourteen years, and now feels a great longing after it.

On the third Sunday of Advent, I found myself very feeble, especially as I could not sleep well the night before. Nevertheless, I preached the forenoon sermon, and published that which was most necessary; and after divine service I also had a conversation with the congregation, which remains standing. (1) Concerning the silver cup and wafer dish, presented from thankfulness to God by one of the church council, who has returned from Europe, and I requested the people to look at these now and not permit themselves to be disturbed in their devotion on the coming Sunday, when first made use of. (2) Concerning the reception of new members of the congregation, as many German Lutherans have recently come into the country. (3) Concerning some arrangement in reference to the salary of the schoolmaster, for the benefit of poor children who are unable to pay the school money, of whom there are many in the congregation. The great cold, however, prevented our perfecting the last matter under consideration. Immediately after returning home, I had a call in reference to the second, so that I could not even eat a little. Then I married a couple, baptized two children of Reformed parentage, and otherwise attended to many calls this evening.

On the 19th of December, after having had various visits, I buried an English woman, at the request of her brother, on the English churchyard according to the English manner, at which many English of various kinds and sects were present. In the house of mourning I took occasion to speak with the company of the sinful custom which the people have introduced here in this country at funerals, of giving as much wine and other strong drink to the funeral attendants as they are willing and able to drink, from which many disorders arose, especially out in the country.

On the 23d of December I preached a

preparatory sermon, and held penitential and confessional services. But, between these services, I, in the presence of the congregation, examined and confirmed the man of twenty-four years mentioned on the 9th inst. He was properly awakened.

On the fourth Sunday of Advent, I preached to a very numerous congregation, and administered the Holy Supper to eighty-four persons. During the administration, a great indisposition often came over me. But the Lord still strengthened me so far that I could finish my work. But as soon as the last communicant had received it, I could contain myself no longer, but hastened to the sacristy; and, after I had recovered a little, I went before the altar again, prayed and blessed the people, in much weakness.

December the 29th. In the past days, I several times visited a very sick member of our congregation, and found his soul's condition improved day after day. As he to-day manifested a hearty longing for the Holy Supper, and I, by further instruction, led him still more to the examination of his heart, amidst much emotion, he described himself in his own words so well that I had no reason to doubt in reference to his true repentance. After prayer, I administered the Holy Supper to him. Singing, prayer, the humble declaration of the sick, and the whole transaction made some impression on those who were present.

On the 2d of January, 1750, I visited the school with the church council and the wardens, and examined the children. I must acknowledge that the children improve perceptibly. After I had closed with prayer, and several verses were sung from a New Year's hymn, one of the wardens distributed a cake to each child for their greater encouragement. The number of children at this time was sixty, who regularly visit the school, and among these there was one negro also.

From the 3d to the 5th of January, I have had almost constant visits from people who announce themselves for the Holy Supper. Several times it became too burdensome to me, especially as the people are mostly wholly spiritually blind and dead, and there is much talking to be done to direct their attention to their deep corruption, and to the necessity of a true change of heart. The new-comers especially are very ignorant. Oh! how I often sigh under this burden!

On the 13th of January, I preached a preparatory sermon in the afternoon, and had penitential and confessional services.

On the second Sunday after Epiphany, the Holy Supper was administered to sixty-eight communicants.

On the 15th of January, I again visited a man of the congregation who has already been sick for a very long time, who in his great weakness of body, among other talk which showed his longing after grace, complained with emotion that he perceived nothing at all of faith, although he called upon God the Lord for it day and night.

On the 16th of January, I heard from the lips of credible witnesses, how the man mentioned yesterday, who died this forenoon, several hours before his death said with joyful lips, that it was now truly well with him, and that he already sees the New Jerusalem, and would soon be set free.

On the 29th of January, the newly-arrived Reformed preacher, a man already advanced in life, and appointed to this place, visited me. We spoke chiefly of the honest and pure object which an evangelical preacher must have, especially here in this country, if anything is to be built up and produce fruit. I rejoiced not a little that the Reformed had now also received their own preacher.

On the 8th of February, at his earnest desire, I examined a fine young English Quaker of twenty-one years, and thereupon baptized him in the presence of two Englishmen as his baptismal witnesses. The man, as well as his sponsors also, was of good understanding, and not a little awakened, on account of which I had uncommon joy. The name of the Lord be praised for the grace shown to this young man. May he keep him constant unto the end.

On the 22d of February, I visited four sick members of the congregation, among whom one begins to come to a knowledge of his former wicked life. My exhortation in the days of his health seemed then to be utterly in vain, but now he is more attentive. In the afternoon, a woman who had been ruined a year before came (whom I had already several times directed to a true repentance of heart) and made acknowledgment of the sins which she had committed, with tears and emotion of heart. She also made known her repentance therefor, and her great desire for the Holy Supper, with the offer, readily and willingly to submit to a Christian church discipline as an example to others.

On the 2d of March, I was early taken three miles from here, to a sick man, who was troubled with all kinds of hard thoughts during the past night (which were published by the people as temptations), and who had a great longing to see me. After having given him instruction, and offered up prayer, I left him, in the hope that these horrible images may conduce to his true repentance, and to the salvation of his soul, with the promise to come again as soon as I could, and to administer the Holy Supper to him, according to his repeated request. In the meanwhile, he should examine himself still more. His sickness did not seem to me to be unto death, but for his radical conversion.

On the 3d of March, I had many calls by the people. In the afternoon I preached a preparatory sermon, and held penitential and confessional services. Sixty were present who made confession.

On Sunday, Invocavit, after I had baptized three children, and preached to an extraordinary multitude of people, the Holy Supper was administered to the above-mentioned sixty persons, among whom some seemed to be very contrite and much affected.

On the 5th of March, I began, with several of our church council, to visit our members from house to house, whereby I was convinced of the necessity of frequent house visitation, by every one especially. If only strength of mind and body could endure all! I resolved in the name of God to do it every week on a certain day throughout the whole summer. In the winter it cannot well be done, on account of the very bad roads, the weather, the wind and snow. The Lord my God grant unto me much time, strength, and a compassionate love. At noon, after twelve o'clock, I went with the same four miles from here to visit some sick, and to administer the Holy Supper to the man mentioned on the 2d inst. He was extremely weak, so that he could speak but little; still he had a great longing for it, and related to me with a weak voice how three angels appeared to him and flew over his bed, from which moment he experienced in himself a special joyfulness of faith and an assurance of the forgiveness of his sins. I directed him from these extraordinary things much more to the revealed Word of God, and showed him several reasons from it whereby he could assure himself of the pardon of his sins, which also must stand forever. After I had held up before him the regular way to attain to grace and salvation, I prayed, absolved him, and administered to him the Holy Supper.

On the 9th of May, I visited a man who had been sick for a long time already, whom I met in the utmost weakness, so that he could with difficulty speak, much as he desired to; still he gradually expressed this much with many tears, that he had not partaken of the Holy Supper in many years, on account of the divisions in the congregation, and now had a great desire for it. To make preparation thereto I went home, and on my return I found him sitting in bed and weeping bitterly. All that was spoken with him, and his humble and penitent declarations, did not pass without emotion, whereby I obtained a fine opportunity to speak to the hearts of the wife, the children, and other people who were present.

April the 5th. This afternoon I held the last preparatory meeting with the young people who are to be confirmed. Immediately afterwards I had to go a mile from here, over the stream, to a sick girl, who serves with Separatists, and has had a great longing to see me. When I came there, I found the maid in great bodily weakness, but also in a fine state of penitence, and longing after grace and the Holy Supper. This I also at length administered unto her, upon her repeated request, after further previous examination and her own declaration, which was very edifying, so that her repentance could not be called in question.

On Palm Sunday, after the sermon, I examined and confirmed twenty-four persons, among whom were two women of other sects, and the rest were for the most part adults.

On the 14th of April, I had an extraordinary press of people from many places, who as yet announced themselves for the Holy

Supper, among whom were some who wept very bitterly. In the afternoon I preached the preparatory sermon, and held penitential and confessional services with two hundred and forty-three persons, who made confession.

On the first day of Easter, I preached to a very large multitude of people; and after the sermon I administered the Holy Supper to the above two hundred and forty-three.

On the 28th of April, the dear brother Brunnholtz, to meet whom, together with one of our wardens, I rode out nine miles, arrived here safely to my joy and consolation.

On Sunday, Misericord, I baptized a child in the forenoon, but Mr. Brunnholtz, weak as he was, preached for me, and not without edification. In the afternoon I preached, and let the schoolmaster, Jacob Löser, instruct the youth, so that Mr. Brunnholtz might also for once hear him. After the afternoon service, we had various calls, and my beloved brother gave himself the pleasure, and distributed passages to the children.

On the 30th of April, I took Mr. Brunnholtz along with me into the prison, where I had to visit two women who had been confined hitherto for infanticide, and upon whom criminal justice was to be held this day. The one whom I had already visited on one occasion, I found in many tears; but the other seemed to be very obdurate and malicious. In the afternoon we went into the school. Meanwhile, Mr. Mühlenberg had arrived. Mr. Schaum, from York, also came in the evening.

Early on the 1st of May we were visited by Mr. Conrad Weiser, and Messrs. Kurtz and Schaum. After having taken fraternal leave, Messrs. Mühlenberg and Brunnholtz rode away again, as the former had promised to hold a meeting forty miles from here, on the Philadelphia road, and to baptize several children, which the people depended upon. Messrs. Kurtz and Schaum accompanied them for several miles. I cannot sufficiently thank God for my dear colleagues. The favor and consolation of standing in brotherly love and unity among and with each other in this country, to see each other together, or only to read a letter from one another, can scarcely be expressed.

On the 5th of May, at noon, I had a funeral and a funeral sermon. The deceased maid had already served as maid-servant for three years with Separatists and scoffers at religion; but still had given God the glory during her illness, and had me called to her on several occasions. She also partook of the Holy Supper in the presence of those who had the mastery over her, in great contrition and simplicity of faith. These people, together with all their neighbors, all Mennonites and people attached to other sects, brought in the corpse, and were orderly and attentively present at the funeral sermon.

In the forenoon of the 15th of May I married a couple, members of the congregation, of whom the bride was in a fine state of penitence last year; and this spark, as I would hope, is not yet wholly extinguished.

On the 16th of May I visited a sick man twice, whom I had already visited several times, and found him in a fine condition of soul. I met him in great bodily weakness, but his soul built upon the true foundation of faith. It seems as if he was approaching still nearer to his end. May the Lord make him still more faithful and trustful every day until his death. My soul must praise the Lord my

God for all grace, patience, health and help which he has permitted me to experience hitherto. I entreat for nothing more than that my office may be blessed to souls, and that I myself may be saved, together with many of those who hear me. Highly venerable fathers, diligently include me and my whole congregation in your faithful intercessions.

JOHN FREDERICK HANDSCHUCH.

INDEX.

	PAGE.
Acrelius, Provost	411
Amsterdam	413
Anabaptists	55, 211
Ancram	350
Andrea, Rev. Mr	271, 306, 366
Archbishop of Sweden, Rescript of	114
Arndt's True Christianity	27, 135, 200, 262, 275, 398
Arthur, Rev. Mr	364
Bagenkopf, Rev. Mr	117
Baptism, Its mode	213
Baptists, Seventh Day	377, 431
Beaver Creek	446
Benefactions from Germany	253
Berkenmeyer, Rev. Christoph William	354, 363
Bethlehem	77, 338
Blue Mountains	339
Brunnholtz, Rev. Peter, 34, 43, 113, 124 148, 168, 247, 258, 278, 285, 386, 440, 470.	
visits Lancaster, York and Tulpehocken	122
taken seriously ill	193
report of Philadelphia Church	228
impaired health	403
Caetus Miserabilium	123

(475)

INDEX.

	PAGE.
Canada, The Indians of	110
Catechism, How regarded	198
Luther's Small	398, 408
Church contentions	73, 79, 108, 149
Cockson, Mr.	454
Consecration of St. Michael's Church in Phila.	187–190
Conewago.	86, 101
Conference meeting at Lancaster	287
Cohansey	401
Conversion of American Indians, How to be done	113
Conversions, special cases, 5–66, 129–140, 172–178, 194–218, 258–276, 313–315.	
2 Cor. v. 16, 17	10
Crypto-Herrnhuthianismus	344
Darmstadt collection.	407
Deut. v. 29	263
Devil, white and black	89
Doctrinal basis stated	87
Dreams, how to be interpreted	44
Early piety, Case of	258
Earltown	166, 415, 418, 420
Ecclesiastical order urged	296
Epilepsy at New Hanover	5
Evangelicals serving out their passage fees	296
Falckner, Rev. Justus	354
Fork	334
Fosseberg.	183
Francke, Rev. Prof.	129, 235, 245
Franklin, printer and postmaster	398
Fresenius, Senior, Doctor, Pastoral collection	240

INDEX.

	PAGE.
Gal. vi. 15	10
Gentiles, Their Salvation	9, 13
Germans, Arrivals of	367, 412
Göttingen	277
Goschenhoppen	334, 366
Halle	60, 118
Hamburg	221
Hamilton, James, Gov	457
Hartwick, Rev. John Christopher	113, 180, 190, 342
Handschuch, Rev. John Frederick,	154, 163, 170, 189, 247 285, 334, 389, 410.
visits York	432.
removes to Germantown	225
Heathen, The, Christ's inheritance	10
Heb. xi. 6	325
xii. 14	326
Heidelberg	334
Heintzelmann, Rev. John Dietrich Matthias	221
visits Brunnholtz,	223, 250
Hofgut	356
House visitation	467
Huguenots	54
Hymns, Reading of	26
Immersion	215
Incendiarism	36
Indianfield	306, 366
Indians, American	110
Isaiah i. 3	42
Inspired, The	51

INDEX.

	PAGE.
Jews, Their salvation	9, 13
John i. 47	270
iii. 18	10
x. 23–28	30

Kammerhof, Bishop.................. 79, 121, 144, 338
1 Kings xix. 4....................................... 289
Kingston, N. Y................................ 342, 352
Kluge, Rev. Samuel........................... 287, 402
Knoll, Rev. Christian.......................... 354, 356
Koch, Mr. Peter...................................... 115
Kraft, Valentin...................................... 147
Kreuter, Rev. Dr.................................... 343
Kuhn, Adam Simon.................................. 453
Kurtz, Rev. J. N., 49, 76, 115, 145, 148, 285, 366, 389, 410, 417, 471.
            is examined for licensure.......... 186
            is ordained...................... 190

Lancaster, Church of 77, 163, 225
        Rev. Handschuch's Ministry at........... 170
Leslysland... 182
Leutbecker, Mr. Caspar............................ 116
Lischy, Rev. Jacob......................... 79, 82, 142
Liturgy of Amsterdam............................. 355
Lord's Supper received unworthily................. 139
London... 222
Löser, Mr. Jacob......................... 393, 418, 423
Luke xiii. 4.. 94
Lutherans, German, in Pennsylvania, their numbers... 242

Magdeburg.. 221
Mageus, Mr. Melchior Joachim...................... 362

	PAGE.
Macungie	334
Manatawny	148
Marienborn	143
Mark x. 16	9
Marriage, a disorderly	34
Matt. xi. 28	106
Matt. xv. 19	195
Mennonites	17, 51, 472
Majority, when attained	176
Moravia	8
Moravians	19, 96
Motecha or Skippack	17
Mühlenberg, Rev. H. M.	25
journeys inland	48
journeys through Pennsylvania	66
visits Upper Milford and Saccum	123, 140, 179, 283
is taken ill	124, 142, 263
wife and children ill	168
visits Raritan	180–186, 292–299, 389
abundant in labors	218, 290
labors in New York	232
method at funerals	262
visits Lancaster	328, 440, 471
visits New York	337–365
called to New York	367–373
Myconius	265
Nässman, Rev. Mr.	189, 411
Nazareth	338
Newborn, The	66, 67
New Hanover, special cases of awakening	5, 23–60
school at	151

	PAGE.
New Goschenhoppen	224
Newlanders	413
New York	231, 353
calls Rev. Weygand	250
uses the Liturgy of Amsterdam	355
Nicky, Mr.	85, 88
Northkill	109
Nyberg, Mr.	77, 103, 115, 151, 412
Oley Mountains, The	126, 282
Opus Operatum	75, 380
Palatinate, The	67
Papists, The French	110
Perkasie	290, 309
Perkiomen Creek, crossed	310
Perlin, Rev. Mr.	411
1 Pet. iii. 1	30
2 Pet. i. 19	44
Phil. i. 6 and ii. 13	29
ii. 12	30
Philadelphia, St. Michael's consecrated	187–190
enlarged	226
prayer-meetings	397
Pneumonia	131
Providence	113, 257, 281
special cases	17, 33, 34, 43, 53
Psalms xiv. 1	40
xciv. 19	274
Quakers, English and German	51, 55, 215
Racheway	183

INDEX. 481

	PAGE.
Raritan................................145, 179, 334, 365	
Mr. Schrenck at...........................	250
church consecrated..........................	366
Rev. Weygand ordained....................	366
Rauss, Rev. Lucas....................... 333, 365, 404	
Reformed congregations pastorless..................	241
Rhinebeck.................................. 342, 347	
Riess, Rev. John Frederick.......................	357
Romans i. 21-32..............................	11
ix. 7, 8..................................	10
ix. 15...................................	9
Rotterdam....................................	413
Rudolph, Carl................. 84, 88, 97, 146, 182, 344	
Saccum............... 123, 257, 280, 289, 308, 334, 338	
Sacony.....................................	334
1 Sam. iv. 20.................................	275
Saudin, Provost...............................	189
Saltzwedel...................................	221
Schlauch, Jacob...............................	453
Schaum, Rev. John Helfrich.. 114, 167, 170, 185, 192, 284,	
389, 401, 410, 471	
ordained at Lancaster.....................	286
Schlatter, Pastor..............................	240
Schleydorn, Mr...............................	354
Schools, want of........................... 55, 251	
Schuylkill...................................	148
Scoffers................ 40, 48, 65, 129, 177, 191, 472	
Schrenck, Ludolph Henry... 277, 285, 290, 307, 329, 338,	
409, 440	
Schulze, Rev. Christian Immanuel...................	221
assists Rev. Mühlenberg....................	221

                                                              PAGE.
Separatists..................... 51, 71, 200, 469, 472
Sickness prevails....................... 128, 132
Silent, The.............................. 71
Skippack or Motecha..................... 17
Spangenberg, Rev. Mr................ 121, 144, 425
Staatsburg.............................. 351
Stendal................................ 221
Studium, Biblico-Catecheticum............. 279
Stoever, Mr............................ 288
Susquehanna River....................81, 108
Synod, organized........................ 190
    meetings of................. 333–335, 402, 440

Tarbush............................... 347
Thomas á Kempis, books of............... 191
Tohickon.............................. 334
Trauberg, Rev. Mr...................... 411
Tulpehocken...................... 77, 116, 334

Unander, Rev. Mr....................... 411
Union churches......................... 73
Upper Milford................. 123, 280, 289, 308

Vigera, Mr................... 157, 258, 400, 404
Virginia....................... 19, 52, 287
Visits, pastoral......................... 469
Vocationis instrumenta................... 285
Voigtland............................. 60

Weiser, Mr. Conrad... 36, 74, 76, 110, 113, 115, 157, 285,
                                                    337, 471.
Wernigerode........................... 221
Weygand, Rev. J. A. 192, 197, 232, 292, 335, 365, 366, 393

INDEX.

	PAGE.
Wilmington	411
Wolf, Mr. Mag	293

York	81, 101, 167, 284, 401, 410
Rev. Schaum, pastor at	170

Ziegenhagen, Rev. Fred. Michael	117, 222, 235, 245
Zinzendorf, Count Von	68, 96, 117, 412
studied at Halle	118

www.ingramcontent.com/pod-product-compliance
Lightning Source LLC
Chambersburg PA
CBHW051846300426
44117CB00006B/286